In Their Own Words

In Their Own Words

Songwriters Talk About the Creative Process

Bill DeMain

Westport, Connecticut
London

Library of Congress Cataloging-in-Publication Data

DeMain, Bill.
  In their own words : songwriters talk about the creative process / Bill DeMain.
    p. cm.
  First published in 2004.
  Includes bibliographical references (p.) and index.
  Contents: Burt Bacharach—Hal David—Ray Charles—Harlan Howard—
Dolly Parton—Isaac Hayes—Donald Fagen & Walter Becker—David Bowie—
Graham Nash—Carlos Santana—Todd Rundgren—Michael McDonald—Stevie Nicks &
Lindsey Buckingham—Billy Joel—Jimmy Jam & Terry Lewis—Amy Grant—
Jane Siberry—John Rzeznik of Goo Goo Dolls—Tori Amos—John Linnell of They
Might Be Giants—Sarah McLachlan—Ben Folds—Seal—Paula Cole—Jewel—Dido—
John Mayer.
  ISBN 0-275-98402-8 (alk. paper)
  1. Popular music—Writing and publishing. 2. Composers—Interviews. I. Title.
MT67.D46 2004
782.42164′13—dc22   2004050079

British Library Cataloguing in Publication Data is available.

Library of Congress Catalog Card Number: 2004050079
ISBN: 0-275-98402-8

First published in 2004

Praeger Publishers, 88 Post Road West, Westport, CT 06881
An imprint of Greenwood Publishing Group, Inc.
www.praeger.com

Printed in the United States of America

∞™

The paper used in this book complies with the
Permanent Paper Standard issued by the National
Information Standards Organization (Z39.48–1984).

10 9 8 7 6 5 4 3 2 1

There are five things to write songs about: I'm leaving you. You're leaving me. I want you. You don't want me. I believe in something. Five subjects, and twelve notes. For all that, we musicians do pretty well.

—Elvis Costello

Contents

Acknowledgments

I would like to thank my friend Lydia Hutchinson, who has given me the opportunity to interview hundreds of songwriters for her magazine *Performing Songwriter* (www.performingsongwriter.com).

Thanks to Eric Levy and all at Praeger for their enthusiasm and support, and Jeff Bleiel for letting me reprint a few of the interviews that appeared in an earlier book of mine (*Behind the Muse: Pop and Rock's Greatest Songwriters Talk About Their Work and Inspiration*, Tiny Ripple Books, www.tinyripple.com), including those with Tori Amos, Burt Bacharach, Hal David, Billy Joel, Sarah McLachlan, and Dolly Parton.

As always, thanks to my parents, Jim and Nettie, and Molly Felder, and also Allison Inman, Brad Jones, Jill Sobule, Griffin Norman, Frank Goodman, Bill Lloyd, Amy Rigby, Boo Hewerdine, Gary Clark, Paul Zollo, Elizabeth McCracken, Stephnie Weir, Andrea Dewese, and Cliff Goldmacher.

And of course, to all the songwriters who talked to me about their art for this book.

Introduction

Like ninety-nine percent of the songwriters out there who will read this, I'm not yet able to make my living by my songs alone. I've had some success—placements in TV shows, the odd cover, a few hits in Japan—but I still have to work a day job.

But as day jobs go, I have a pretty cool one. I interview songwriters, mostly for a magazine called *Performing Songwriter*. I've been doing this for over ten years. In that time, I've talked to a lot of well-known writers (David Bowie, Burt Bacharach, Dolly Parton) and a lot of less well-known but by no means less talented ones (John Linnell, Jane Siberry, Ben Folds). Under the guise of professional journalist (I still feel like a dilettante most days), I'm able to get up close and personal with the creative processes of these writers. It's an amazing thing. These discussions have brought me an enormous amount of insight into my own work as a songwriter. It's almost like having an ongoing master class with some of the most successful and innovative songwriters of the last fifty years as my instructors.

Here are a few things I've learned. No matter how frustrated and insecure you may feel at times as a songwriter (and if you don't occasionally feel this way, there's something wrong), you are not alone. Billy Joel feels this way. So do Sarah McLachlan and John Rzeznik. Feel better? Even though they've had Top 10 hits and have sold millions of records, these songwriters are still in awe of the process. John Mayer hit it on the head when he said, "The game is the same no matter what you do and who you are. When you're alone in a room, it doesn't matter how many records you sold, how many people you've got around you. It's you and the possibility and what are you going to do to find it."

I've also learned that in order to write songs, you have to *write* songs. Sure there are tricks and shortcuts (many of which you'll find in these pages), and sure it's essential to listen and read voraciously, but you still have to log the necessary hours with pen in hand. Here's what lyricist Hal David has to say about it: "I work very hard. I work on every word. I spend inordinate amounts of time deciding whether 'and' or 'but' is the right word. To a certain extent, lyrics flow easily, but no matter how much they flow at a given time, by the time you really get it put together and finished and refined to the best of your ability, it's a lot of work."

Another thing. As Yoda once said in a distant galaxy, far far away, "There is no try." That would seem to contradict what I just said about logging the necessary hours. Well, songwriting is full of contradictions. We all know the feeling of working for an entire afternoon and not catching a single line under our nets, then that evening, when we're in the middle of washing the dishes or watching *Law & Order*, a whole verse appears out of nowhere. A combination of work ethic and the Yoda no-try philosophy. Both are necessary to be a songwriter.

I could go on about what I've learned, but instead I think I'll cut to the chase and let you hear from the songwriters you know and admire.

Thanks for reading the book. I hope it inspires you to write a great song of your own!

CHAPTER 1

Burt Bacharach

Interviewed 1998

Hits: "Walk on By," "The Look of Love," "(They Long to Be) Close to You"

"I think in terms of making miniature movies," says Burt Bacharach of his approach to songwriting. "Every second counts. Three-and-a-half-minute movies, with peak moments and not just one intensity level the whole way through."

For over forty years, his unforgettable miniature movies have been enjoying a near-continuous run with listeners the world over. "Walk on By," "Anyone Who Had a Heart," "Do You Know the Way to San Jose?" "Alfie," "A House Is Not a Home," "The Look of Love," "What the World Needs Now Is Love," "I Say a Little Prayer," "Windows of the World," "Promises, Promises," "I Just Don't Know What to Do with Myself," "I'll Never Fall in Love Again," "Raindrops Keep Fallin' on My Head," "This Guy's in Love with You," "That's What Friends Are For," "God Give Me Strength"—the list of classics is long and illustrious.

Burt Bacharach was born in Kansas City on May 12, 1928. As a kid, he was a typically reluctant piano student who eventually warmed to the instrument thanks to the sounds of romantic classical music and bebop jazz. After studying theory and composition at Mannes School of Music, he embarked on a long apprenticeship—nightclub piano player, arranger for Vic Damone, musical director for Marlene Dietrich—that finally delivered him into the halls of songwriter central, the Brill Building in New York City. There he met the lyricist who would become his partner, Hal David.

Of writing with David in the early days, Bacharach recalls, "We'd work together in a room with a window that didn't open and a kind of beat-up piano, both of us smoking. You know, your typical image of how songwriters wrote in a room at a publishing office."

From that small, smoky cubicle came the music that along with the Beatles, the Beach Boys, and Motown would help define the era of the 1960s. It was a breezy sound, gently propulsive, irresistibly melodic, and full of sensuality. It was a sound that challenged listeners with its time changes and dynamic shifts. It was a sound to stir the imagination.

In all, the successful duo penned a string of thirty-nine consecutive chart hits, most of them for their voice of choice, Dionne Warwick. Their songs have been covered by an A to Z of artists, including Aretha Franklin, Tom Jones, Barbra Streisand, Dusty Springfield, the Carpenters, the Fifth Dimension, Rick Nelson, and Herb Alpert. Beyond that, Bacharach and David also wrote a hit musical (*Promises, Promises*) and several award-winning movie soundtracks (*Casino Royale, After the Fox, What's New Pussycat?*, and *Butch Cassidy and the Sundance Kid*).

After Bacharach and David split in 1973, Burt kept a low profile through the rest of the decade. He reemerged in the 80s with a new lyric partner (and his third wife), Carole Bayer Sager, charting with MOR hits such as "On My Own" and "Arthur's Theme (The Best That You Can Do)."

In the 90s, Bacharach enjoyed a huge revival, which resulted in a three-CD box set, a TV special and, most significantly, a collaboration with Elvis Costello on 1998's *Painted from Memory*, an album of new material that echoes Burt's best work of the 60s.

In 2003, Burt Bacharach teamed with legendary soul singer Ronnie Isley on *Here I Am*, an album of classic Bacharach-David songs cut live with a forty-piece orchestra.

What was the first piece of music that made an impression on you?

I heard a couple of things that really influenced me very much, attracted me more than influenced, and one was Ravel's *Daphnis and Chloe Suite*. I thought it was very beautiful and very different from the kind of classical music that I'd been listening to on drives with my parents—Beethoven, the heavier kind of sounds, Richard Strauss. Suddenly I was hearing something that was really lyrical and beautiful. That kind of turned my head around. Of course, then I heard Dizzy Gillespie's big band in New York at one of those clubs and Jesus, I'd never heard anything like that. Miles in front of everybody else, what they were playing. It was like a window opening.

Had you written your first song at that point?

No, that was still high school. I don't think I wrote my first song until I was in college and that was not a very good song. That's when I tried it.

Do you feel like there are things that you learned in your college composition courses that applied to your pop songwriting?

I think all the technical study, whatever, the solfeggio and learning how to be able to read music and write it down—it's all very helpful. It's like the situation if I was hearing something in my head and I couldn't get to a keyboard to check it out, but I could take a scrap of paper in a hotel or a restaurant or something and just write it out. I think that's very important. It certainly is for me. To read and to be able to write music. I think you learn the rules so you kind of break the rules. What else did I learn? It's hard to teach classical composition, I think, because I don't know that there any set forms that one has to follow or how key that is. You know, you still learn it. With Darius Milhaud, that was an important thing with me. He heard this one piece I was working on and told me that it was very good. It was very melodic and the rest of the class was writing very dissonant music, and he really encouraged me to tap into the melody. It's nothing to be ashamed of, he said.

When you're given a title or a bit of a lyric, what are your first steps in approaching a melody?

I think I just try to see what it means to me, first of all. If it's an attractive thought, an attractive idea. I don't dislike writing to a lyric. It takes you in another course that you might not go into if you were just writing a straight melody, then giving it to a lyricist. It kind of sets [you] out on a road and then you sort of have to follow it in a general direction. Sometimes that's a very attractive direction.

I know you've said you like to get away from the piano as soon as possible when you're composing. What are the main advantages of that?

You can hear a long line that way. You can hear the whole song. You can hear it evolve. And not to be as concerned with what the fingers and the hands are playing, where they're going. It's short term with my hands on the piano. It sounds really good for that one bar but I'm trying to hear the whole thing, and hear how it would sound just coming at you as a song, as a listener. You can hear the long line. I can anyway. Certainly that applies to orchestration as well, to hear what comes in when. I just get a better picture when I get away from the keyboard and just try to hear it that way. You can also get trapped by pretty chords when you're at the piano. I mean, guys have written great songs and continue to do so while sitting at their instrument, whether it's guitar or piano. Not to say I don't sometimes start at the piano, then get away from it. But I have to have a long-range picture of the whole scope of a piece. I get a sense of balance that I wouldn't get if I were sitting at the piano. I can't say enough about where your hands tend to go, because they've been there before.

If a songwriter wanted to improve his or her melody writing, what kinds of things would you suggest?

Try to get away from your instrument and work that way. It's very tough nowadays, because you can be duped by the technology we have. I can have my two-and-a-half-year-old go to one of my MIDI keyboards and play a couple of notes and it'll sound great. If you have a keyboard that's MIDI'd with a couple of synthesizers, so you have strings and horns, you can sound glorious. But when you take it all apart, when you peel back the cover, what do you have? Do you really have a song, do you really have a melody? It's like the same principle when you take something you've recorded and play it on a little, cheap tape machine. If it's there, it's there. I remember Quincy Jones playing his album *The Dude* one night at his house for a group of friends, and he played it on a small boom box. I guess Quincy was thinking, "If it's good, it's going to sound good on the least expensive equipment."

All those great intro figures you've come up with—"Walk on By," "I'll Never Fall in Love Again"—did you compose them as part of the songs?

Very often they came as part of the songs. Very often when I wrote those songs, I was hearing everything that went with it—the drum pattern, the bass. I never liked to go into the studio with just a chord sheet and a rhythm section. I liked to write out a drum part, a bass part, a guitar part. At least it would be a framework, a structure so they would know what I had in mind. It would change, but at least it had a start. The drummer would know where I wanted a cross stick. For me, if I just went in with a chord sheet, it's too loose.

I've read too that you would often write words under the notes of an instrumental line.

Yes, even if they didn't make any sense. It had a word and if you sung the word on your flugelhorn, it would be more than just a note by itself.

I've always been a big believer in words with notes. I used to write for the trumpet players, or the reed players, anybody that would have a singular statement to make on a record, I'd write the lyric underneath. So they'd be playing melody notation but they'd try to speak through their instrument the actual lyric. People that I worked with in the studio who knew me didn't think it was so crazy, and whether they thought it was crazy or not was unimportant to me. There was a reason I did it. There are certain things that can't really be notated, I find, in an orchestration. It's maybe two eighth notes, a sixteenth note, and another eighth note and that's the way it should be notated, but that's not the way it totally feels. But if you put words with it, or even vowel sounds, it does make a difference.

Do you have an ideal environment for composing?

No, but the more beautiful a setting is, the more beautiful an environment, the harder it is to write. We used to write in the Brill Building with a closed window, no view, no air, and Hal smoking all over the place. Then you get into a dream setting, and it's like the Ian Fleming thing, where he used to go to the Bahamas and he'd close the curtains so the light wouldn't come in and he wouldn't know where he was, and therefore he could write.

Have you found over the years that you're more effective at certain times of the day, or do you write at night?

I try not to write at night. Sometimes I can't help it, because I just find that it kind of stimulates me and I'm hearing it all night long. I hear the music all night. It just keeps going around in my head. It wakes me up, keeps me awake.

The records that you've produced of your songs always have great dynamic range.

It's about the peaks and valleys of where that record can take you. It's to a different dimension than you might be able to get. You can tell a story and be able to be explosive one minute then as kind of a satisfying resolution. I think one-level records always made me a little bit uncomfortable after awhile. They stayed at one intensity. It kind of beats you up, you know? It's like a smile. If you have a great smile, you use it quick, not all the time.

Do you have any recollections about writing "Wives and Lovers"?

It was an assignment for a movie. It was a song for hire. I don't know what we got paid, not much. Without an assurance or much of an assurance that it would go in the picture. It was just a promotional film. So Hal and I wrote it. It's a shame it didn't make the picture but it has probably had way more value than the picture in the long run. It's the same with "The Man Who Shot Liberty Valance." That again was a song that wasn't anything other than a promotional song.

Had you written anything with that jazz waltz feel before?

Maybe not. It might have been the first.

Whose is the definitive version in your opinion?

I'm not sure I have one. I like Dionne's record. I think she did it more like I thought it should be. I like Jack Jones' record too, though I had to get used to it. It was very different than what I'd imagined. But it started to do really well and became a hit, so I thought, "I can get used to it that way."

How about "The Look of Love"?

"The Look of Love" was really targeted for that one character in the picture [*Casino Royale*], for Ursula Andress. It was really written just watching her on my Moviola. Very sensuous, sexual theme. I treated it as an instrumental first, then Hal put lyrics on it. We got the ideal singer for it, went in and made that version for the picture with Dusty.

When you gave a melody to Hal, would you be careful not to have the dummy words in there?

Not really. The dummy words have to be in there so you have the right length, the right amount of syllables, the right amount of words, all to take home with him. I know one example, on "Raindrops Keep Fallin' on My Head," I kept singing that title. Even though Hal tried to change it, we never came up anything that felt as good. He made it make sense overall, though he tried some other ways first because it's not the most natural way one would think to write that lyric.

I'd like to ask you about a few of your contemporaries in the 60s. Were you a Beatles fan?

Moderately. You know, I was on the same bill with the Beatles in London, I think when they did the Royal Command Performance. I was conducting for Dietrich. They had already recorded "Baby It's You" on their first album, but you know they just were happening. My recollection is that I talked to one or two of them, but not much, in rehearsal that day. I'd seen posters in Sweden when I was there a couple of months before when I was there with Dietrich. I didn't know who they were. But I soon did.

I interviewed Jimmy Webb, and he cited you as a major influence, especially when he first started writing. Did you guys have much contact?

I admired Jimmy. I thought that album he did with Richard Harris [*A Tramp Shining*] was one of the great, great albums. I think the songs are just unbelievable on it. The production was great. He made Richard Harris sound just fantastic. I have a lot of respect for Jimmy. We never communicated really. He was on the West Coast, I was on the East Coast.

So many groups from that time, when I listen to them now, like Eric Burdon and the Animals or Paul Revere and the Raiders, sound very stuck in that time. Yet the stuff that you and Hal did with Dionne still sounds fresh to me. Any thoughts about that?

I can't say it was a little ahead of its time, because it wasn't. It was right in the time. It's like clothes maybe. Clothing gets outmoded. I'm not sure I know the reason why hairdos get outmoded. You look at them and you feel it's very off, because it is very off. It's just another time. It's the same thing with records. I think the, I don't want to say cheap songs or less substance songs, or more like rock 'n' roll or what was going on at the time, or simplified songs have less of a chance to survive. Take "The Long and Winding Road"—it was incredible then and it's incredible now. Maybe it's got something to do with a substantial song to start with. What the song says and how it's treated, and if it's not surrounded by a dated arrangement, or just an arrangement that would work at the time. Maybe then it will hold up thirty years later. That's my only read on it. Ballads, you know? Up-tempo tunes, maybe because of the very framework they had to be in, maybe didn't have the same chance to grow.

I wanted to get your impression on the difference between Hal and Carole Bayer Sager as lyricists. Do you feel like Hal's lyrics brought different kinds of melodies out of you than Carole's did?

I'm not sure. I think it's very possibly a different time as well. They're both great lyricists. Carole is one of the fastest lyricists I've ever seen. Too fast for me the way she writes, just because I'm that far behind. I'm still working on one note or something like that, and she's basically got the song done. Hal was more like the one who would take it home, work on it, bring it back the next day, and we'd look at it. Then he'd go back and I'd go back and we'd work alone a lot. Then together.

Hal seems like he might be a less sentimental person than Carole. Is that true?

You know, one is a woman, a beautiful woman, and the other is . . . if you look at Hal, then you listen to the lyrics, you've got to be stunned at the insight that Hal has in those lyrics. Brilliant stuff. And Carole too. I was lucky to have worked with them both.

I was really knocked out by "God Give Me Strength," the song you wrote with Elvis Costello for **Grace of My Heart.** *It sounds more like the stuff you were writing in the 60s. Was that a conscious choice?*

No, not at all. I'm not sure that was so. The picture was about that time, so I think that influenced the way people think too. I don't think I was writing backwards or trying to put it in a time-set.

When you think of your songwriting, do you ever see it in the way a painter might recognize different periods in his work?

Yeah, I think it's got to be in periods. Certain things I did then, there's no way I could do now. There are songs, like the first couple of hits I had, "Magic Moments" and "Story of My Life"—that's another way of thinking than I've certainly thought the last twenty or twenty-five years.

Do you have the sense that some of what you wrote with Hal for Dionne will be around a hundred years from now?

I think there's a chance that some of it will because it lasted thirty years. I think at that time you could make songs that had a chance to last.

I don't think we would be having hits with songs like that now perhaps in today's market.

What's the most difficult thing for you these days as a composer?

I think the market is very tough for good songs. It's very difficult because there's less space for good songs. There's a very youth-oriented radio format, much rap on urban stations. You know, artists that you could count on to make an urban hit then have a pop hit, like Aretha Franklin, Gladys Knight, Dionne, or Patti LaBelle, it's no guarantee anymore. You used to be able to have a Top 5 urban hit with them, then it would cross over into the pop market. But they don't necessarily get played or accepted at radio like they did. It's a shame. There are terrific singers out there like Toni Braxton, Tony Rich, and Babyface. They make great records, great songs.

If you were hired to teach a workshop on composing, what kinds of things would you stress to your students?

It's hard to teach composing. I studied composition and I think you should learn the basic stuff, like to be able to write music down. If you hear it in your head or you play it, you should be able to notate music and write it. I think it's helpful. It's so easy now, you just play something and dump it onto a tape machine. I'd have my students learn to read and write music. I think it's important. I think that you learn to try to listen when you're writing your own music, to get a long picture of it, as I said before. It's a discipline to be able to do that. Hear where it's lacking, where it's good, where it's boring, where it's overkill. The same with a record. You try to hear the record in your head, then hear it again. It's a fine-tuning thing.

What are three things that you haven't done yet as a songwriter that you'd still like to do?

I think I'd like to do another musical. I'd like to write something for a symphony orchestra, other than the way I did with the Houston Symphony [the *Woman* LP]. And I don't know, that would be sufficient, those two.

Do you have any thoughts on pop music in the next century?

I have no idea what's going to happen, if it's going to get better or worse, with more machines or live musicians. All I know is this. If I was a young musician, a violinist, and I went to a music school like Julliard, I would think that things would look very bleak, because there wouldn't be recording dates to play. The synthesizer takes the place. And if I wasn't up for a symphony orchestra—which isn't easy for a young musician—a violinist coming out of Curtis or Julliard, maybe they wind up in Oklahoma with a city orchestra, but they don't wind up with the Philadelphia Orchestra, not yet anyway. Also, French horn players. The samples are so unbelievable on the synthesizers. I like it, but I don't like it, you know? You can make a perfect record even if you're not a good bass player. You can play four bars of a bass part on a synthesizer, copy it, paste it. So it's good and it's bad. I don't like it that live musicians don't work as much as they used to do. Like drummers. There's the drum machine. It never slows down, it's perfect for dance, perfect for techno. But no matter what happens, I have to believe that there'll always be room for a good song.

CHAPTER 2

Hal David

Interviewed 1996

Hits: "Alfie," "What the World Needs Now Is Love," "I Say a Little Prayer"

"Above all, I try to create an emotion to which others can respond," says Hal David. "Unless I can create an emotion to which I can respond, I throw the lyric away. I assume that if it moves me it may do the same for someone else."

David's modest assumption has been proven correct with hundreds of three-minute masterpieces, especially those cowritten with composer Burt Bacharach. Few lyricists have expressed themselves on the subject of love with the grace, empathy, and simplicity of David. Whether sensuous ("The Look of Love"), spiritual ("What the World Needs Now Is Love"), romantic ("This Guy's in Love with You"), humanitarian ("The Windows of the World"), or David's specialty, broken-hearted ("Anyone Who Had a Heart," "I Just Don't Know What to Do with Myself," "A House Is Not a Home"), he always achieved that goal of making a deep emotional connection.

Hal David was born May 25, 1921, in Brooklyn, New York. Inspired by his older brother, renowned Tin Pan Alley lyricist Mack David ("I'm Just a Lucky So and So"), Hal began his lifelong passion for writing when he was a teenager. While serving in the army during World War II, he wrote lyrics for military revues. After he got out, he wrote special material for nightclub acts. In 1949, he scored his first hit when Mel Torme took "The Four Winds and the Seven Seas" into the Top 10.

During the 50s, David collaborated with a number of composers and made the hit parade with "American Beauty Rose" and "Bell Bottom Blues." In 1956, while a staffer at Famous Music in New York City's Brill

Building, he met Burt Bacharach. After collaborating intermittently for four years and scoring a few hits (most notably "Magic Moments" for Perry Como), the pair discovered the perfect voice and vehicle for their material in Dionne Warwick.

Along with the Beatles, the Beach Boys, and the Motown Sound, Bacharach and David wrote the songs that defined the 60s—with Burt's dynamic, daring, rule-defying melodies always anchored by Hal's insights and heartfelt sentiments.

As Dionne Warwick says, "There are some of Hal's lyrics that I can listen to and cry to and then feel a sort of release. It's my voice, but it's not just me. There's a universality about what's being said. Listening, I know I'm not alone in my feelings. Everybody has felt that way. And knowing that, I feel better."

After Bacharach and David split in 1973 (they've since mended fences and written a few songs together), David went on to collaborate with several different composers, turning out such hits as "Almost Like a Song" and the Willie Nelson—Julio Iglesias duet "To All the Girls I've Loved Before." From 1980 to 1986, he was president of ASCAP, and continues to serve as a member of the society's board of directors.

What were some of the things early on that attracted you to writing lyrics?

Firstly, my older brother Mack David was a very successful lyricist, so that became part of our family life early on. What may have seemed like an odd profession to someone else seemed quite normal to me.

How much were you able to learn from watching and listening to your brother?

I grew up listening to songs, being involved with music, playing with little bands. I played violin. I guess I learned an awful lot, but it's hard to know what you learned. I don't recall watching my brother write. I don't know to what extent he did that at home, at least when I was around. I think I learned by osmosis, by listening and watching, and I probably did ask questions, but I don't recall. I learned by writing. The best way to learn how to write songs is by writing songs [laughs]. Most of us are collaborators—there are very few Irving Berlins and Cole Porters and Frank Loessers around—so we learn from our writing partners too.

When you were first starting out, what kinds of things did you do to get your foot in the door?

I did what was the usual and normal thing in those days. Music publishing and writing took place, for the most part, in New York City, except if you were doing films, then it was Los Angeles. The publishers were, to a large extent, in the Brill Building on Broadway and Forty-ninth Street. So you wrote your songs with various collaborators. Most of the publishers had piano rooms, and you usually had some kind of relationship with a publisher where you'd be able to work in one of their rooms. Then you'd go and play your songs around from publisher to publisher. There were eleven floors in the Brill Building. You'd start at the top and work your way down, playing your songs as if you were selling your wares.

Nowadays you bring a CD to a publisher, and if they don't care for it, they can shut it off. Back then, when you were playing live, were you ever stopped?

Firstly, everything was live in those days. I guess it may have happened here and there, but no, I think there was too much courtesy to do that. I don't think anyone would stop you in the middle of a song.

The songs were probably shorter then too.

Not necessarily. Songs today aren't necessarily longer. The records may be longer, but the song itself isn't. Very often you're just repeating and going to different keys.

How did you meet Burt Bacharach?

We were both working up at Famous Music in the Brill Building, and in those days, everyone in the music business seemed to know everyone else. There was always a great mixture of people writing together. You'd write with one composer in the morning and another in the afternoon. Pretty much a lyric writer wrote with a lot of composers over a period of time. So I met Burt and we liked each other, and we liked the songs we wrote, and that's how it happened. We had a room at Famous Music and we'd meet around eleven, twelve o'clock every day. I was very hardworking, as he was. I was always writing lyrics. He was always writing melodies. The question asked repeatedly was, "What do you think of this?

What do you think of that?" Either my lyric would set him off to write a melody or vice versa.

You were both very prolific.

Even as we worked together on one song, he'd give me another melody or I'd give him another lyric, and very often we were writing three songs at a time—a song together, a song to his tune, a song to my lyric. So we had a number of things going.

I've read that you didn't have one set way of writing with Burt. But say it was a song where you were given a complete melody first. Can you describe your first steps in approaching a lyric?

The first step is to listen to the music very closely, not so much to learn what the notes are, but to see what the music was saying to you. If you're a lyric writer, you should hear the music talking to you. That's what I'd be doing initially.

While you were doing that, would you be taking notes or scribbling ideas?

I'd often write dummy lyrics, and I still do that. It helps me retain the melody, and particularly if the melody is a little complex.

How about finding the placement of the title?

Well, I think a title is where you ordinarily go first. But very often I'd start off with lines that would take me to a title. The placement of it very often was obvious, and sometimes, with Burt's melodies, not so obvious. I think "I Say a Little Prayer" was like that. The chorus section goes [sings], "Forever, forever you'll stay in my heart and I will love you." That's ordinarily where the title would fall in that song, but for whatever reason at the time, it seemed to me that the title should come in the less obvious place of the verse, after "The moment I wake up, before I put on my makeup." That's where I decided to put the title.

Do you keep a log of possible titles and lines?

I don't know if I keep a log, but I have notebooks full of lyrics, lines, titles. But it's not something that when I get an assignment, I go through and look at them, no. Every once in a while I do look at them to stir my memory and energize me, but I don't use them as a log in that sense. I pretty much attack everything very much in a fresh manner.

Do you use a rhyming dictionary?

Yes. I also use *Roget's Thesaurus*.

When you were writing a song with Burt that began with a lyric, like "Alfie," how would you decide on form and rhyme scheme?

I wouldn't decide, it would decide for me [laughs]. I think that's what happens when you write. You have a whole background of experience, and that comes into play, but essentially, very often you start to write and the work creates its own form. I don't think too often I thought of what form it was going to be then set out to write within that form.

How did you hook up with Dionne Warwick?

There was a Drifters session she was working on, and we were there—we had a song on the date—and she came over and said, "Could I do some demos for you?" We fell in love with her right away, and she started doing all our demos. Then she did one entitled "Make It Easy on Yourself." And that led to her deal on Scepter Records, and her first hit with "Don't Make Me Over."

How was writing show songs for Promises, Promises different from writing pop songs?

Show songs, to a certain extent, for me anyway, are somewhat easier to write because you had a story to deal with. When you're writing a pop song, you've got air to deal with, blank paper to deal with [laughs]. You have to create out of nothingness. When you do a show, there's a story, there are characters, there are scenes. There's a tree on which you hang your songs. Writing a show song, of course, while in some respects it may be easier, is also more challenging because it deals with subjects that you wouldn't deal with very often in a pop song.

That was such a wonderful show. Why didn't you and Burt do more?

Well, I've sometimes wondered the same thing [laughs]. Burt lost his feeling for writing shows after that. His experience was different from what he had expected it to be. He came out of a record background, and every time you play a record back it comes out the same. It doesn't change. But if you do a show, the tempo can be too fast, too slow. The singers or actors can change lines or notes. The audience doesn't know these things, but you do. And if you're a perfectionist, and of a mind to let it drive you crazy, you don't enjoy it. So Burt didn't want to do another one.

There's a song from the show called "Whoever You Are" that I think is one of my favorite ballads you've written. I really admire all the inner rhyming. How much do you labor over a lyric like that?

I do labor over my lyrics. That's one of my favorite songs, to begin with. I think it's a great melody and I like the lyric a lot. But I work very hard. I work on every word. I spend inordinate amounts of time deciding whether "and" or "but" is the right word [laughs], and I work very, very hard. To a certain extent, lyrics flow easily, but no matter how much they flow at a given time, by the time you really get it put together and finished and refined to the best of your ability, it's a lot of work. It'll probably go through two or three drafts. You may even go back to something that's close to the very first draft you had, but you're trying the others just to see whether it can be improved or not.

What inspired "Do You Know the Way to San Jose?"

I wrote that to the melody. People have asked me, and I'm not really sure. Most times I'm not sure [laughs]. I think your work is obviously influenced by your life experience. I did spend time in San Jose during World War II. I was at Fort Ord, California, and possibly because I had spent time in San Jose in those days, that may have been the natural outgrowth of that.

How about "One Less Bell to Answer"?

There's no question about that one. Burt and I were in London working on a project, and I was invited to a dinner party at his house. His wife Angie said to me, "When you arrive, don't ring the bell, just come in. It'll make one less bell for me to answer." And at least I was smart enough to know it was a good title.

"What the World Needs Now."

That one took me a long time to write. I don't think I've ever spent as much time on a song. I had the chorus. It was very clear to me, but the verses I couldn't get. "Lord, we don't need another mountain" is the opening line of the verse. Once I got that line, I knew where I should go with it. There was a oneness to the idea and the language that flowed from chorus into verse. But that took a few years to reach that point [laughs]. I love that song.

When you listen to today's music, do you hear any lyrics that impress you?

Yeah, I'm sure I do, but I couldn't name specific ones. Lyrics seem to be less important today than thirty years ago. I wish I didn't think so, but on the whole, lyrics seem to be less important. Very often the melodies seem to be less important. More often than not, the sound and production seem to be more important, but I'm not sure. There are certainly some terrific songs written today. There just don't seem to be as many of them.

Can you tell me the names of a few songs you wished you wrote?

"As Time Goes By," "Mack the Knife," "September Song," "Night and Day," "By the Time I Get to Phoenix." That's just a few.

What advice would you give to an aspiring songwriter?

First, make sure it's what you really want to do, because there's an awful lot of rejection that takes place, particularly early in your career, and that you want it enough to live with the rejection and get past the rejection. And secondly, what you've got to do is get yourself to the places where the music is written and published—like Los Angeles, New York, and Nashville, depending on what you write. Meet the people there, start writing and I think you learn by writing, and you succeed by being where things are happening.

CHAPTER 3

Ray Charles

Interviewed 2003

Hits: "Hit the Road Jack," "What'd I Say," "Busted"

Ray Charles is behind the grand piano, swaying from side to side, head tilted back, wraparound shades catching the light, smiling, grimacing, and singing in a voice that is part cry, part gleeful shout, and all soul.

For over fifty years, this picture has been a constant in popular music, an iconic image, a beacon of integrity. Styles change, trends come and go, but Brother Ray, the "genius of soul," is still there at the grand, swaying, singing, doing what he does best. The legendary pianist-singer-songwriter-arranger-bandleader said, "Music isn't something that's separate from me. It *is* me. I can't retire from music any more than I can retire from my life. I believe the Lord will retire me when He's ready. And then I'll have plenty of time for a long vacation."

He was born Ray Charles Robinson on September 23, 1930, in Albany, Georgia, but was raised in Greenville, Florida. His parents were poor—his dad a handyman, his mom a washerwoman. When Ray was four, his younger brother George drowned in a washing tub before Ray could call for help. Shortly after, Ray started to lose his eyesight to glaucoma. By age six, he was blind, but that didn't stop him from banging on a neighbor's piano every chance he got. His parents enrolled him in a school for the deaf and blind, where he studied music and learned to read and write in Braille.

Ray left school at fifteen. Now an orphan, he drifted around the South, eking out a living with his music. In 1947, he moved to Seattle, where he soon established himself as a polished nightclub crooner in the style of his idol, Nat King Cole. Imitation may be the highest form of flattery, but it won't get you noticed, as Ray discusses in the following interview. Finally, in the early 50s, he found his own voice. Gone was the polite croon, in its place a raw, unrestrained exuberance that went straight back to Ray's childhood Sundays in church. The historic sides he cut for Atlantic Records fused this gospel fervor with the blues and rock 'n' roll into a style all his own, one that would lead directly to the R & B and soul music of the following two decades. Influential? Ray drew up the blueprint for at least a hundred careers.

In 1959, Charles left Atlantic for the greener (and greenbacker) pastures of ABC. One of his first releases there was *Modern Sounds in Country and Western Music*. With covers of classics such as "I Can't Stop Loving Her" and "You Don't Know Me," the album sold millions and helped Charles cross over to a white audience. Though it seems natural to mix and match styles these days, back then it was almost unheard of. "I wasn't singing country and western. I was singing it like *me*," said Charles with a laugh.

Singing it his way is what this legendary performer continued to do, until his death on June 10, 2004, at the age of seventy-three. Whether it was a Beatles favorite, a Broadway show tune, a Pepsi jingle, or "America the Beautiful," he made it a Ray Charles song.

His final album, a collection of duets with artists such as Willie Nelson, Elton John, and Bonnie Raitt, is being released in August 2004.

In the late 1940s you were singing in the style of two of your heroes—Nat King Cole and Charles Brown. Then when you signed with Atlantic, you left the imitations behind. What was going through your mind, and how did you make the leap into your own style?

One morning I woke up and I was just laying there in the bed with thoughts running through my mind, when all of a sudden it hit me. I began to realize that people would come up to me and say, "Hey kid, hey kid, you sound just like Nat Cole!" Or "Hey kid, you sound like Charles Brown!" It was always "Hey kid." And I began to tell myself, "You know one thing? Don't nobody really know your name. They don't know who the hell you are. You're just a 'Hey kid.' " And then my thoughts went back to my mom. She used to always tell me, "Boy, be yourself. I don't care what you are, but be yourself. Don't try to be something you're not." So I started telling myself that. Although I was scared to do it because I could get work sounding like Nat Cole. I said, "Oh man, I don't know what I'm gonna do. Suppose I fail?" But I thought, I can't keep going around imitating. I have to sound like myself, good, bad or indifferent. If I make it, I make it. If I don't, I don't.

Did you ever meet Nat Cole?

Oh yeah. I loved him. He was such a mild man. Just like his voice sounds to you. He was a very warm person, and he knew I loved him. He was very genuine with me. He said, "You know, I appreciate it, and it's really really nice that you've patterned yourself after me, but I have to tell you, in the end, you're gonna want to find your own way." That's the way he put it. "You're gonna want to find your own way." There's nothing wrong with admiring people. We all admire people. I don't care what you do in your life. You got it from somebody. That's why you admire that person. If you're a writer or a musician or a newspaperman. There's somebody that made you feel good about what you do. He understood that, Nat Cole.

It seems like you became a songwriter almost out of necessity. Do you feel like it's something that came naturally to you?

Well, it had to come natural. You used the right words when you said "out of necessity," because that's really what started me writing. Atlantic would send me songs and I didn't like them, and yet I wanted to record. So I finally said to myself, "If you don't like what they're sending you, maybe you should write your own stuff." And so I just started doing that. But I'm not a genuine writer. I've seen guys that could write a song in five minutes. It would take me two or three days to write a song. I'd write it, tear it up, rewrite it, tear it up, until I got it to where I thought I wanted it. But as it turned out, the things I wrote, the majority of them were very successful. Writing is something that I enjoyed doing, but it was not the kind of thing that I wanted to pursue. I was blessed in the sense that I knew how to write. I just sort of put it to good use. But as soon as I got to the point where I could go out and hire people to write good stuff for me, I almost stopped writing completely. Now I may write an arrangement once every year and a half, two years, just to keep in practice. But otherwise, I don't do any writing anymore.

One of my favorites of your early songs is "Greenbacks." Was it a tribute to Louis Jordan?

Oh no. What I did in tribute to Louis was "Let the Good Times Roll." I was crazy about him. He was very unique. He had his own style. That's what I love about the musicians of the past. They had their own thing. Today you find people and everybody's trying to sound like who had the last hit.

But you know, when I came up, you heard people like Sinatra and Ella Fitzgerald and Dinah Washington. All of these people, Nat Cole, Charles Brown, every one of these people, if they sang two notes, just two, you knew who they were. That's what I don't see today, and that bothers me. I don't see creativity like it used to be, where everybody stood on their own.

Talking about your own style, you caught some flak in the 1950s for combining gospel and blues. Did you think you might be onto something new and revolutionary?

I didn't even bother about it. I didn't even think about it when I got the flak. You see, that was one of those things where I said, "If I'm going to be myself, I got to be myself." If some people don't like it, I cannot help that. Why wouldn't I sound like that? That's the way I grew up. Listening to the blues, and I grew up in the church. It came very natural just to sing the way you sing. It wasn't like something that I created. I was just being myself. I was around the blues and heard Big Boy Crudup, Tampa Red, Big Joe Turner, and all those people, and yet I went to all the revival meetings, the Sunday services, Sunday school. All the things that had to do with the church, I was involved with. Naturally, I was influenced by that. So if you're influenced by something, it's going to come out in you, isn't it? There you are.

What's the story behind "What'd I Say"?

I said to my band, "Look, I don't know where I'm going, so you follow me." And I told the Raelets, "Whatever I say, just repeat it after me." When I ran out of things to say, I started to moan and go "uhn, uhn." After a minute or so, the crowd was moaning right along with us. Then they came up to me after the show and asked where they could buy the record. I just laughed and said, "What record?"

How do you keep your voice in shape?

I'm very fortunate that my voice has held up over the years. I just made seventy-three this past Monday. But I don't do anything special. Of course, as you grow into what you're doing, you learn how to do things a lot easier. It's like a ballplayer, like a pitcher, for instance, you know? When he first gets into the league, he throws the ball. Then after a while, he learns how to *pitch*. So that's the same thing. When you're young, you don't know how to really use your voice, so you tend to holler instead of sing, if you know what I mean. But as you mature, you learn how to take care of your voice and you know how to sing the notes without straining yourself. So I just sing very natural and very easy. I don't put no strain on my voice. I just let it do what it's gonna do [laughs].

When you're singing "Hit the Road Jack" or something you've done many times, how do you stay emotionally connected?

It's the easiest thing in the world. You take a song like "Georgia," I've sung it thousands of times. But what happens is when I sing something, I never ever sing it the same way twice. And that's not because I'm trying to be different, but it's because I sing according to what I feel that night. Every day of our lives we feel different. You don't feel the same way today as you felt yesterday. You may come close, but there is a little difference, and what difference there is, makes the difference.

You've always been a sharp dresser. How do you pick out your clothes?

I'm kind of a plain person. I don't get too far out. I just like the major, main colors. The blacks and the browns and blues and grays. I'm not into all this high fashion stuff. I just want something to fit me. One thing about clothes. If you wear good clothes that fit you, you never go out of style.

You've been singing and writing about love for sixty years. Has it affected your own love life?

No more than it affected anybody else, I guess. I just sing about it. To sing about something—that's your art, that's what you do. What you do from your artform is one thing. Your private life is another. The two don't mix. At least I don't think so. I play piano, but that ain't got nothing to do with my private life.

CHAPTER 4

Harlan Howard

Interviewed 1996
Hits: "I Fall to Pieces," "Busted," "Heartaches by the Number"

The typical songwriter who rolls into Nashville is an unknown hopeful with an acoustic guitar and a notebook full of titles and half-finished songs. When Harlan Howard arrived in 1960, he was already famous, with his first number one and a $100,000 royalty check in his pocket.

Not that he hadn't paid his dues. After a stint in the early 50s as a paratrooper in the Army, he touched down in Los Angeles. There he spent most of the decade working in a printing factory and writing songs in his spare time. Though he landed a few records with West Coast country acts like Tex Ritter, Freddie Hart, and Buck Owens, his big break came when Charlie Walker took "Pick Me Up on Your Way Down" to number one.

Howard recalls, "I'd had my first hit, but I'm still working at this factory, and I still haven't received any money yet. One day, I'm on the job and I get a long-distance call from Nashville. It was Ray Price, and he says that he's recording and he liked 'Pick Me Up on Your Way Down' and do I have any new songs? So I sent him a tape of three songs, one of them called 'Heartaches by the Number.' To this day, that is still the biggest hit I've ever had."

Arriving in Music City with an illustrious freshman class that included Willie Nelson and Roger Miller, Howard soon established himself as a one-man hit machine. "I Fall to Pieces," "Busted," "Mary Ann Regrets," "Tiger by the Tail," "The Everglades"—these were all penned in his first few years in town. By 1965, his songs had been covered four hundred times.

In the decades after, Howard came to be regarded as the King of Music Row, with an annual birthday bash picking party in his honor. The hits kept coming too, with number ones such as "Blame It on Your Heart" and "Don't Tell Me What to Do."

Harlan Howard died March 3, 2002. He was seventy-four.

Were there specific events that made you want to write your own songs?

How it happened is that I was living on a farm in Michigan with these older folks, helping with the chores and going to school. I was twelve or thirteen years old and these folks would go to bed at eight o'clock at night, and this was before TV, so I got to listen to this little roundtop radio. One Saturday night, I had my ear up to the radio and I discovered WSM and the Grand Ole Opry. Ernest Tubb happened to be singing. He had the richest, manliest voice I'd ever heard and I flipped out. These songs he'd sing on the Opry, I got to writing them down. By the time he was done, I might have half the song, because I couldn't write that fast. I'd turn the radio down and I'd just mentally sing it until I had the melody in my mind. I'd sing these things and then—they were kind of short—so I got to writing another verse or two, to his song. I got me a title, the melody, the phrasing, so I'm just copying what's up above in terms of syllables and rhymes. It's not really writing, but in a roundabout way, it sure as hell is teaching you structure. I wrote a couple of verses for the song "Born to Lose" that to this day, I think are as good as what they already had [laughs]. I was touched by the words of the songs that Ernest Tubb sang. He was singing about serious relationships, and that blew me away because, for some reason, I think that's what I wanted to do. I was a kid on a farm, but I knew I wanted off that damn farm when I got big enough. That had more impact on me than anything since.

Did you have a favorite songwriter early on?

Cindy Walker, probably the greatest country music writer I've ever heard, lives in Mart, Texas now, and she's getting kind of old. She was my favorite writer. She's worth a book. She wrote one of the best country songs ever written—"You Don't Know Me." She also wrote for Roy Orbison. She wrote "Watching the Bubbles in My Beer" for Bob Wills. She'd mail them to singers, one lyric, one song, and a little homemade demo with piano and her singing. Another country singer I discovered back when I was listening to Ernest Tubb was a guy named Floyd Tillman. He wrote, "I Love You So Much It Hurts Me" and another huge hit called "Slippin' Around." He coined that phrase for cheating. He was very impressive and a very unusual singer. Those two and Ernest Tubb and their kind of music is my favorite.

Did you learn songs by these writers and take them apart?

When you want to be a writer, you listen close. I still do. It's just like everybody else. Most of the songs, even back then, weren't worth listening closely to. You hear the beginning, and your thoughts would drift away. Just like they do now. The song doesn't impress you. But I did learn a lot of songs.

Do you have favorite ways to get started when writing?

I like titles, and I can show you [he pulls out a restaurant napkin with a few scrawled titles]. Restaurant napkins, bar napkins, whatever. Of course, I never have a pen, because that would be getting too serious [laughs]. I doodled around the other day on a pretty neat song, which I need two more lines for, called "Looking Back Down Life's Road." It's just kind of reminiscing. It was about life and love and friends and all that, and it feels like a pretty good song. I don't think I'm necessarily going for the jugular vein of the hit parade with this song, but it's fun to write anyhow. I'm sixty-eight. I look back down a lot of roads. It doesn't matter as much now if I write a hit every time. I just want to enjoy it. So in order for me to try to write one for the hit parade, I have to allow myself to doodle around in between. All these years, from age twelve to now, I've trained myself to listen to everything that's said. I read the paper from front to back. Even there in the news, you might find something that's interesting. A title, an idea. All these things are floating around. You write it down if it's interesting and then you think about it.

In the early days, you wrote mostly by yourself. Now you're more of a cowriter.

I've got three buddies. Mostly Kostas lately. We are so good together and we write so quickly. I've got a legal pad with song titles. When my buddy comes over, I'll do the shuffle, as if the titles were cards. He might have something he really wants to write. He'll throw that at me. If I don't feel it or it isn't something that excites me, I'll say, "Well, I don't think I can get into that." A real honest conversation, an exchange of ideas. They're thinking of writing this or that. I'm thinking of writing a handful of things. A lot of times these things you think are titles really just wind up being a line in a song. In other words, you can't hang your hat on it. It isn't strong enough for three minutes, but it's a neat line someday to make your verses not be so trite. We're always looking for those. Every good song ought to have at least a couple super interesting lines besides the title.

Love is usually something that's idealized in pop songs, or expressed in a codependent "I'll die without you" sort of way. What do you try to do with the concept of love in your songs?

The toughest songs in the world to write are love songs. "I love you and I will forever and blah blah blah." Occasionally, I'll hear something like "Wind Beneath My Wings." That was a great idea and a great title and they wrote it well, and how could any woman not love that song? It's totally commercial and totally beautiful. But those are hard to find. I'd rather get into a song about a relationship that's a little bit shaky or even tragic or even over. That in my mind represents country music and the drama of the man-woman thing. That to me is the most fun to write. But country music has gotten away from that. The truth of what's going on with people is being ignored. People drink, they cheat, they do all these things. Fifty percent of all marriages end in divorce. It's almost like fifty percent of the country fans are not being represented, people whose marriages fell by the wayside. And that's where I come in.

Let me ask you about a few of your hits—"Don't Tell Me What to Do."

I've been married and divorced several times, and nothing will irritate me more than an ex-wife giving me advice, and telling me, "You'll be happy. You'll love again. You're a fine man, blah blah blah." That's pretty sickening [laughs]. I know I'll love again. I'm normally quite happy to be free of a situation. But I sure as hell don't want advice from them. If I want to roll in the gutter, I'll roll. If I want to fall in love again, I'll do that. Even if it's a mistake. But that's the place I wanted to get into with this song. One of the things that I'm really proud of as a writer is a lot of my buddies have always told me that I might be the best at squeezing a lot of stuff in one line, and a lot of them liked the first line of that song. It says, "We tried and we failed and it's over / I didn't fit the image in your mind." I got rid of a bunch of clutter, two verses worth at least. We got married in Massachusetts and moved to Boston, blah blah blah. The first line tells you that the relationship has failed and why it's failed, so the situation is over. I condensed the hell out of that and it flowed like a river. Max [D. Barnes, his cowriter] had some good lines in that song too. We both sat there giggling like schoolkids, getting rid of space. Roughly you got three minutes. So when you can condense a whole bunch of history of a relationship and get that out of the way and get to the heart of the matter, it's so much fun to do. You can't do it all the time, but it's fun to try to do.

I've heard that the song sat around for a few years.

Max did a demo, and it laid around Sony/Tree for like six years, then Pam Tillis discovered it somehow and they recorded it the next night. Imagine it taking six years. I heard so much crap on the radio in the meantime. I heard some great songs too, but a lot of flops. But here's a really killer song a boy or girl could do, with an interesting story and melody and the whole thing, and to take that long. You can live with it if you're writing constantly. In other words, the old songs will catch up with you, even though it's several years down the road. By that time, you've written a bunch of newer songs. It's not like you've forgotten it, but you've pitched your butt off and you think, "Maybe I was wrong and maybe this kind of song isn't in." That's stupid also, because hit songs should always be in. I don't care how country they are, or how pretty, or how loving, anything.

"I Fall to Pieces."

It was Hank Cochran's idea. This was back in the summer of 60. He had like maybe the first two lines and the title. He had it started, and man, I'm a lyric-writing son of a gun and I heard it and said, "I'd love to help you." And so we went out to the garage, he grabbed the guitar and I grabbed the legal pad, and it really didn't take us very long. The one thing I remember is that we wrote half the song and we thought it was done. After Hank left, I got to timing the song, like I usually do, wondering how long or short it is, and it wasn't long enough. I thought about the tricks we sometimes use, repeating a certain section over again. But the juices were flowing, so I wrote the second half just copying the way we wrote the first half. I took it out to Hank and he liked it, and we might've changed a line or something. But we made it twice as long. He put down a little work tape, and that was it. It was a nice song, a good song, but I have to believe that Patsy Cline, her treatment of the song, made it better than I thought it was. I always wrote in batches, and to me, it was in the middle of a batch of like fifteen songs. There were some others I thought were just as good or maybe even better. But man, when you get a record like that, wow! Plus the public really liked it. It was a hit for about a year or something. It surprised me. I was writing some weird little songs at the time, being a new writer in town, and I was probably more interested in those. But "I Fall to Pieces" was where I learned to be a commercial slut [laughs].

If you were to teach a class on songwriting, what would you tell your students?

If you really want to be a songwriter, you do it. Maybe the way to learn would be to pick out a classic or something that you really love and is the type of song you want to write. Where they have a title on their lyric, you put your own title. It would be great if it even had the same number of syllables. Take the first verse and just sing it out, count the syllables. You write a new lyric to their melody. You duplicate the structure, but totally different lyric. Then try to throw away their melody. Go to a different key. Write your own melody. What have you got? You've got a song. This is like growing up and learning the methods and the styles. If the first person wrote it perfectly, you've got your idea with a perfect structure. Then you can do what I've been doing all my life, make the melody fall with the lyric. Throw the other melody away. That would be a neat exercise. It's a challenge. You can learn all this stuff from the radio. What did you steal? You didn't really steal anything. It's showing you how simple it is. We all write differently. Some guys like to go out driving. Dallas Frazier, that's how he wrote. I couldn't do that. I'm too tense when I'm driving. I'm more like a home writer. I've got a little corner of the house and a big old Gibson guitar that makes me sound good. I'm totally content just being a writer. I'm here to do one thing. I just love a great song, as a listener, as a writer.

CHAPTER 5

Dolly Parton

Interviewed 1996 and 2002

Hits: "Jolene," "Down from Dover," "I Will Always Love You"

Dolly Parton has no doubt about her priorities.

"If somebody said to me, 'You can only do one thing in show business for the rest of your whole life. What will it be?' I would say, 'I'll write songs.' To me, it's like putting something in the world today that wasn't there yesterday that will still be there tomorrow. That's my favorite thing I do."

Though she's played many roles over the last forty years—country music superstar, wisecracking comedienne, movie actress, tabloid trash queen, savvy entrepreneur, multimillionaire, warm-hearted philanthropist, pop culture icon—Dolly is, behind it all, a songwriter, and a great one at that.

Her far-reaching accomplishments are more incredible when you consider her beginnings. Dolly Rebecca Parton was born January 19, 1946, in a one-room cabin in the mountains of east Tennessee, the fourth of twelve children born to poor sharecropper parents. While Dolly grew up without electricity, running water, a telephone, or indoor plumbing, she was surrounded by a loving family who instilled in her a sense of humor, a good dose of common sense, and a passion for music. "I'm proud of the humble beginnings," Dolly says, "the fact that dreams can come true for just ordinary people."

After singing for "my brothers and sisters and chickens and the dogs with a tin can as a make-believe microphone," Dolly got her first break at ten years old when she landed a job singing on a radio/TV program called *Farm and Home Hour*, broadcast from Knoxville ("I was on TV before we owned one," she says).

This led to her first recording, at fourteen, a one-shot appearance on the Grand Ole Opry, where she brought the house down, and a songwriting deal with Tree Publishing. In between, she found time to attend high school classes. In her autobiography, *Dolly: My Life and Other Unfinished Business*, Dolly writes of taking trips to Nashville with her Uncle Bill, also a tunesmith. The two of them lived in "an old junked-up car," writing songs, washing in gas station restrooms and, on the sheer gumption of both uncle and niece, meeting everyone they could.

On the day after she graduated high school, Dolly boarded a bus and headed for Nashville. What happened over the next thirty years is the story of the American Dream, rags to riches, from holler to Hollywood transformation of a country bumpkin into Dolly Parton, one-woman industry. The clear sound of her lovely mountain tremolo voice and her hillbilly glam image have become a permanent part of the tapestry of twentieth-century American popular culture.

In recent years, Dolly has recorded three critically acclaimed bluegrass records—*The Grass Is Blue, Little Sparrow,* and *Halo and Horns*—that have been nothing short of a songwriting bonanza and a career reinvention. Embracing her Smoky Mountain roots—Dolly jokingly calls the style "hick-hop"—she is writing and singing with a fire and conviction you might expect from a new artist with something to prove.

While many of her fifty-something contemporaries have headed for easy-money meccas like Vegas or Branson, or worse, ended up in an *Entertainment Tonight* "Whatever Happened To" segment, Dolly has kept moving forward. She says, "Just because the times are changing, you can't stop. You have to find a way to change with them. It's inevitable that things are going to change. The business, the nature of the business changes, but the songs and the talent don't ever change."

In your book, I like how you talk about the importance of maintaining a wonder for life and learning new things. Are you always learning new things about writing?

I think that learning new things about life and living and people automatically gives me new things to write. So yeah, I do think I learn everyday about writing better. But you know, I never was one of those writers. A lot of people write a formula. They write what's commercial. "You have to have this, you have to have that, you've got to have two verses and a chorus." That's what I was taught when I was young and started in Nashville. It was pretty much two verses and a chorus, but I never could get everything I wanted to say in two verses and a chorus [laughs]. So to me, some of the best songs I write just ramble on and on and on. They're more like stories. People say, "Oh, you shouldn't write a song more than three minutes long because they won't play it on the radio." But some of the songs I've written are like four and five minutes long. So I don't know if I'm really learning anything that I should learn, but I think I write better and better because I live more and more.

When you first came to Nashville in the 60s, were there certain songwriters that you looked up to or that helped you?

Well, most of my influences as singers and as writers were in my family. My family was very musical. My grandfather was a wonderful writer, and he was also a minister. But he used to write some of the most beautiful songs. All my uncles wrote, my mother wrote, my grandma wrote. On my grandpa Owens' side, his mother, who everybody called Mammy, she played the autoharp, she played the banjo, she smoked a pipe [laughs], and she wrote all these incredible songs. So I got to hear all these songs handed down. Of course, my own mother played the guitar and she used to sing. So I don't remember being influenced by anybody in Nashville. I was just young when I first started coming here. I started on radio and TV when I was ten, and I was making trips back and forth with my Uncle Bill. So it wasn't that I was swept up with other people's writing. I was just swept up with the idea of being in Nashville where the music lived, where the records were made and where the songs were written. I just wanted to come as my own writer and be my own singer.

In the early stages of writing, do you like to have a title or a storyline?

It depends. That happens to me different ways. I do write titles all the time and song ideas, things that come. I'd love to be able to write them that second, sit down and write it, but I don't always have the time when a great title will fly into my mind. So I'm always writing titles down, and a lot of times when I do have the opportunity to sit down and write, I'll often look through my list of titles and pick out a great title that's really outstanding, and I'll think, "Oh yeah, I remember, that was gonna be great," and I'll basically remember what I was thinking. So I'll use that. But, by the same token, sometimes when I'm not even thinking about writing at all, I'll just be walking through the house and I'll always have my guitars sitting around different places. Sometimes my hand just automatically reaches for my guitar and I'll pick it up and without thinking, I'll say, "I'm just going to hit a lick here just to hear the sound of music." Sometimes it sounds really good and it'll hit a chord in me and I won't have anything in mind and it'll all come out at one time. I'll just start playing and I'll just start singing some words and all of a sudden, something will pop out, then before I know it, I've started a song.

I'd like to mention a few of your songs to find out what inspired them—"Jolene."

My husband's really good looking, and he's one of those people who gets sweet crushes. He had his girl at the bank that he liked. It's perfectly fine with me. This girl was a redhead. Her name wasn't Jolene, but I'd always know when he'd go to the bank, and I'd always kid him. "Now I know we ain't got that damn much money. What are you doing hanging out at the bank?" He'd say, "Oh, I'm just going to see my girl." So I just took that idea as far as the love interest. As for the name itself, there was a little girl that had come to a show that I did with Porter Wagoner. We used to sit on stage afterwards and sign autographs. And there was this one beautiful, little redhead girl. She must've been eight or nine years old. She was wanting an autograph, and I said, "You are the prettiest thing I've ever looked at. What is your name?" And she said, "Jolene." I said, "That's a beautiful name, and I'm going to remember that and write a song about that someday. So if you ever hear a song on the radio called 'Jolene' that I'm singing, then you'll know it was about you." I never heard from her though. I thought maybe through the years I might. On stage I used to say, "Here's a story about this little redhead girl that was trying to steal my husband. Years went by, and now I wish to hell she had" [laughs].

"Daddy Come and Get Me."

That was one of those songs that I wrote with my Aunt Dorothy Jo. We were just sitting and writing, and she had this aunt who had a lot of emotional problems. Mostly because her husband drove her crazy. He was a real cheat, a womanizer and everything. She was so in love with him, but he just treated her terrible. He tried to make her think she was crazy because she cried so much, and that she was imagining all this stuff. She wasn't crazy, of course. But at one time, he was trying to get rid of her to go with this woman who he'd really taken a shine to, and he put her in a damn mental institution. Of course, the family got her out and all, but we just based the song loosely on that.

"Coat of Many Colors."

That's my favorite style of writing. That's more natural for me than trying to just do a few words in a simple song. To tell a story, I can rhyme words really good, and to me, it's the same as writing a book. So I really enjoy it. Usually, I just start out writing and I think, "I'm going to write and I'm not going to think about how long it is or how many verses I got before I get to the chorus, or how many times I go back to the chorus. I'm just going to write what I think and what I feel, then if I have to tear it down and fix it up to make it commercial, then I'll do that." But it's much easier for me to write the story songs. Boy, I can tell you a story in a minute. Honestly, I can sit down and write a big long story song much easier than I can the other kind—the more commercial, typical songs.

"Down from Dover."

I was on the bus one day with Porter and we were riding through Dover, Tennessee, and I was sitting at the window of the bus, and what really made me write that song was that this cloud went across the sun and it swept a shadow across this field I was looking out at through the window. I just saw this crawling shadow across this field—it wasn't clover, but it rhymed with Dover and we were in Dover [laughs]—but whatever was in that field, the shadow swept across it. And I sang, "And the sun behind the cloud just cast a crawling shadow over the fields of clover." That was the first thought that came to my mind, and then I thought, "Time is running out for me and I wish that he would hurry down from Dover." It was like little word triggers. All of a sudden, I thought, "This is great and it's a pretty tune. What'll I write about? Who would live in Dover? Some simple girl would live in Dover, because it was like a simple, country town." So automatically I started thinking about, "What would I write about?" And the next thing I knew I was writing about this pregnant girl. Anyhow, it just came and boy, once I got into it, it was one line after another. I love to stay in there when I'm writing the story [laughs]. I don't want to get out until I'm through with that movie.

As somebody who didn't know much of your older material until recently, that song really surprised me because it was so dark.

Back then, most of the stuff I wrote was dark and sad. There were story songs like "Daddy Come and Get Me," "Jeanie's Afraid of the Dark" and all those sad-ass songs. "Down from Dover"—that was so ahead of its time, but nowadays that would be very tame on the radio. You certainly could talk about a girl having a baby. We released that as a single and they wouldn't play it on the radio. They wouldn't play it because it was so suggestive and it was about a pregnant girl and it was so against what country radio was at that time. I just thought it was great. But now, boy, they can just say everything in a song [laughs].

Do you feel like those dark songs go against the grain of your image as Dolly Parton?

It goes against my image, but it don't go against who I am. There are many sides to me. But everything I ever wrote, I'm proud of. I was that girl. I didn't get pregnant, it wasn't a true story about me as many of my songs are based on things that I've experienced. But I had had numerous nieces and relatives that had gotten pregnant and their daddies wanted to kill the boy that done it. I was just trying to find a way to make it as sad and pitiful as I could. It's not against my nature at all. In fact, when I hurt, I hurt all over and I've been through some major sad things in my life. But I also have that other cheerful side and I try to show my best. This is my image. I'm a very positive person. In fact, I've often said that you have to work at being happy, just like you have to work at being miserable. And when I'm working on those sad songs, I'm working at being miserable [laughs], and I can do it. I've been to all them places in my emotions with broken hearts and feeling all those things.

"Just Because I'm a Woman."

It was after my husband and I had been married for a year, he asked me if I'd ever been with anybody else, and I didn't feel like lying, and I had been. But he'd never asked me before, so I certainly wasn't gonna volunteer any information [laughs]. So I said yes, and he was really hurt, he was crushed with that, and he was in a terrible mood for two or three months over that. And I just felt terrible, so I wrote that from a very personal place. Not just about women in general or how they're treated. It was just about that relationship, that moment in time—like my mistakes are no worse than yours just because I'm a woman. That all cleared up later, and that was all fine after I'd said enough times, "You can kiss my ass." I did it, and I can't say I'm sorry I did it because that was part of my growing up and part of my life. I'm just sorry that you're acting like this about it, because I could've lied to you and then done it too. If I had to do it over, I would, so I just said, "My mistakes are no worse than yours."

"Your Ole Handy Man."

It was not about me, period. I remember my Mom used to work like a dog and she'd sometimes say, "I'm getting tired of being the handy man around here." She was talking to us kids too, and Daddy, where she was having to do everything, and here with a house full of kids twice as strong. I just thought that was funny—Mama saying, "I'm getting tired of being the handy man." That's where that came from, but of course it fits so many people. But that's what you do when you're a songwriter. I can write for everybody, but a lot of songs that I've written that are totally different than what somebody thinks they are appeal to a broad audience. I'm surprised sometimes to hear all the ways that people interpret things.

"Eagle When She Flies."

Male DJs on the radio would not play that song. They hated it. It didn't do well with me singing it, because they thought it was against men and not about women. It is really a great man's song to sing, but for a woman to sing it . . . When I wrote it, I wrote it for a theme for *Steel Magnolias*, which they didn't use. But I based it on my relationship with my mother and my sisters and both my grandmothers. Because it's about the strength of women and the stuff that they had gone through, and what we went through together. It was really just about the life of women. It had nothing to do with men. It was about me, like "being a sparrow when she's broken, but an eagle when she flies," meaning you're so sensitive, but yet when it's time to fly, when Dolly Parton has to be Dolly Parton, she has to go out there and shine and smile and do positive interviews and things that people ask. But when I hurt, and when I have my personal problems to deal with, they're hard to bear. My burdens are very hard to bear. So it was really about that. It was a very personal song.

How about "I Will Always Love You"?

I wrote it when I left Porter Wagoner. [They'd been performing as a duo.] So it was so full of every kind of emotion you could imagine. You know, seven years of fighting and creativity and our success and our relationship, it was just all those things. When you are able to write all those feelings, that's what I think truly makes the classic songs. But I remember exactly where I was sitting when I wrote it, I remember the time of day, I remember the fireplace. It was in my husband's and my first house, and we had a den that was part music room. The fireplace was right in front of the couch, and I always had my writing spot when I would write there. I always sat in the very corner of the couch. You remember those days when you really wrote something great. But I pretty much remember where I was and what I felt with every song I ever wrote. Even with the thousands of songs I've written, I almost remember what time of year it was, what time of day it was, if I was inside or outside, if I was on the porch, if I was in the car. You just remember those things when you allow yourself to feel that deeply. They leave an impression.

Those simple, straightforward love songs are sometimes the hardest to write.

That one was easy because the times were so hard. And it was so hard for me to communicate with Porter . . . He wouldn't listen to nothing at that time because he was so angry and so spiteful and so mean about the whole thing that he wouldn't allow me a conversation to try to explain why I was doing what I was doing. I thought, "Well, the only way I'm going to be able to express it is to write it." Everybody can understand a song. There were so many things I wanted to say, there was so much emotion, feeling and heartache on his part and on my part. Once I started it, the song seemed to pour out.

What's the story about Elvis wanting to record the song?

Elvis loved the song. I never met Elvis and there were many times I could have. I don't know why I didn't. I think I just wanted him to always be the way he was in my mind. I had met some people that I wish I hadn't, you know what I mean? Not that you wish you hadn't, but he was just so special, he was so spiritual and out there anyway, I didn't want nothing to blow the image. But at any rate, he was here recording and he wanted to do the song, so they notified me and I was so excited. So, the next thing they said was, "But you know Elvis has to have half the publishing on the song. Everything he records, unless it's already a standard, he has to have half the publishing." I said, "Well, I'm really sorry, but I don't give my publishing to nobody. Not half of it, not ten percent of it, not any of it." I had just started my own publishing company, and I said, "If he loves the song and the song is that good then he'll record it anyway, and if he don't, well just say that I'm flattered with the thought." But I would not give up the publishing, and thank God I didn't, because that song made me more money than all of the others put together. If I'd given up half the publishing then I would've made half the money, plus I would've lost half the pride in it. It's the fact that I wrote the song by myself and published it myself just made the whole thing more special. It was not something you had to share. It wasn't the selfishness of the money, it was just that I was offended because the song was already out. I thought, "I'm not giving up the publishing." No lawyer told me not to do it. In fact, everybody else told me I was crazy. "Elvis Presley? You're saying no to Elvis Presley?" [laughs]. I didn't say no to Elvis personally. I don't even know the man [laughs].

Are there things you haven't done as a songwriter that you still want to do?

Yeah, have more hit records [laughs]. I'd love to write more songs like "I Will Always Love You," which I've written. I just wish somebody would pick them up and do them, which I think somebody will. But I'd also like to just be able to write more and have bigger records, like I said, by myself and with other artists.

You've been making records and performing for nearly forty years. What can today's new artists do to achieve that kind of longevity?

It's hard to say. Who can ever predict what good things or bad things are going to happen to you, or who's going to last, or who's going to fade? A lot of it has to do with personality, with character, your background, timing. There are so many elements. But I would just say that, certainly in my case, I've been around a long time because I've never let my business slip. I've never lost motivation. Even at times when they weren't playing me on the radio because I was an older country artist. A lot of the artists like me just threw up their hands and gave up. They thought, "Well, they're not going to play my damn record on the radio . . ." I didn't think like that. I thought, "How lucky have I been? I've won every award anybody could hope to win, I've had all these songs, I've had this wonderful career, so I'm grateful and thankful for that." But I'm not done! I never stopped writing songs, even when nobody was listening. I knew that I was going to sing and I knew I was going to write, even if I just recorded stuff and sold it out of the trunk of my car. I've often joked about that, but it's basically what I'm doing with these last three albums. I paid for them myself, then leased them to Sugar Hill. I own the masters. I'm responsible for everything. I thought, you can't give up, you can't lose momentum. You get something going. Even though somebody stops on you, you can't stop yourself. You've got to stay in the mainstream, know what's going on. You've got to do your quality work and you can't get down on yourself, you can't get depressed. If you've got a gift, you're gonna always have that gift. So just find new ways to place it, find new ways to market it. You have to always be thinking and working.

If you were going to teach a workshop on songwriting, what kinds of things would you stress?

I'm best at just having people ask me direct questions, so I don't know. I've never taught a class. I wouldn't know how to teach somebody how to write a song. I think first of all, it has to be born of you to be a great songwriter. I think you have to have that gift and that burning desire. You can learn to write a song, as we was talking about, a formula song. But I think to be a true songwriter, I think you have to really allow yourself to feel and allow yourself the freedom to write it the way you want to. I don't think you need to get yourself locked in. You might mix and match. If people are just looking to be commercial, you can still be a great song-writer and still follow a form or a formula. But I think the best thing to do is be true to yourself as a songwriter. I'd think you'd need to set aside some time to do it if you truly are serious about it, even if you have another job. I would think that sometime during the week—you know how everybody has a hobby—I'd let that be my hobby until it became my job. I would set aside a few hours a week to just devote to that, and I would listen to other people's things and see what the trend is, if, like I say, you're just going to be commercial. If you're just going to be a songwriter, do it. Just do it.

One thing about the struggle to make it as a songwriter is it can be pretty hard on the ego. You always seem like a person who has a surplus of positive attitude. How do you maintain that?

Well, I know I have a gift that God gave me, and nobody can take it away. I have to be true to the God-given gift and cannot allow for some-one to hurt my little ego and my little feelings to the point where it crip-ples what God has given me. So I have to rise above that, as all people do. You're going to get rejected. I've certainly sent more songs out than I've ever got recorded. You may send a thousand songs out or three thousand, but if you get one recorded, it was worth it. You just never know. It's a gamble anyway.

CHAPTER 6

Isaac Hayes

Interviewed 2003

Hits: "Soul Man," "Hold On, I'm Coming," "Theme from *Shaft*"

If you were born in 1970, there's a one in five chance that the soundtrack to your conception was by Isaac Hayes. While it may be hard to prove this scientifically, it's no secret that Hayes almost single-handedly invented the makeout album with his landmark *Hot Buttered Soul* LP. With four lengthy songs—including an eighteen-minute-plus cover of "By the Time I Get to Phoenix"—Hayes created a sonic aphrodisiac of smooth soul, spoken word, and suggestive sighs. "The best part about it is the foreplay and the contemplation," says Hayes.

Of course, being the high priest of carnal love is only one of his achievements. As a staff songwriter at the legendary soul label Stax Records in the 60s, Hayes wrote (with partner David Porter) such enduring classics as "You Don't Know Like I Know," "B-A-B-Y," "I Had a Dream," "When Something Is Wrong with My Baby," "Hold On, I'm Coming," and "Soul Man."

Over the next forty years, his deep-dish resume would come to encompass twenty-nine solo albums (including the groundbreaking blaxploitation soundtrack to *Shaft*), duets with Dionne Warwick and Millie Jackson, three Grammy Awards, an Oscar, an induction to the Rock 'n' Roll Hall of Fame, television ads for Pepsi and Burger King, a top-rated radio show as a DJ on New York's KISS-FM, roles in such films as *Escape from New York* and *It Could Happen to You*, the voice of Chef on the popular animated show *South Park*, a successful restaurant in Memphis (with a chain planned), spokesman for World Literacy Crusade International, and head of the Isaac Hayes Foundation (a nonprofit organization that supports various global causes). And if that doesn't make Hayes a Renaissance man, how about this? He is also an honorary African king and member of the royal family in Ghana.

Born August 20, 1942, in Covington, Tennessee, to a sharecropper family, Isaac Hayes was raised by his grandparents to a life of hard work in the fields and worship in the church. It was before the congregation that a five-year-old Isaac made his singing debut. By the time he hit his teens, the family had moved to Memphis and he'd taught himself to play piano, organ, and saxophone. He dropped out of high school to pursue music (he later earned a diploma) in bands such as the Teen Tones and Sir Isaac and the Doo-Dads.

One constant of his upbringing was the exposure to a wide variety of musical styles. "I was like a sponge when I was growing up," Hayes says, "so when the time came to really squeeze that sponge out during my creative process, I tapped into those things that influenced me—the jazz, the blues, the R & B and classical."

"Theme from *Shaft*" along with many of Isaac's other songs are now R & B staples, and have been sampled by over 140 artists, including Dr. Dre, Snoop Dogg, Destiny's Child, and TLC. Beyond Isaac's writing and performing, his Afrocentric style and political activism have set standards for black artists over the past thirty years. As director John Singleton (who did 2001's remake of *Shaft*) says, "Isaac Hayes changed the way black men saw themselves."

Though Hayes is juggling many careers these days, he says that making records is still important to him. "This fall, I'm scheduled to start doing a new album. I'm going to try to give people songs of substance, songs that stir the emotions. That is, if I'm not sabotaged by the record industry. I have to keep some artistic integrity in my music."

You've been writing songs for a long time. Has it gotten easier?

It's about the same. It's all about inspiration.

What is the most mysterious part of the process to you?

When you've been writing as long as I have, I don't think there's no mysteries about it. There's *magic* about it. You get an idea and you start working on it and it starts coming to life. That never goes out of it. That's the fascinating part about it. There are sections in a song sometime where it flows faster. When you go through the rapids, it flows very fast. Then when you get in the quiet waters, it's a little more slow coming. Sometimes it's rapids all the way and the song comes very fast. I don't know what it depends on. That's the way creativity goes. Sometimes it's fast, sometimes it's moderate, sometimes it's slow.

A lot of songwriters draw a distinction between writing consciously and writing unconsciously. How do you feel about it?

I've had that feeling where I'm like a channel. That's what I call the magic part. It just comes so easy. When it happens, it happens. You're along for the ride [laughs].

Do you remember your first week at Stax?

Man, I was scared stiff. Here I am, in this place I've always dreamed of being where all these greats have been. I'd been playing a lot of small clubs and [Stax president] Jim Stewart heard me and said, "Hey, do you want a job?" Booker T. had gone to school and Stax needed a replacement keyboard player. I'd actually been there a few times before with other bands, but they'd always turned me down. My first session was for Otis Redding. Talk about being scared. But it was a very loose vibe. We worked up the arrangements around the piano and the drums. In those days, we recorded to one track, so everybody had to really get the parts down. There were very few written parts. A lot of room for spontaneity.

When you started writing songs at Stax with David Porter, did it take a while to find your groove?

We wrote a lot of songs. When we first started, we'd be up at Jim Stewart's office every two or three hours, saying, "We got a hit!" Jim said, "Back to the drawing board, fellas." Eventually we found our groove and then we started writing just one after another. And when Sam and Dave would come to town for a session, we would meet with them a couple of nights before and write with them sitting there. And they would learn the songs as we wrote them. It came so freely and so easy. We'd go in the studio and David would work with Sam on vocals and I would work with the band on the music. It was a hell of a team.

One of your first big hits for Sam and Dave was "You Don't Know Like I Know."

That came right from the church, from a gospel tune. [Sings] "You don't know like I do what the Lord has done for me." I thought, "Well, if the Lord can make you feel good and do things for you, why can't a woman do the same?" [laughs].

What inspired "Soul Man"?

I was sitting in front of the television watching the riots on the evening news. They were protesting and burning buildings in Detroit. One of the commentators said, "Well, your building would be passed over if you've got the word 'soul' written on it. They won't torch it." Blacks were running around the streets with their fists clenched in rage, screaming, "Yeah, soul brother, yeah!" I said, "Wow, they're coming together as one." Whether it's right or wrong, they are united, and they are taking pride in the word *soul*. I thought, "Soul man, that's it."

How about "When Something Is Wrong with My Baby"?

David and I had been working in the studio all day and we got tired, and I said, "Man, let's go home." So I'd been home about fifteen minutes and the phone rang. It's David. "Man, I got it!" "What do you mean you got it?" He said, "Man, I came home and I was tired and I sat on the sofa, and my lady came around me and started to massage my shoulder. She said, 'What's wrong? Is there something wrong with my baby?'" He jumped up and said, "That's it!" [laughs]. He started writing those lyrics on a brown paper bag. We went over to a friend's house who had a piano, and he started reciting those things, and I started playing the triplets, just a simple progression. It flowed so good.

Hot Buttered Soul *was groundbreaking, in that it helped change the emphasis in R & B from singles to albums.*

I was given a free hand when I started recording my own stuff. When I was a songwriter at Stax, we had limitations because Jim wanted us to sound a certain way. If I put a nice chord in a song, he'd say, "No, no, I don't want that. Stop." But when I had a chance to do my own album, it was different. I asked [Stax business manager] Al Bell, "Can I do it the way I want to do it?" And he said, "Carte blanche, however you want." Then I was given the freedom to exercise my creativity with no boundaries. That's when I started putting the strings and horns together with the funky rhythm underneath. I didn't feel the pressure to come up with a hit record, because there were twenty-six other albums being released that spring. But doing so, I stretched and I trusted what I felt and it outsold everything at the label that spring, and a star was born [laughs].

It's been said that a lot of babies were conceived to that album. What do you think about the way the subject of sex is addressed in today's R & B?

Some of the lyrics are kind of raw. I don't want to sound old-fashioned, but they're raw. When I talked about things that I considered sexy, you didn't just lay it all out. You left a lot to the imagination. You did it with better taste. You didn't have to name body parts. Whatever happened to foreplay? These kids want to jump in and get it over with, like rabbits. The best part about it is the contemplation and the foreplay.

How did the "Theme from Shaft" come together?

Gordon Parks, the director, said, "All you have to do was zero in on the character." Shaft was a relentless guy. He was always in pursuit, he was always on the move. Gordon said, "That's what your main theme should denote." And that's where I got the idea about the sixteenth notes on the high hat. It just fell in place from there. Before I even presented it to Skip [Pitts], the guitar player, I had the wah-wah in mind. I always had a fascination with the wah-wah. I tried early on to put it on a tune that David Porter and I produced, so I liked the way it sounded, and of course, I'd heard Hendrix use it. When Skip played, I got on my knees and worked the wah-wah pedal with my hands, then he got the feel and took over from there. The lyric came easy. I did censor myself though. "This cat Shaft is a bad mother . . . shut your mouth." I did it that way—otherwise somebody would have told me to shut my mouth [laughs].

A lot of classic soul artists from your generation are struggling to stay current and reach a younger audience by using more modern beats and sounds. What do you think of the records that are being made by your contemporaries?

The best of them don't come across, unfortunately, and I blame the record companies for that. I'm not knocking hip-hop, but there's not enough depth to it. If you think about it, on the charts now, whoever has a hit record, it lasts for a week. Then next week, it's somebody else there. And people can't remember two months ago. But back in the day, when we had hit records, they'd stay at number one for three or four weeks. It stayed in the minds of people because it had more depth, had more meaning. And like I said, I blame record companies, because they're trying to make quotas. How many did we sell this week? But the art itself is suffering. These kids don't even know who their predecessors were. They don't know whose shoulders they're standing on.

I don't hear any influence in modern R & B from the great vocal groups like the Spinners and the O'Jays.

You don't, you're right. The ironic thing about it is that today's gospel is more R & B than the old R & B was [laughs]. It's got more funk to it. It's amazing. But that's the way it is.

In the late 90s, you had a second career as the voice of Chef on South Park. What did you think when you first took the part?

I was reluctant. When my agent told me I had a job doing a voice-over, I thought it was for Disney. But when I read the script it was really funny. I remember saying, "I hope you guys got insurance because you're going to get sued." The more I did it, the more fun I had. But at the beginning of *South Park*, I thought that I'd ruined my career.

If you were going to teach a class on songwriting, what would you tell your students?

I learned that a song has three areas. The opening, the middle part, and the ending. And you have to explain it. Why this? Why that? You lay your case out first, and then you explain why. To justify all of that. And you always have to make it simple. You know now, when they write songs, they take one line and repeat it over and over. I mean, I did repetitive stuff too, in the vamps of songs. I just kept grinding it out, but I was mood setting. I'd made my point already, and then I'd just keep repeating the end because it's a mood. Nowadays they take one line and going over and over and over, and that's the song. And how much was said? It makes you wonder, "Where is it going?" Also, there's so much electronic stuff going on in the marketplace. I do it too. I was forced to because promoters don't want to pay for a full orchestra anymore. So I create the same songs electronically, to simulate an orchestra, but it's nothing like the real stuff. But what you get nowadays is kids doing these various things with drum machines and samples. The record companies love it because they put very little in. Low investment and a high yield. I guess they're so insecure in their jobs that they don't think about the art. They don't think about the quality. You hear it so much, and society begins to accept it, and you begin to think, "That's the way it always was." But it's not. The reality of real songs with substance can have a profound effect on the human psyche. People don't know they're deprived of it until they hear it and feel it and it starts stirring up the emotions within them.

CHAPTER 7

Walter Becker and Donald Fagen of Steely Dan

Interviewed 2003

Hits: "Rikki Don't Lose That Number," "Deacon Blues," "Hey Nineteen"

To interview Donald Fagen and Walter Becker is to accept that at least a third of the answers you'll get will be delivered with a kind of shtick. Non sequiturs, arcane references, wry observations—since they met in the late 60s at Bard College in New York, the two friends have been volleying them back and forth with the timing and practiced nonchalance of Bob and Ray.

This affectionate give-and-take is also part of what has made them one of the most unique songwriting teams in pop history. Drawing from jazz, hipster movie soundtracks, Brill Building pop, rock 'n' roll, and the blues (Fagen says that their approach is often about "subverting the blues"), they trade ideas, building up compositions that are both harmonically complex and catchy—a delicate balance mastered by very few. Any danger of preciousness in the music is tempered by a wicked sense of humor in their lyrics. Eschewing the typical you-and-I love scenarios, they create worlds in their songs, alive with colorful characters and telling details (consider the delicious opening lines of "Hey Nineteen" "Way back when in sixty-seven/I was the dandy of Gamma Chi"). Drop the needle (or laser beam) down anywhere in their recorded works—"Bad Sneakers," "Any Major Dude Will Tell You," "Kid Charlemagne," "Peg," "Babylon Sisters," "Cousin Dupree"— and you're instantly transported to a place that could only be Planet Steely Dan.

This interview coincided with the 2003 release of *Everything Must Go*, their second album after a ten-year hiatus.

You've been writing songs for over thirty years. Has it gotten easier?

Becker: We have sort of an ongoing thing, almost a pipeline situation, where we have titles and bits of music, spare parts, ideas and songs that we wrote that we didn't use on a previous album. So we were able to ramp up pretty quickly and get the writing done for this album. We did it, for the most part, in about the half the time that it took for the one before. Partially that's because we were already up and rolling.

Fagen: That was like a start-up, *Two Against Nature*.

When you revisit these fragments and ideas, is it difficult to reconnect?

F: We'll be writing something in the present and something will remind us of something we've already written. I'm playing the piano and I'll have a chord, then my hand will go to some other chord that seems right, and it turns out that it's something we wrote but put aside a while back. We've been piling up years worth of stuff.

Are the fragments mostly musical?

B: We have lyric things, we have titles. Songwriters realize that the thing that comes at the beginning, the sort of seed idea for the song or the story or whatever it is, is really important, even if it's just a fragment. Just having a list of possible names for songs that we thought we might write someday is really very helpful.

Donald, you've said that you feel like most artists only have a few years when they're at their most inspired, then it becomes a matter of maintaining some kind of standards. As songwriters, how do you fight against that inevitable slide that seems to affect so many artists?

F: You don't put out material just to put out material. If you have some years where you don't have anything percolating, then it's best not to put anything out. You have to sort of stand by that, even if you're broke [laughs].

B: Although, in my experience, the years that you're broke are the years that you do put something out [laughs]. The other thing is, we don't write songs for other people, for the most part. Donald has had a few tunes done here and there, but sort of our entire output pretty much goes into the Steely Dan records and the solo records that we've done. And we throw away a lot of stuff. We have a lot of songs that we've deleted. I think that other people who are producing more probably include more of those things that we have the luxury of not including because we make as few records as we do.

F: I think when we weren't together or weren't writing, we took other kinds of jobs. I was working on various things, writing for movie scores, and Walter was producing jazz records. You have to find something to do during the daylight hours. I think your unconscious is working anyway and you just have to wait. As Walter says, sometimes when you get really desperate, your mind will get working. Desperation is a great motivator.

Also, maybe just having a songwriting partner helps to challenge you to do your best work, keeps you honest.

F: I think you're right about that.

B: It also keeps you productive in a way. Whereas you could sit by yourself and be stumped or blocked, or you could go off on a lengthy self-indulgent tangent of some sort—in a way that is your personal thing. If you're doing it with a partner, you're less likely to get off on those tangents, and you're less likely to keep going back and sitting there day after day if you're not producing anything. If nothing's happening, you stop doing it. I think also, with a partner, it makes it more amusing. You're not just confronting problems. On the days that you have where you don't get a lot done, you do something else. You have a few laughs. You go for a walk, or otherwise console yourselves one way or another.

F: Or write little screeds for the Web site.

B: That's right. Nurse our petty grudges against various members of the human race [laughs].

F: Also, there's always someone there to say, "You know, that idea is psychotic. Let's go onto the next one, okay?"

B: "That's not a chorus, that's a cry for help."

Have your roles in the cowriting relationship changed over the years?

F: I think when we first started writing in college, maybe Walter was initiating more music. I think now it's sort of like, there's usually some kind of kernel that's developed before we start. The input on lyrics seems to be about the same as it always was.

B: Also, I'm a computer programmer now, because when we're writing, we're essentially making the demo at the same time. It's a relatively superficial element to the job, but it does somehow bridge those things together—the writing and recording.

Let's look at the opening track on the new album, "The Last Mall." How did that evolve?

F: It started as an idea and we came up with the basic storyline. It defined itself as a blues early on.

B: Once you know that, in a general way, you sketch in the details later. I think at one point we had on our idea list something about the "Three Sad Malls."

F: "Three Sad Malls" was another idea we had. Near where Walter lives, there were these three malls, right next to each other. The one that was originally built there in the 50s, then there was kind of an updated mall, a little more modern, then there was a yet more modern and grand mall. It was interesting, because the first mall from the 50s had a mostly ethnic population and it was the lowest economic level, and it increased going up to the most modern mall, where the more upscale people shopped. So we had this song called "Three Sad Malls" that was going to talk about that, but we never wrote it.

That song and others from past records like "Chain Lightning" often sound like blues progressions, but there are all kind of interesting things you do to subvert it.

F: We've used a lot of blues to start with. I think every once in a while college kids get into blues—urban blues, Chicago blues, Delta blues. And one of these movements happened in the early 60s when we were in school, and both Walter and I were in pickup blues bands here and there, doing Muddy Waters songs. Out of that movement came Eric Clapton and all these white guys who learned to play blues guitar. It's always been one of our favorite things. Within jazz, blues is the core of many jazz compositions and blues is what guys can play when they meet each other for the first time. Just for practical reasons. They may not know certain songs, but everyone can play the blues. There's something very satisfying about it. It doesn't get boring. And there's also a tradition of subverting the blues within blues and within jazz. Duke Ellington was an amazing blues subverter. He used to love to start with the blues and then add a section.

I noticed that when you were on **Piano Jazz** *recently, you covered "Mood Indigo" and "Star Eyes." I assume that as listeners you're drawn to those kind of classic, sentimental love songs. Have you ever tried to write that way?*

F: I don't know if I'm drawn to sentimental love songs. I think the literature of jazz has always been the standards of the 20s, 30s, 40s, and 50s—most of which have romantic lyrics. I think we're drawn to those mostly because they are the bones of what you improvise on when you're studying jazz.

B: By and large, the lyrics of those songs are the least interesting and ultimately the most limiting aspects of them as songs. I think, for example, one of the things that's hard for me listening to most any jazz song is, "Now we've got to sing 'Body and Soul' or 'I Can't Get Started.'" I don't want to make another journey through that lyric. I've heard it so many times, and it's only so good to begin with, in many cases, and it was stylized to the traditions of the day. There are some spectacular exceptions, of course. But I think some qualified people, as a group, should undertake the job of getting permission, then rewriting the lyrics of the standard songs, so that some new jazz singer can sing "Stella by Starlight" with another set of lyrics. In my opinion, you're not tired of hearing the music, but you are sort of tired of the lyrics in many cases. So I propose that as an endeavor. It wouldn't take much. I think other composers would soon start to follow in our footsteps, don't you? [laughs].

F: I think it's part of the impulse of singers like Jon Hendricks and people who improvised and scatted over the choruses to songs and wrote lyrics to fit the scat ideas. That's part of what Charlie Parker did too, writing melodies over chords. It's boring to play the same melodies. So one of the functions of jazz is a kind of rescue operation to keep these songs interesting and fresh.

B: Operation: Jazz Rescue [laughs].

Steely Dan songs are always harmonically rich. If songwriters wanted to liven up their chord progressions, what would you suggest?

F: Look to another genre, and start your search there.

B: Realizing that chords may have more than two or three notes in them would be one way. Another way would be to use chords with two or three notes but don't use the right bass notes.

F: Read Schoenberg's harmony book. It's very enlightening.

B: Joni Mitchell developed quite an elaborate system of playing triads with different bass notes to achieve a certain effect.

F: We used to be big fans of Laura Nyro, and she would substitute bass notes in a great way. She had a way of combining soul music with more interesting chords. You'd also hear it in Motown records. It's funny, because with classical harmony, they'd already gone through this, with Stravinsky and Bartok and Hindemith, but pop music started doing it a little bit later.

B: One of the problems with more sophisticated harmony is that it has a lot of unwelcome baggage for pop music, in many cases. So you want to avoid the associations that people have with major seventh chords and diminished chords with other kinds of music that tend to make the thing not sound like pop music or not sound tough or whatever. One of the things that we've worked a lot on is trying to get that richness without getting all of the negative sonic connotations that people seem to have in connection to that stuff. That's why I think Joni Mitchell or Laura Nyro, instead of playing a C major seventh chord, they would play a G triad over C, eliminating the E, and you get some of the lyrical feeling of a major seventh chord, but not so much of the sentimental feeling.

F: If you take the third out, it's not as saccharine. It's more austere sounding, and yet has the major seventh. When you hear Laura Nyro's music, you wouldn't think lounge. Although of course now, lounge players do that too.

When you guys finish a song, is there a checklist you go through to make sure it's the best it can be?

F: I don't think it should ever be boring. Sometimes you can just let the track go with nothing on it and if the track's sufficiently entertaining, that's fine. As long as your mind doesn't drift, you know?

B: There are definitely times when we write a song and take it in and try to record it, and then realize that "Oh, this doesn't really work." It needs another section. There are a lot of times when we think a song is finished and then work with it a little bit or live with it a little bit, then go back and change or add to it.

F: Sometimes you have to thin it out. Sometimes we've got too many chords in it. Like if you write a song with a thousand chord changes, it would be the most boring thing you ever heard, because it has too many chords.

You once said that a successful song is one that would make you laugh when you listen back to it. Is that still true?

B: I don't feel it as necessary that other people's songs make me laugh, although I like it when they do, in the right way. But I definitely like it when our songs have a humorous component to them.

F: Sometimes with music that is really great. I don't think there's anything particularly funny about it, but my response will be to laugh at it. Even something like Stravinsky. I don't know exactly why. Something about seeing the way a great artist controls all the elements in a certain way and causes something to happen—it somehow causes a laughter response.

B: It's a complicated thing in general about why people laugh.

F: I'll laugh at the sad parts of Fellini movies.

B: Part of that has to do with the idea that you're not entirely engulfed in the reality of the work of art. You're also looking at it simultaneously from a slight remove and you're thinking about the artist making that work of art. And when you see him pull off an incredible trick, even if the essence of the trick is to produce a powerful sad emotion or something like that, you're amused and delighted that he did it.

F: You want to give the artist a right-on handshake.

Let me mention a few more of the new songs to get your reaction. "Godwhacker" is interesting. Putting a hit out on the big guy upstairs.

B: It seems like a natural thing to be thinking about at this point in time, especially in light of recent history.

F: I think the state of global affairs and so on and the condition of man is a good enough reason to want to make some changes.

B: At the top [laughs]. I think it reflects a legitimate dissatisfaction. Musically, it has a certain hunting-down quality.

F: Cop show jazz, for many years, has been one of the elements that we like to draw on. I think we've mentioned in previous interviews that we were not only jazz fans but fake jazz fans as well. Fake jazz sort of followed modern jazz with amazing rapidity. Almost as soon as bebop had established itself, a kind of fugitive bebop appeared on television.

B: That's why they say the white man is the devil.

F: Fugitive jazz is just jazz with a visual association to go with it.

B: Usually originating somewhere in California [laughs].

"Lunch with Gina."

F: About a scary but interesting girl. Especially celebrities sometimes have to deal with obsessive fans or stalkers. I think anyone who's been in a relationship has realized that there's something imbalanced about it at times.

B: You can see that this is completely crazy, but still not be able to dismiss it.

"Pixeleen."

F: There's an element of Japanese animation in the lyric.

B: Think of it as a pitch for some television series/game show/computer game tie-in.

F: I remember when we wrote it, we thought, "Maybe someone will make a Pixeleen show." Teenagers now, their lives are just so saturated by media, it appears that they have no life left. It's all about tie-ins with other various formats, none of which include actual real life [laughs].

How about an old song—"Doctor Wu"?

F: I used to know what that was about, but I don't anymore. I used to have a girlfriend from Florida and that relationship kind of permeates that song, but we added a lot of other stuff to it.

B: That was a song that it was never easy to say what it was about.

"Peg."

F: "Peg" has a kind of psycho chick thing about it, a little bit. It's kind of a combination between "Pixeleen" and "Lunch with Gina."

B: Psycho chick lite [laughs]. The girl in the song is more shallow than predatory. A garden-variety climber.

F: It's about someone who's not obsessed with you, but they're obsessed with success.

If you were going to teach a class on songwriting, what would you tell your students?

B: A writer writes [laughs].

F: Never buy a hat through the mail [laughs].

B: I would advise them—borrowing from John Gardner—to avoid the "frigidity of Longinus" [Cassius Longinus, c. 213–273, a Greek rhetorician and philosopher].

F: The frigidity of Longinus? You mean when your watch has stopped? [laughter].

B: John Gardner describes frigidity as failing to sympathize with your characters in a way, being false to your characters in a way that your reader understands.

F: Don't ever get involved with technique to the point where it becomes too important. It's the least important thing to have. Some people think it's the most important, at least conventional technique. Make up your own technique.

Are there things you haven't done as songwriters that you'd still like to do?

B: We still haven't invented an entirely new kind of music, which was an ambition we had briefly sometime around our third or fourth album.

F: A lot of times we think, "Let's just throw out all the stuff that we know and what we want to hear and what we would want to make." The stuff that you know is like part of your body. There's something contrived about most people's revolutionary works.

What are some records that influenced you most as songwriters?

All Duke Ellington records
Bob Dylan records from the 60s
Miles Davis Quintet from the 50s and 60s
Dionne Warwick records with Burt Bacharach/Hal David songs

Stax records

Sam and Dave

Otis Redding

Howlin' Wolf

Stravinsky

Ray Charles

CHAPTER 8

David Bowie

Interviewed 2003

Hits: "Space Oddity," "Fame," "Let's Dance"

"I'm not just looking to write a good song," says David Bowie. "I'm looking for something else. I'm looking for reharnessing energy somehow. And often an album will have good songs on it, but it's not enough for me. The song is merely a by-product, often, of what it is I'm really trying to do."

Ever since 1969, when he first appeared on the radar as a marooned astronaut named Major Tom, David Bowie has engaged fans and critics with those creative reharnessing efforts. Half the fun of following this chimerical artist has been trying to fathom what he'll look and sound like when he emerges from his next creative cocoon.

To be a Bowie fan in the 70s was to be continually astonished by each new incarnation. In 1974, he released the apocalyptic rock 'n' roll of *Diamond Dogs*. In 1975, the Philly soul-influenced *Young Americans*. The next year, the jagged, noisy *Station to Station*. The year after that came the chilly minimalism of *Low*. Despite the stylistic zigzags, Bowie regularly landed singles on the charts. And of course, each album was accompanied by a completely different physical style for the singer. The obvious difference in today's release schedules aside, there is nobody in contemporary music (with apologies to Beck and Radiohead) who even comes close to this kind of successful artistic reinvention.

Though the physical transformations in his recent work have been more subtle, Bowie continues to surprise with his sonic explorations (in the last decade alone, there was the drums 'n' bass of *Earthling* and the concept art of *Outside*). He has also diversified to pursue other interests: Web host, journalist for an art magazine, wallpaper designer, photographer, painter, actor and one-man corporation (in 1997, he became the first pop star to offer himself as a share issue).

The one constant through all of his changes is brilliant songwriting. His claim that songs are "by-products" aside, there's no denying the enduring power of songs such as "Life on Mars," "Changes," "Ziggy Stardust," "Suffragette City," "Rock 'n' Roll Suicide," "Jean Genie," "Rebel Rebel," "Fame," "Young Americans," "Station to Station," "Golden Years," and "Let's Dance."

In 2003, David Bowie released his twenty-third album, *Reality,* and embarked on his first world tour in over a decade.

When you're writing songs, how important is it for you to return to a kind of beginner's mind about it?

I understand that very well, and it is terribly important for me to do that. It's absolutely essential that I get surprised and excited by what I'm doing, even if it's just for me. I think process is quite important; to allow the accidental to take place is often very good. So I trick myself into things like that. Maybe I'll write out five or six chords, then discipline myself to write something only with those five or six chords involved. So that particular dogma will dictate how the song is going to come out. Not me and my sense of emotional self. Of course, I'll cheat as well. If I've got the basis of something really quite good coming out of those five or six chords, then I'll allow myself to restructure it a bit, if I think, "Well, that could be so much better if it went to F-sharp" [laughs] or something like that. But to define the rules, then take it as far as you can go with that little rule, then break it, I find is really a way of breaking writer's blocks as well. I don't have writer's blocks in that way.

Do you still use the cut-up methods from Burroughs to write lyrics?

Absolutely. I'll use them to provoke a new set of images for me, or a new way of looking at a subject. I find it incredibly useful as a writer's tool. And I'm amazed these days at the amount of cut-up sites that are now on the Internet. It's quite phenomenal. There are at least ten, and two or three of them are excellent. I've used them too. I've put a bunch of pieces of text into the thing, then hit the "cut-up button," and it slices it up for me [laughs]. In 94, when I was really starting to get into the computer in a major way, I had a program devised so that I could specifically do that. And most of the lyric content of the *Outside* album came out of that program. But now, they're all over the place, especially on poet sites. There are a lot of poets who still work in that method, so I'm not alone.

This idea of juxtaposition and pasting together has been kind of fundamental to what you do as an artist.

I think that was my premise for writing and making music when I was a kid. When I'd gotten a little more sophisticated and had a more rounded idea of what I was as an artist—and it wasn't immediate by any means—but around the late 60s, early 70s, it really started to all come together for me as to what it is that I like doing, and what satisfied me the most. And it was a collision of musical styles as much as anything else. I found that I couldn't easily adopt brand loyalty [laughs], or genre loyalty. I wasn't an R & B artist, and I wasn't a folk artist, and I was this artist or that kind of artist, and I didn't really see the point in trying to be that purist about it. What my true style was is that I loved the idea of putting Little Richard with Jacques Brel and the Velvet Underground backing them. What would that sound like? [laughs]. That for me was really interesting. It really seemed for me what I was good at doing and what I enjoyed was being able to hybridize these different kinds of music somewhat.

"Rock 'n' Roll Suicide" from Ziggy *Stardust is a great example of that.*

Right. To go from a 50s rock-flavored thing with an Edith Piaf nuance on it produced that. There was a sense of French chanson in there. It wasn't obviously a 50s pastiche, even though it had that rhythm that said total 50s. But it actually ends up as being a French chanson. That was purposeful. I wanted that blend, to see if that would be interesting. And it *was* interesting. Nobody was doing that, at least not in the same way. The same approach was being adopted by a certain number of artists from that era.

It's something you definitely shared with Roxy Music in the early 70s.

Yes, we came from art school–based thought, and I think we were all very aware of George Steiner and the idea of pluralism, and this thing called postmodernism which had just cropped up in the late 60s, early 70s. We kind of thought, "Cool, that's where we want to be at. Fuck rock 'n' roll! It's not about rock 'n' roll anymore. It's about: what is content, and how do you distance yourself from the thing that you're within?" All these kinds of things were terribly exciting. Both sides felt that we were on the cusp of something absolutely new, a new sense of dualism. There were no absolutes. Nothing was necessarily true, but everything was true. It was all this sense of "Wow, you can do anything!" [laughs]. You can borrow the luggage of the past, you can amalgamate it with things that you've conceived could be in the future, and you can set it in the now. And it was like, "Wow, this is no longer rock 'n' roll. This is an art form. This is something really exciting." We got off on that, kind of knowing that there weren't too many people thinking in that way. I think certain things had been done that were not dissimilar, but I don't think with the sensibility that I had. We knew that our sensibility was right on the money in terms of the 60s were so over, and this 70s thing was a harder, more cynical, ironic place, and the attitude was a whole different thing. It wasn't love and peace and beads. This was something else, like "What a fucked-up society. Let's see what it sounds like" [laughs]. The sense of pulling away from it all.

I'd like to ask you about a few of your songs to get your reaction—"Space Oddity."

In England, it was always presumed that it was written about the space landing, because it kind of came to prominence around the same time. But it actually wasn't. It was written because of actually going to see the film *2001*, which I found amazing. I was out of my gourd anyway, I was very stoned when I went to see it, several times, and it was really a revelation to me. It got the song flowing. It was picked up by the British television, and it was used as the background music for the landing itself in Britain. Which I'm sure they really weren't listening to the lyric at all [laughs]. It wasn't a pleasant thing to juxtapose against a moon landing. Of course, I was overjoyed that they did. Obviously, some BBC official said, "Oh, right then, that space song, Major Tom, blah blah, that'll be great." "But he gets stranded in space, sir." Nobody had the heart to tell the producer that.

"Heroes."

I'm allowed to talk about it now. I wasn't at the time. I always said it was a couple of lovers by the Berlin Wall that prompted the idea. Actually, it was Tony Visconti and his girlfriend. Tony was married at the time. And I could never say who it was [laughs]. But I can now say that the lovers were Tony and a German girl that he'd met whilst we were in Berlin. I did ask his permission if I could say that. I think possibly the marriage was in the last few months, and it was very touching because I could see that Tony was very much in love with this girl, and it was that relationship which sort of motivated the song.

I have a friend who said he saw you perform the song in Berlin in 1987 at the wall.

I'll never forget that. It was one of the most emotional performances I've ever done. I was in tears. They'd backed up the stage to the wall itself so that the wall was acting as our backdrop. We kind of heard that a few of the East Berliners might actually get the chance to hear the thing, but we didn't realize in what numbers they would. And there were thousands on the other side that had come close to the wall. So it was like a double concert where the wall was the division. And we would hear them cheering and singing along from the other side. God, even now I get choked up. It was breaking my heart and I'd never done anything like that in my life, and I guess I never will again. But that was so touching. When we did "Heroes" it really felt anthemic, almost like a prayer. I've never felt it like that again. However well we do it these days, it's almost like walking through it compared to that night, because it meant so much more. That's the town where it was written, and that's the particular situation that it was written about. It was just extraordinary. I was so drained after the show. It was so wonderful. We did it in Berlin last year as well and there's no other city I can do that song in now that comes close to how it's received. This time, what was so fantastic is that the audience—it was the Max Schmeling Hall, which holds about ten to fifteen thousand—half the audience had been in East Berlin that time way before. So now I was face to face with the people I had been singing it to all those years ago. And we were all singing it together. Again, it was powerful. Things like that really give you a sense of what performance can do.

"Rebel Rebel."

There's a new recording of it that they're using in the *Charlie's Angels* movie. It's the version that we've been playing on the shows this last year. I hadn't done it in quite a few years, so we restructured it and made it more minimal, and it works really well.

When I was high school, that was the riff by which all of us young guitarists would prove ourselves in the local music store.

[Laughs] It's a real air guitar thing, isn't it? I can tell you a very funny story about that. One night, I was in London in a hotel trying to get some sleep. It was quite late, like eleven or twelve at night, and I had some big-deal thing on the next day, a TV show or something, and I heard this riff being played really badly from upstairs. I thought, "Who the hell is doing this at this time of night?" On an electric guitar, over and over [sings riff to "Rebel Rebel" in a very hesitant, stop-and-start way]. So I went upstairs to show the person how to play the thing [laughs]. So I bang on the door. The door opens, and I say, "Listen, if you're going to play . . ." and it was John McEnroe! I kid you not [laughs]. It was McEnroe, who saw himself as some sort of rock guitar player at the time. That could only happen in a movie, couldn't it? McEnroe trying to struggle his way through the "Rebel Rebel" riff.

Had you met Warhol before you wrote the song "Andy Warhol"?

No, and I took the song to the Factory when I first came to America and I played it to him, and he hated it. He loathed it. He went [imitates Warhol's blasé manner] "Oh, uh-huh . . ." then just walked away [laughs]. I was kind of left there. Somebody came over to me and said, "Gee, Andy hated it." I said, "Sorry, it was meant to be a compliment." "Yeah, but you said things about him looking weird. Don't you know that Andy has such a thing about how he looks? He's got a skin disease and he really thinks that people kind of see that." I was like, "Oh, no." It didn't go down very well, but I got to know him after that. It was my shoes that got him. That's where we found something to talk about. He liked my shoes. They were these little yellow things with a strap across them, like girls' shoes. He absolutely adored them. Then I found out that he used to do a lot of shoe designing when he was younger. He had a bit of a shoe fetishism. That kind of broke the ice. He was an odd guy.

"Fame."

Fame itself, of course, doesn't really afford you anything more than a good seat in a restaurant. That must be pretty well known by now. I'm just amazed how fame is being posited as the be-all and end-all, and how many of these young kids who are being foisted on the public have been talked into this idea that anything necessary to be famous is all right. It's a sad state of affairs that it's that way round. However arrogant and ambitious I think we were in my generation, I think the idea was that if you do something really good, you'll become famous. The emphasis on fame itself is something new. Now it's, to be famous you should do what it takes, which is not the same thing at all. And it will leave many of them with this empty feeling. Then again, I don't know if it will leave many of them with this empty feeling, because I think a lot of them are genuinely quite satisfied if they get that. I know a couple of personalities over in England who are famous for being famous, basically. They sort of initially came out of the pop world, but they're quite happy being photographed going everywhere and showing their kids off and this is a career to them. A career of like being there and turning up and saying, "Yes it's me, the famous girl or guy" [laughs]. It's like, "What do you want? Is this great?" It's so Warhol. It's as vacuous as that. And that to me is a big worry. I think it's done dreadful things to the music industry. There's such a lot of rubbish, drivel out there.

The song has its roots in something by James Brown, right?

It was a guitar riff that Carlos Alomar had. He used to play in James Brown's band and he'd come up with this riff for a piece called "Foot-stompin'." When we were in the studio, I asked Carlos, "What was that riff you had?" And it went from there.

Had you been having conversations with John Lennon about fame before the song was written?

Yes. Actually, much more to the point, we'd been talking about management, and it kind of came out of that. He was telling me, "You're being shafted by your present manager" [laughs]. That was basically the line. And he basically was the guy who opened me up to the idea that all management is crap. That there's no such thing as good management in rock 'n' roll, and you should try to do it without it. Which I did start to pull together, and it was at John's instigation that I really did without managers, and started getting people in to do specific jobs for me, rather than signing myself away to one guy forever and have him take a piece of everything that I earn.

During the 80s, you spent a lot of time on your own. You've even said that you were content to go whole days without speaking a word to anyone, just working on whatever project you were involved in. I think a lot of artists and writers struggle with this question of solitude versus companionship. Your thoughts?

That's a difficult question. Better for me is to have a family. But better as a writer, I'm not sure. Obviously it does tend to shift one's focus as a writer, having a family. Unless you make an active decision to ignore one's responsibilities as being part of a group, and kind of artificially put yourself back into an isolationist stance. I'm not keen on that anymore, because I don't think there's anything terribly impressive about being alone. I don't find it to be nice, and I don't really want to go back to being like that again. So I'd have to say it's better now. Maybe it served its purpose for me in the later 70s. I probably reached a peak of a certain kind of writing at that time, where it worked for me being that sort of pulled back from things. But what started off as being pulled back in a kind of bemused fashion started to become more—because of my addictions and all that—I think things took on a different nuance. What started off as more of an arty exercise ended up as myself almost ostracizing myself from the rest of whatever society I was in. It became more of a mental health concern [laughs]. And I think it led, actually, to a depression in my writing during the 80s. I don't think my writing in the 80s was rewarded for being in that position. And in fact, when I kind of re-emerged as being part of something, a group, or willing to have more of an affinity with the people around me, and obviously with my marriage, my writing actually improved beyond belief. From the late 80s into the 90s, and onwards, I really like what I've written. I feel that it's very strong material overall. I can't say that about the 80s. So I have to say that being in the midst of others is a better thing for me as a writer.

Does having a solid marriage with a new baby help you maintain a more optimistic outlook?

There's no way I can look at the world and say to my two-and-a-half-year-old daughter, "Oh, it's all over. Good luck, kid" [laughs]. I can't do that. I've got to find some positivism in the future. Maybe I wouldn't have bothered so much, or maybe this album wouldn't have had that half-hearted attempt to find the silver lining, if I didn't have my daughter. Because it's very easy for me to be quite nihilistic. I'm not absolutely committed to the idea that there's an evolution of any kind [laughs]. I think that things are pretty much as they always have been for the last twenty-five thousand years. I don't think we're really evolving much above the caveman sensibility. It's still about surviving and killing and looking after one's immediate family. Not much more than that has happened, frankly [laughs]. Technologically, obviously things have moved along at a speed that we don't understand, nor can control, because our emotional and spiritual sides are so far behind our abilities to manufacture stuff. So I'm not very positive, but I have to change all that.

Have you written a modern-day equivalent of "Kooks" [a song from 1971's **Hunky Dory** *that he wrote for his son Zowie] for your daughter?*

No, I haven't. I think rather than doing it in song these days, I'm actually doing it in physical actions. I might have written a song for my son, but I certainly wasn't there that much for him. Maybe I don't feel the need to have to do that this time around. It's not like my offering. I don't need one, because she's right there with me all the time. I'm not on the road to the extent I was when I was a kid. I was ambitious, I wanted to be a real kind of presence, I wanted to be something. And I had Joe, my son, very early, and with that state of affairs, had I known, it would've all happened a bit later. But these things happened. Fortunately, everything with us is tremendous. But I would give my eyeteeth to have that time back again to have shared it with him as a child. One does a child a great disservice by not being there. However, that's what it is. It just won't be like that with my daughter.

You've been making records for almost forty years. Do you remember what made you want to be a musician in the first place?

Little Richard. If it hadn't been for him, I probably wouldn't have gone into music. When I was nine, and first saw Little Richard in a film that played around town—I think it was probably *Girl Can't Help It* or *Disc Jockey Jamboree*—seeing those four saxophonists on stage, it was like, "I want to be in that band!" And for a couple of years that was my ambition, to be in a band playing saxophone behind Little Richard. That's why I got a saxophone. A good story about that. I got a saxophone and I thought, "Somebody should teach me." So I went through very early copies of the *Melody Maker* and found that one of the best saxophone players around at the time was Ronnie Ross. So I looked him up in the phone book and I found he lived in Aubington. He was the best baritone player in the jazz scene in Britain. I was like nine or ten years old, and I phoned him up and I said, "Hello, my name is David Jones, and my dad's helped me just buy a new saxophone and I need some lessons." And he said [in rough working-class accent], "I don't give lessons. I'm a jazz player." I said, "But I really want to learn." He said, "Well, what are you doing Saturday morning?" "Nothing." "If you can get yourself over here, I'll look at you." And he taught me for about three or four months on Saturday mornings. I'd get the bus to his house. Many, many years later, I did the Lou Reed album *Transformer*, and we decided that it would be very cool to have a baritone sax on it. So I phoned Ronnie up, booked him for the session, and he came along and played this fantastic solo at the end of "Walk on the Wild Side." Then at the end I went out, and at the time, I was Ziggy Stardust—red hair, no eyebrows, boots sky high, the whole thing—and I said, "Hello, how have you been?" He said, "Uh, all right, you're that Ziggy Stardust, aren't ya?" I said, "You know me better as David Jones." He said, "I don't know you, son." I said, "See if you remember this: 'Hello, I'm David Jones and my dad's just helped me buy a saxophone . . .'" And Ronnie goes, "My god!" [laughs]. That was so great that I was able to give him a gig. He had absolutely no idea that I had been that little kid who had been over to his house. He's no longer with us unfortunately, but he did talk about it in a couple of interviews in Britain. He said to me, "You should've kept at it, you would've been all right."

What records affected you most as a songwriter?

"Inchworm" by Danny Kaye [written by Frank Loesser]—it was a song that he sang for the film of *Hans Christian Andersen*. I loved it as a kid and it's stayed with me forever. I keep going back to it. You wouldn't believe the amount of my songs that have sort of spun off that one song. Not that you'd really recognize it. Something like "Ashes to Ashes" wouldn't have happened if it hadn't been for "Inchworm." There's a child's nursery rhyme element in it, and there's something so sad and mournful and poignant about it. It kept bringing me back to the feelings of those pure thoughts of sadness that you have as a child, and how they're so identifiable even when you're an adult. There's a connection that can be made between being a somewhat lost five-year-old and feeling a little abandoned and having the same feeling when you're in your twenties. And it was that song that did that for me.

The Rite of Spring by Stravinsky—it's not so much a song as a piece of music that hipped me to the idea that stuff could be really odd and still draw you in. I thought when I first heard those opening notes, "Wow, this is great!" And it had the ultimate bass riff at the end. It was like, "Man, if Jack Bruce played that, how incredible!" [laughs]. That really motivated me, that piece of music. I even tried to play it on stage once with one of my amateur bands.

"Waiting for the Man" by Velvet Underground—a friend of mine came over to the states to do some work with Andy Warhol at the Factory, and as he was leaving, Andy said, "Oh, I just made this album with some people. Maybe you can take it back to England and see if you can get any interest over there." And it was still the big vinyl test pressing. It hadn't got a company or anything at the time. I still have it. There's a white label on it, and it says "Warhol." He signed it. My friend gave it to me and he said, "This is crap. You like weird stuff, so maybe you'll enjoy it." I played it and it was like, "Ah, this is the future of music!" I was in awe. I thought, "This is the new Beatles." For me, it was a whole new ballgame. It was serious and dangerous and I loved it. And I literally went into a band rehearsal the next day and put the album down and said, "We're going to learn this song. It is unlike anything I've ever heard." We learned "Waiting for the Man" right then and there, and we were playing it on stage within a week. I told Lou that, and he loved it. I must have been the first person in the world to cover a Velvet Underground song.

"My Death" by Jacques Brel—it's very important to me as a song.

"Sure Know a Lot About Love" by the Hollywood Argyles—it was a combination of the baritone sax and the piccolo on the solo which I thought, "Now there's a great thing to put in a rock song" [laughs]. Which I nicked, then put in "Moonage Daydream" later.

CHAPTER 9

Graham Nash

Interviewed 1997

Hits: "Teach Your Children," "Just a Song Before I Go," "Marrakesh Express"

The Two Teens, the Fourtones, Ricky and Dane. You'll be forgiven for not recognizing these musical groups that rocked—or more accurately, skiffled—the schools of Manchester, England, in the late 1950s. But in the fourth band he started, known as the Hollies, Graham Nash (born February 2, 1942) found the right vehicle for his pleasantly nasal tenor voice and melodic songcraft. Along with Allan Clarke and Tony Hicks, Nash penned memorable mid-60s psychedelic pop hits such as "Carrie Anne," "Jennifer Eccles," and "Dear Eloise."

Then in 1968, a restless Nash, wanting to explore deeper issues in his writing, left to start a group with two Americans, Stephen Stills and David Crosby, and one Canadian, Neil Young. With their rich four-part harmonies and socially conscious songs, Crosby, Stills, Nash, and Young helped spearhead the acoustic-based singer-songwriter movement of the early 70s.

In the 80s and 90s, Nash devoted much time and effort to charities and political projects, including No Nukes and M.U.S.E., while rejoining his cohorts for the occasional onstage and in-the-studio reunion. In recent years, Nash has shown himself to be a talented photographer and sculptor (check out his work at www.nashnet.com), and also wrote a fine book, *Off the Record*, which explores the stories behind many well-known songs of the rock era.

You've been writing songs for over thirty years. What about the process still mystifies you?

That I'm not sure where it comes from. I've lightly tried to analyze it, but I don't want to analyze anything that's so mysterious. People have often asked me, "How do you write songs?" and to me, it's "How do you not write songs?" Open up your eyes, take a look at what's going on around you and surely, you've got to scream inside to let your thoughts out, and the way it comes out in me is music, sculpting, art, collecting, my own personal photography, and all that kind of stuff. I'm not sure what it is, but I'm so glad that it goes on constantly in my life.

Other songwriters I've talked to have said they feel like songs come through them. Does it feel that way to you?

Absolutely. That's one of the reasons I don't know where they come from. In my wildest nights, I think that some power way higher than any of us is running this whole show and I do know that I thoroughly believe that music is incredibly healing and therapeutic. So I have to think that someone wants music in this world to make people feel a little better.

Listening back to songs from different periods of your career, I was struck by how you've managed to avoid patterns in your writing. Do you think much about that?

I try not to ever repeat myself. There are songwriter friends of mine who I criticize because they do repeat themselves, and I think that's laziness in a way. I'm trying to remain as simple as possible. I've seen so many people who've studied piano for fifteen years and then I say, "Sit down and play me something," and they say, "Well, I can't. I don't have any music." Wait a second, don't you know how to play the piano? I find that mystifying, that they just can't sit down and play something. So I try to keep as simple as possible. I've never learned to read music—and that may be a failing on my part—but it seems to have worked for me. I have no problem handling large orchestras and letting them know exactly how I feel and what kinds of chords I want them to play. But it's mostly in colors and emotions rather than dots on a page. So I try to remain as simple as possible, almost childlike.

I was reading comments you'd made about your songs "Cathedral" and "Marrakesh Express," and you said that both came out of experiences with drugs. With the perspective you have now, do you think doing drugs helped you as a songwriter?

I don't think so. I don't think it helps me as a person. It hasn't for many years, because I stopped a long time ago. I think it takes up too much time—the search, the preparation, the taking of—and we don't have that time.

I think that human beings have always tried to elevate their consciousness. That's why they used to sit in rings and smoke the bark of trees in the jungle, and crush certain herbs and spices in bowls and drink it—to get higher. That's why alcohol was invented. We've always tried to get higher than our lot here, but after a while that becomes a self-defeating game, so I stopped.

What do you remember about writing "Southbound Train"?

It was the very first song that I really thought that I might be a writer. I'd done "King Midas in Reverse" earlier, with the Hollies, and I'd written some songs that I thought were deeper than the normal kind of moon-June-spoon kind of songs. But "Southbound Train" was kind of different. I liked that song, and I liked it for one reason. When I played it for Bob Dylan, he asked me to sing it twice. That was in the penthouse suite of the Warwick Hotel in New York City, in 1971. One time after another I sang it. Now it may have been that he thought it was the worst song that he'd ever heard in his life or it could have been that it was an interesting song and he wanted to hear it again. I prefer the latter.

How about "Wounded Bird"?

I wrote that for Stephen when I saw him going through some deep emotional changes involving a lady. You must understand one thing—all my songs are written for me. It doesn't matter if I wrote "Wounded Bird" for Stephen, there's a wounded bird inside me. I write for myself, period. If somebody else gets it, or likes it, or if somebody else says that's a song about so-and-so, that's fine. But there's a bit of me in every one of my songs. I recognize that fact in my writing, that there's a great deal of me. I find myself to be a very normal person who is struggling as well as he can with a very tough life. Yes, I'm privileged. Yes, I have the love of my family and friends. Yes, I have an art that I do that pays well. But it's still a tough life. You still have to get up in the morning and get your kids off to school and hope that they're safe all day, and deal with your own insanity. It's not an easy life, even if you're Bill Gates. And so, I think that with any song I write, if I can please myself, I stand a good chance of pleasing you.

In the years you spent with Joni, do you feel like there was much competition between the two of you as songwriters?

I never was in competition with Joni. I think that would be a very foolish thing to undertake. There was a short time there where she was writing and recording her second album, and I was with David and Stephen recording our first album, and Joni and I were living in Laurel Canyon that she'd write "Willie" one day and I'd write "Our House" the next day, then she'd write something, then I'd write something. But you can't compete with Joni Mitchell. She's brilliant.

How do you think your sculpting has affected your songwriting?

There's a tremendous parallel between sculpting in stone and photographing in black and white and writing songs. It's just, "Where do you want to point your energy at this particular time?" Sculpting helps my mind in the exercise of filling out and in the exercise of taking away. Sculpting is really an amazing art because you are adding by subtracting. You're discovering as you go along. You may look at a small block of stone and think it's going to be a gorilla, then you make one mistake and the stone will shatter and change your mind as to what it is. Now it's a shrimp. You have to go with those changes, you have to work with that. If I want to put a nose on the face of you, I can't stick a nose on there. I have to take everything away at the cheeks to make the nose stick out. It's very strange. If I'm stuck on a song, I'll just go to one of my other mediums. But all the time, it's on the conveyor belt in my mind being worked on and then something clicks and I go back and finish it.

If you were going to teach a workshop on songwriting, what kinds of things would you stress?

To teach my students to see. There's a big difference between looking and seeing. Looking is being able to avoid the chair in the middle of the night when you get up to take a pee. But seeing is something very different. Looking is a surface thing, while seeing is a search for the reason why it looks like it does. Why is this situation like this, why does this painting look like this, why is this happening? If I was to teach a workshop, I would start everybody seeing. Once you start to see, that action permeates the rest of your consciousness. When you see, you start making your tea better, you start looking after your children better, you start appreciating life better and deal with the depth of whatever is in front of you, instead of just casually looking at things. So much of my input is visual. As a sculptor and a photographer, too, it's visual, so I relate it a lot to seeing. For instance, watching PBS for an entire year is seeing. Watching 90210 for a year is looking. There's not much you're going to learn on that show. There's probably a lot you'll learn on PBS. So it depends on what kind of depth you want to look at your world with. There was a fabulous story told once about Duke Ellington going to play for the Queen of England. He wanted to do something really fresh and new, but he hadn't written anything in the past forty-eight hours that he thought was worth a shit. So he's in the car, and they pull up to a light, and he winds the window down. A sparrow lands on the wall next to him and squawks some improbable riff, and Duke thinks, "Wow, what a beautiful tune." By the time he got to the Queen's place, he'd already gotten his new tune that he was going to play live for her that day. That's seeing, that's listening, that's opening up every pore of your body for melody. There's melody in everything. There's songs all around. Everything's music. Enjoy the show of life. If you allow yourself to go on the journey, you will be well rewarded.

CHAPTER 10

Carlos Santana

Interviewed 2002

Hits: "Soul Sacrifice," "Samba Pa Ti," "Europa"

In 1969, he stole the show at Woodstock. In 1999, at the unfashionable age of fifty-two, he stole the show at the Grammy Awards. In the thirty years between these landmark events, Carlos Santana has trodden a career path as full of twists and turns as one of his epic guitar solos.

A quick tour: he introduced Latin rock to the masses, got famous, sold millions, fought drug problems, found a guru, made free-form jazz records with John McLaughlin and Alice Coltrane, reformed his namesake group many times, once even into a Journey-REO sound-alike band (remember "Winning"?), dropped out of sight for much of the 90s, re-emerged bigger than ever as a duet partner with young guns like Matchbox 20's Rob Thomas and Michelle Branch, then sold even more millions.

Santana, always a spiritual seeker, credits his comeback to a visit from an angel called Metatron. In ancient lore, Metatron is the first of the archangels, the one who sits nearest to the throne of God. He's sometimes known as the Chancellor of Heaven. He also occasionally does career counseling. He came to Santana in 1997 and announced, "You will be inside the radio frequency for the purpose of connecting the molecules with the light."

This cryptic message arrived just as Carlos was renewing his bond with Clive Davis, who signed Santana to Columbia back in 1969. Davis was now head honcho at Arista. After watching Carlos headline a show at Radio City in New York, the impresario called him the next day with the offer of a contract and a game plan for the guitarist's return to the charts. Davis envisioned a new album with a combination of contemporary sounds, hip guest artists, and the vintage Santana vibe. "I knew Clive would never ask me to do anything or play anything crass," Carlos says. "So I felt safe."

Big-name Santana fans eagerly jumped on board: Dave Matthews, the Dust Brothers, Eagle-Eye Cherry, Wyclef Jean, Eric Clapton, and Rob Thomas. The song that Thomas cowrote and sang, "Smooth," would be the ubiquitous calling card for *Supernatural*, an across-the-board smash that spent eleven weeks at number one. The molecules were definitely connecting with the light.

But for all his recent material success, what remains important to Carlos are the very things that he found at the Woodstock festival where he made his name: love, happiness, peace, spirituality, and music.

"Music transcends everything," Carlos says. "Music transcends Arista, Columbia, Elektra, Phillips, and Warner Brothers. It transcends all the marketing guys and all the bosses. Music transcends all that. So it's nice to work in a field where you might be around for a while, if your intentions are correct. Especially now when we have an opportunity to create a new bridge for the new millennium. We are the architects of tomorrow."

When Carlos talks, he will sometimes close his eyes and reach deep inside for his words. If some of what he says occasionally strays into precious New Age–speak, you get the sense that he believes every word. And he's very self-aware. At one point, he told me, "You know, people, sometimes they say, 'Santana has illusions of grandeur.' No. I just don't have a small ceiling. I don't put a roof on my aspirations or dreams."

What you've achieved over the last three years is remarkable. A complete revitalization of your career. Aside from the recognition, the sales, and the Grammys, what's given you the most pleasure from all that's been happening?

Renewing the bond with my wife. We're almost thirty years married. Because of *Supernatural*, I was able to stop at the peak of it and spend a year and a half just being a daddy and a husband, just doing normal, everyday things, without being Santana or Carlos or having a guitar. I got to just become a full-time person. It's very rewarding. I recommend it to people—to taste and enjoy and savor their relationship with their wife and children. There's nothing more sacred. Not Jerusalem, not the Vatican, not the Pyramids. There's nothing more sacred than your relationship with your family.

Did the time off influence your vision for the new record, **Shaman?**

Yes. I've felt more replenished. Fortunately, I'm too naive and I'm just not wired to feel pressure or to compete with *Supernatural*, or compete with anything. It was easier to be patient, and be full-on again with every artist. There was a parade of writers and singers, musicians and engineers, producers, accountants, lawyers, managers. You have to be able to honor each one, validate each one, so that that person can say, "Hey, I'm emotionally invested in this." This is why *Supernatural* became very successful. There was a lot of people who are emotionally invested, and we are all one together. It had nothing to do with Santana or Carlos, in my opinion. It had to do with reminding people that all of us are capable of feeling totality and absoluteness.

The music and lyrics on the new record are very positive. I think it's interesting that teenagers are getting into it, given that they naturally tend towards stuff that's more rebellious, like Eminem.

When I was a kid, we used to watch Boris Karloff and the Mummy and Dracula. And then there was the difference between Elvis Presley and John Coltrane. Eminem to me is like Dracula and Boris Karloff and Elvis Presley. It's more like entertainment or social commentary. But *don't* confuse it with music. Music is John Coltrane and Miles Davis and Bob Marley and Jimi Hendrix. I validate Boris Karloff and Bela Lugosi. I got a lot of joy from them, because they made Halloween every day, and it was cool to get scared. It's like raising your hands up when you go down a roller coaster. And I do validate Eminem. I'm sure he has a beautiful, gifted way to rap, different than Snoop Dogg or Notorious B.I.G. There's a place for that. I'm not saying that it's better or worse. It's just different. But for me, I was conditioned to use music to uplift and to complement and to transform and to illumine. I don't play music to bullshit anybody or con anybody, or sell anything. I utilize music basically to compel people to feel like Evel Knievel, and sit on that motorcycle and ride and dare to jump your own Grand Canyon. I relate to music from a more challenging and daring place. I dare Eminem to utilize what God gave him to take the masses into a new place. A new place where people can stop suicide, where people can stop wars, people can stop the sickness of separation between divine and evil. I dare myself every day.

That daring seems like a key to longevity as an artist.

Exactly. That's what I learned from Miles Davis and Jimi Hendrix. What are you going to do later on when you start getting like Elvis Presley where your belly's too big and the next thing you know, you're not Elvis Presley anymore. You're like a joke. Make no mistake, man. If you're not into spiritual principles, you will become a caricature of yourself really quick. I'm into having fun, but also growing spiritually. Because I only have so much time while I'm visiting this planet. We come from the light, we're going to return to the light. I push beauty, elegance, excellence, grace, dignity. I don't push guilt, shame, judgment, condemnation, or fear. That's what rappers do a lot. I'd rather push beauty and purity and innocence. All of us have those things. You might misplace it but you never lose it. So *Shaman* and *Supernatural* are successful because we're touching on something that the Beatles used to do. "All You Need Is Love," "Give Peace a Chance," "Imagine." Those songs are bigger than the Beatles now. Songs by Bob Marley are bigger than him now. Songs by John Coltrane are bigger than Coltrane now. That's what I want to be. I want to be in their company. Those are the people I equate my existence with. I never got into music to be Elvis Presley, to get attention, and to get girls. That's okay, but it's not it.

Thirty years ago, when you had to follow up the commercial success of the first three Santana records, you went in what could be said was the opposite direction, playing more free-form instrumental music. Was it a reaction to the pressure of being on top?

It played with my head, but even at that time, I was into John Coltrane, so he was showing me the difference between monetary success and spiritual success. He was showing me that there's the big picture, then there's the small ego picture. The ego always says, "Me, me, me, me, me." The big picture says, "Do re mi fa so la ti do" [laughs].

It's healthy for musicians to find validation for what they do in the music itself.

Yes. For a long time, everybody ignored me at the Grammys. That's okay. Because my phone was ringing and it was Miles Davis, Wayne Shorter, Pharaoh Sanders, Stevie Ray Vaughan, and John Lee Hooker. You can have the Grammys. Look who's calling me, man! At this point, I'm fifty-five, and I feel really grateful, because we are creating a celebration now, towards the dreams that we want to accomplish. Dreams that benefit life and people and the planet. I don't wrap myself with the American flag like Bon Jovi or Bruce Springsteen. I say, "God bless humanity" rather than "God bless America." I believe that's a better way for people on the planet in the new millennium. It's more important than the flag at this point. People are afraid to say what I'm saying, believe me. It's like the McCarthy era and the Nazi thing. The Republicans are really kicking it hard right now, and a lot of people are really afraid to say, "My passion is for the highest good of people on the planet." They say, "Oh, you're anti-American." No, I'm not. I'm more pro-humanity. If you can't see that, then you're prehistoric. You are T. Rex. I'd rather be with the angels than with the T. Rex. The angels see the highest good for humanity and life on the planet. That's my agenda. It's more fun to hang around with the angels than T. Rex. T. Rex smells funny and he's very loud and very obnoxious and very predictable.

As a songwriter, you've commented on the importance of listening to the inner radio. Can you elaborate?

Consider that Beethoven didn't get to "da-da-da-dum" [sings opening of Fifth Symphony] right away. He had to search for that phrase. Every time he did it, he kept looking at the ceiling. The same thing with Bob Dylan or Miles Davis or John Coltrane. They always look at the ceiling and listen to this radio up here. Then they bring it down. One time Louis Armstrong was in the CBS studio, and everybody had big charts of music all over the console, reading it. And they noticed that Louis just had a handkerchief and his trumpet and he wasn't reading. This guy goes, "Hey Satchmo, how do you know where we are in the song?" And Louis says, "It's very simple to me. I just close my eyes, and the whole song becomes like this beautiful tree with fruit in it, and I only play the notes that are ripe." I can relate to that. If you see it, you paint it. If you hear it, you play it. Birds don't read charts. Look how beautiful they sing. Now, if you have both, like Wayne Shorter, who can see it and hear it and read it, then you got something else. That's what Miles can do. But it's not essential. Wes Montgomery didn't read. Neither did Charlie Christian or Django Reinhardt. And they would beat out Leonard Bernstein in a second if it came to improvising [laughs]. It's all equated. If you can bring balance, then that's even better. The main thing is to hear and to play.

Are there ways to get clearer reception on the inner radio, so you can really tune in?

In the old days, you kept moving one dial until it was clear, because you get a lot of static. Your dial is your breath. Four breaths in, from your stomach, seven out. Now if you want your notes to penetrate the molecules of the listener in their heart, think of French-kissing the first time. You think, "Ooh." Because when somebody French-kisses you the first time, especially when it's a beautiful lady, everything stops, and you're in the fullness of the moment. Well, play music like that. I'm giving people a lot of clues they're not going to see in *Guitar Player Magazine* [laughs]. A lot of times, it's not about the amplifier or the guitar or the strings. It's about, "What are you thinking when you hit the note?" That's the clue right there. If you want to get clear, get your breathing together. Four in, hold it. Seven out. First, you're correcting your body attunement to the zone. The zone that John McEnroe and Michael Jordan zone into, physically. Then you got to tune in your brain to the light. You say, "I am, I am, I am the light. Holy, holy, holy is the lord of hosts." When you correct your breathing and you correct your thinking, now you can receive the other voice, that is not the little voice—the penis voice or the mind voice. But the big voice. You get that voice, everybody goes, "Damn." Jew, Hebrews, Palestinians, Apaches coming at you, they all stand at attention, because your voice becomes something that they all need to hear. Like Desmond Tutu. When you listen to him, you become quiet. You know he's saying something that will benefit everything—from your body to your family to all the people on the planet. He's not just making idle chat, man. Desmond Tutu is a deep guy. Music should be played, as much as possible, in that consciousness.

Still, I think there's something to be said for music with more modest aims—just to make you dance and sing along.

I validate 'N Sync and Elvis Presley. There's room for all that. There's room for you to lip-synch and spend four hours in [front of] the mirror learning to dance. But if you want to make a difference in the world and get paid for doing something that you love, that's something else. And that's the field that attracts me. I love Evel Knievel and I like the bullfighters and race car drivers. I like daredevils who defy gravity and time and space. I adore these people, man, because they remind me that I am also capable of grandness and greatness, and that's the best thing that you can pass on to the younger generation. Everybody's capable of higher heights. Create a masterpiece of joy out of your life. Use your adversity problems. Emotional this and that, use them as colors, use them as tools. We live in a free-will planet, but you are accountable and responsible for your choices. Those are big clues for people in junior high school and universities. You can not behave appropriately unless you perceive correctly. So we are the light. Perceive that you are the light and then you will behave like that. You'll make a difference in the world. They're not clichés, man. They're formulas. There is a formula for you to correct your thought patterns, and be successful, whether you're a plumber or a musician. The key to being successful is that you have to find something that people need a lot. Bread. Electricity. Lovers need what? Flowers and chocolate and beautiful songs. You're in demand [laughs]. I don't have a problem with commerciality and pop songs, as long as you present them in the right way.

Is there a reason that you're less represented as a songwriter on the two latest records?

It wasn't my immediate necessity to write. There'll come a time where I'll make it a priority to write all the songs and play all the instruments. But right now, I don't have that immediate necessity. Just putting "Victory Is Won" and "Novus" on there is good enough for me, because those songs seriously kick butt.

What inspired "Victory Is Won"?

Again, Mr. Desmond Tutu. He said, at the peak of brutality in Africa in the early 80s, "When the enemy was stealing our children so they could work in the diamond mines, the enemy had its knee on our throat, suffocating the life from us. We looked at the enemy and said to him, join us in our celebration. You've already lost, we've already won. Victory is won. Celebrate with us." I thought, "Wow, victory is won." I immediately heard the song. Just from one statement he made. I should give him royalties [laughs].

You seem to be drawn to people, like Tutu, who have the ability to unite. Wasn't your father a musician with a gift for bringing people together?

Yes. He was a very charismatic person. Women adored him, men adored him, children adored him. He basically sang and played the violin, but he had a lot of power. He could look you in the eye and play for you, and you felt like, "This is great." To this day, I travel around and I hear, "Man, your father, he played for our wedding or he played for my baptism," or "I met your father on this bus or I met him here, and what a lovely man, and I miss him." Wherever I go, my father already did it. And he never even got to record, except for one time when I invited him to play on a song from *Havana Moon*, with Willie Nelson, Booker T., and the Fabulous Thunderbirds. So like I said, Santana and *Supernatural* and *Shaman*—I've been doing this for a long time, and interacting with a lot of people. Sometimes people say, "This is new for you." And I go, "No, if I give you a list of all the blues players and jazz musicians that I've played with, you wouldn't believe it." I feel like I've played with just about everybody. The only ones left are Tina Turner and a few women. But I can start the circle again. There are a lot of young people, who I don't know their names, but they are just as important and I'd like to work with them also. The main thing is to honor and celebrate people and life on this planet. We're not selling beer, we're not selling anything. I respect Joe Montana and Bill Russell and people who sell beer, but that's not what I want to do.

The sound of your guitar is unmistakable. In the group, it almost takes the place of a lead singer.

Since the beginning, when I first heard B. B. King, I was always more interested in the stories that he told with his guitar than what was coming out of his mouth, with all respect to him. So not until I heard Peter Green do "Supernatural," or Jimi Hendrix create a whole song with just guitar, did I know that there was a way to have no lead vocals, just instrumental, and let the guitar tell the story. On songs like "Samba Pa Ti," "Europa," and "Victory Is Won," they tell a story more eloquently than Spanish or English or French or Japanese. Melody is immediate to the molecules. Molecules don't need ABCs to understand. Melody goes right to the cells. It rearranges the molecules, and those are the melodies that I like.

When I see pictures of you on stage playing guitar, you often look like you're in the middle of a kind of transcendent moment.

All of us are capable of having orgasms all the time. That's really holy and sacred. Orgasms. You don't just get them out of people's sexuality, you can get them in many, many ways. That's why people, when they roll their eyes and they go, "Oh, my God." There goes one. The sensation on this planet of being able to French-kiss for the first time, or every time, and feel notes like that, feel notes like Jimi Hendrix or Bob Marley or Willie Nelson. It's a wonderful thing to be alive and experience sound and notes and resonance and vibration. It's like acupuncture, and those are the needles that correct the equilibrium in people's bodies and in families and in the world and in nations. Sound is a very, very immediate tool to correct and bring balance, between good and evil, between the halos and the horns. By sound, you can correct the sickness of this planet. Not by religion or by politics. By sound. I am honored to work with sound and vibrations. Those are my fields. I don't play guitar, man, to pay the rent. I play the guitar to be like the person who created the Golden Gate. It took a lot of guts for him to submit the plans, because a lot of people told him, "It's going to cost a lot of money. It's going to take a long time, and people are going to die building it." There it is.

Can you offer any encouraging words for young songwriters and musicians?

I would say that you've got to get your connections together. You've got to get out of the bed, out of the chair, and learn where the switches are in the house, so you can turn on the lights and see what you're doing. By that metaphor, I mean, learn to implement, activate, ignite, and infuse spiritual principles in your everyday life. You say, "What the hell does that mean?" It means for you to get off your butt and don't let somebody else do it for you. It means to make the effort to correct your thought patterns, correct your breathing, and connect. Just like you connect with your electricity, you turn on the light. Well, talk to your angel, talk to God. Tell him what your intentions are. Why do you want to play music? I'll give you a clue. If you want to, like a quarterback, go deep and long, you've got to go to a higher God and a simpler God. Go to the same God who made Jesus Jesus, and Buddha Buddha, and Krishna Krishna, and Allah Allah, and Rama Rama, and Jehovah Jehovah. There's one God who made all of them who they are. In other words, connect with your own light. Daily. And then you will see how synchronicity comes to you, with enthusiasm. People want to help you manifest your dreams. It's great to hear Clive Davis on the phone. He's just as enthusiastic about working with me on this one as on the next one. Why? Because I'm not a high-maintenance pain-in-the-ass egotistical guy. He gets excited knowing that working with all those prima donnas, he's working with a guy whose dreams can also be higher than just selling records. So connect to your life. Why are you playing music? You want to be rich and famous? That's lame. You can become rich, only to rip people off, like Martha Stewart. You can become famous by shooting the president, like Oswald. But if you really, really want to make a difference in the world and do something where you have respect everywhere you go and you feel good about yourself in the morning and the evening before you go to bed, then work with your music for the right reasons. It's not how fast you play, or how slick, or how hip. Use music to complement life, to raise people's consciousness. That's the most important thing that you can do.

CHAPTER 11

Todd Rundgren

Interviewed 2004

Hits: "Hello It's Me," "Love Is the Answer," "Bang the Drum All Day"

Todd Rundgren reached a crossroads on November 10, 1973, when his ballad "Hello It's Me" rose to number five on the Billboard singles chart. One way pointed to superstardom, the other to the shadowy land of cult status.

But for Todd, it wasn't a matter of choosing. While *Something/Anything?*, the double album that spawned "Hello It's Me," was catching on a year after its release, for its creator it was already a speck in the rearview mirror. He had followed his muses into new experimental territory, releasing the ambitious *A Wizard, A True Star*, an eclectic tour-de-force on which the twenty-five-year-old wunderkind wrote, arranged, engineered, produced, and played every instrument. Though *Something/Anything?* was chock-full of potential hits, Todd refused to backtrack. "No fucking way am I releasing anything else off that album," he told his label.

He did, however, concede to perform "Hello It's Me" on Wolfman Jack's TV show, *The Midnight Special*, a move that sealed his commercial fate. Fans who were seeing him for the first time must have been shocked. Sporting blue-orange hair, eyes painted with glitter teardrops, wearing dark lipstick and a skimpy top made of iridescent feathers, Todd looked like a cross between a drag queen and the NBC peacock.

This incident typifies the erratic career choices that Todd would make over the next three decades and thirty albums, choices that would test the allegiance of even his most faithful followers. Looks, bands, labels, philosophies, styles—if it was a skin that could be shed, Todd would shed it.

The constant in this fascinating evolution has been his masterful songwriting. No matter if he was writing beautiful love songs like "It Wouldn't Have Made Any Difference," thirty-minute prog-rock pieces like "The

Ikon," ferocious rockers like "Trapped," or silly pop ditties such as "Bang the Drum All Day," he couldn't hide his enormous gift for tuneful melodies (Todd once wrote in the foreword to a songbook collection of his, "These are songs that would've been hits if I hadn't subverted them") and lyrics that addressed the human condition with an open mind and heart.

Aside from his prowess as a composer, Todd is feted as one of pop's most original producers, with a resume that includes Badfinger, New York Dolls, Grand Funk Railroad, Cheap Trick, the Tubes, XTC, Jill Sobule, and his biggest success, Meat Loaf (the *Bat Out of Hell* album helped finance many of Todd's audio and video projects through the 80s and 90s). He has also been a pioneer for enhanced CDs and online delivery. His 1995 album *The Individualist* was one of the first CDs to be offered over the Internet, where subscribers could download the music before it was released in stores. Todd was doing the file-sharing thing years before anyone had ever heard of Napster. Currently, Todd lives and works in the balmy climes of Hawaii. In April 2004, he released *Liars*, both in the form of a traditional CD and downloads to subscribers of his Web site (www. tri.com).

What was the first song or piece of music that moved you?

It would have to be some orchestral music of some kind, very early on. I was aware of the work of Richard Rodgers or Leonard Bernstein before I was aware of Elvis or Patti Page [laughs]. The first thing I ever tried to pick out as a player or musician, where I got out a pencil and drew out staves on a piece of paper and tried to actually figure out what a melody was, was probably one of the songs from [the Leonard Bernstein musical] *On the Town*. It was a sort of Latin thing and it had a flute line in it. I would try to copy the flute part, and I was actually inspired to try and learn how to play the flute. I was about five years old. This was before my love affair with the guitar.

Were you doing that with the thought that you wanted to make your own music?

I don't know whether that was my intention at the time. I'm sure I had some vague idea of eventually composing something. But at the time I think it was just a mysterious new thing to me. Not music, because it was omnipresent, but the concept involved in how music was transcribed and the ideas transferred to other players so that they could perform them.

Did your parents encourage you?

My dad was encouraging, but it was in a sense that it was a certain kind of music. Like, for instance, when pop music did happen, in particular, the Beatles and other acts that I was interested in, my dad had this hi-fi player that he built himself. He wouldn't allow any sort of pop music on there at all. It had to be only his classical long players and the other kinds of music he liked to listen to, which would also be from musicals. He was fairly high-brow in his tastes in terms of musicals. I don't recall hearing *Music Man* being played a lot in the house, but *Kismet* all the time. Even though he wasn't a musician himself, he did have fairly erudite taste in music.

By the time the Beatles came along, did you have it in mind that you wanted to write your own songs?

Yeah, but I don't think I had a good idea of how to go about it. I was well into high school before I came up with anything that resembled an original musical thought [laughs]. It probably wasn't until my senior year that I started to mess around with chord progressions that would eventually become my songwriting style. So no, I wasn't really serious as a songwriter until I was more or less sort of forced into it. It wasn't until I actually put the Nazz together that I came to the realization that "Now you actually have to start writing music" [laughs] because I had a band that I was fronting and the band had to have original material.

You've said that "Hello It's Me" is the first song you ever wrote. That's pretty accomplished for your first at bat.

As I say, I was an avid listener to all kinds of music. So, as far as my influences, even though the Beatles were the biggest thing happening, I still had all of this other music in me. The main influence for "Hello It's Me" was an eight-bar intro that Jimmy Smith played on a recording of "When Johnny Comes Marching Home." He had this whole sort of block chord thing that he did to set up the intro of the song. I tried to capture those changes, and that became the changes underneath "Hello It's Me." I then had to come up with melody and words, but the changes are actually almost lifted literally from something that was from Jimmy Smith's standpoint a throwaway.

When I interviewed Becker and Fagen, they talked about how their approach to chord voicings and harmony was influenced by Laura Nyro.

I know you've said you were influenced by her too early on. What kinds of things about her writing affected you most?

I think there is that more sophisticated R & B thing or the Burt Bacharach side of pop music that involves not just chords that are richer—major and minor sevenths and suspensions and things like that—but the sort of melodic movement and the classical counterpoint elements. That's one of the things that attracted me. But I know for a fact that her influences are the more sophisticated side of R & B, like Jerry Ragavoy and Mann and Weil and Carole King. That is Laura Nyro's lineage. She was a source for that, in a sense, and she also had her own very original and very jazz-influenced way of seeing things. It was that extra layer that made her influential. A lot of those chords she got from other people. But beyond the elements of her composition, I always thought it was the way she played her own material that really sold it. Nobody ever did a cover version of a Laura Nyro song that was as good as her original version.

At the time of Something/Anything?, *you've commented that you hit upon a formula to write songs in twenty minutes. What was your process like?*

A few years before that album, there was a point where I thought I was not going to be an artist in my own right. I thought I was mostly going to work with other artists in production and possibly be writing songs for them. As it turned out, after doing a couple of productions, there were just some sounds I wanted to hear and some musical experimentation I wanted to do, so the label indulged me and let me record my first solo album [*Runt*]. It's a real potpourri of different kinds of styles, and in some ways is a signature of the things I would do later. A lot of the songs evolved backwards, from the production that I wanted to do. I wanted to do a certain kind of thing, so I had to come up with a song so I could do that thing. By the time I got to the second album [*The Ballad of Todd Rundgren*], the significant difference in my thought processes was the introduction of pot [laughs]. A lot of people, they talk about the effects that drugs have and often think of them only in the context of them being recreational and of making you goofy and stupid. But the effect it had on me was to give me an overview on what I was trying to accomplish as a songwriter. Suddenly, I was able to write to something that sounded like a style of my own. I was writing things that were adapted to my own vocal range and capabilities, rather than trying to do it backwards. If you listen to the first album, then the second album, the second album sounds like a songwriter. The first album sounds like a producer. By the time I got to *Something/Anything?*, the kind of overview that I'd gotten about my songwriting became nearly formulaic. I remember the moment that it dawned on me. The very first song on the record, "I Saw the Light," took me approximately twenty minutes to write, from top to bottom. From the time I sat down and started banging out chords until I had all the lyrics done and I was ready to record it. It took about twenty minutes, and I said to myself, "You're not even thinking about it now" [laughs]. It's getting too easy. They were all basically starting out with C major seventh, and I'd start moving my hand around in predictable patterns until a song came out. I thought, I don't want to be that kind of songwriter.

A Wizard, A True Star *was a big departure.*

The significant development in that particular evolution was the introduction of psychedelic drugs into the mental mix.

While you were actually writing?

Well, writing to me isn't sitting down at the piano with a pencil in your mouth, the typical movie style of how songwriters write songs. I'm a terrible collaborator. I can't sit down with someone and start pulling chords and rhymes out of the air. It's possible that up until the moment I started taking psychedelic drugs, I could've been a perfectly good collaborator, because I'd sit down and those chords would just start to happen. But after that I came to realize that what's actually in my head is far more complicated than the songs that I finally come up with, because I'm still allowing myself to be constrained by basic formulas of songwriting that I didn't come up with. Somebody else invented them and capitalized on them, and everybody else realized, "Oh, that's how you write a song." And the songs are always about your relationship [laughs], and you use the word "love" all the time, whether you're thinking about love or not. All of these things came to me, and no matter how I might be improving as a songwriter, I was improving according to somebody else's yardstick, not my own.

Your process started to change?

Yes, that was the point where I realized that the studio was becoming my compositional tool. It wasn't a piano. I don't sit down at the piano with a pad or something like that. What I do is I gestate musical ideas and lyrical ideas and hope that they will, sort of like DNA, match themselves up by the time we get to the end of the process [laughs]. Eventually, my process of writing lyrics has become, for the most part, all after the fact. I completely record everything before I ever get to the vocals. That's because the studio became my compositional tool. I can continue to flesh it out until it sounds something like the final musical bed. The more I do that, the more it suggests to me melodies that belong in the song and also what the most appropriate lyric approach is for the music I'm creating. My process is completely backwards. I have a completely vague idea of the things that I'm going to write about. I figure, why do I have to come up with an actual idea first? All I have to do is just be thinking all the time, and keep an eye on what I'm thinking. And that's the subject of what I'm going to write about. The challenge for me is going to be to come up with a proper bed for ideas that are eventually going to make themselves clear to me. In a way, it's more like sculpture than it is like typical prose. It's more subtractive than it is additive. In a way, when I start out, a song could be anything. It could sound like anything and it could be about anything [laughs]. For me, it's more a process of figuring out all the things that don't apply, and don't juxtapose as I move along through this process. I'll say, "Maybe they'll work better in this other thing that I'm growing over here."

I'd like to mention some of your songs to get your thoughts about what inspired them and how they came about—"Love of the Common Man."

From a musical standpoint it may have some influence from folk rock. It's got shades of the Buffalo Springfield and other sorts of things, and possibly early Eagles and Jackson Browne. But from a lyrical standpoint, it's part of a whole kind of class of songs that I write, which are about filial love. That's what that song, and songs like "Love Is the Answer" and "Compassion" are supposed to be about. I'm not a Christian, but it's called Christian love [laughs], the love that people are supposed to naturally feel because we are all of the same species. That may be mythical, but it's still a subject.

"Bread."

As I said, I'm not a Christian and I am also not a materialist. Unfortunately, I'm in a country full of Christian materialists. I still have the sensibility that makes a lot of people think that I am born again or something like that. In fact, a lot of my songs are covered by Christian artists in the mistaken assumption that if I say "he," "it," or something like that, that I'm referring to their God or their prophet. But my religious beliefs, in some ways, are much more simple and they're much more strict, at least from my standpoint. One is, in my religion, you don't take the name of the Lord thy God in vain, which is, you never, ever align yourself with the so-called Almighty. Because you have no fucking comprehension of what that is, and how dare you assume to know [laughs] what the Almighty, whatever the hell that is, is thinking. And so whenever people say, "God wants this" or "God tells us to do this," that to me is profane. So in that sense, I'm only asking people to do what people are capable of doing. And in any one of those songs I mentioned, I have derived it out of the good book. My basic philosophy is very simple. We can solve our problems. Why? Because we created them. Stop bringing God into it [laughs]. We've got plenty enough knowledge and plenty enough resources that we can create any sort of paradise that people think they can imagine. We just don't. And that's what I'm writing about.

"Bag Lady."

There are certainly eras in which I'm not looking to do much more than write a song that's clear and concise and simply and directly performed. On an album like *Hermit of Mink Hollow*, my objectives weren't much beyond that. I was writing songs that were intended to be performed on the piano, and that didn't require a huge amount of extra embellishment beyond the bass and drums. Most of the arrangement was done with voices. Of course, there were guitars and other things, but most of the embellishment was with vocal arrangements. In a case like that, the songwriting process can appear to be fairly conventional. But I would say that I probably still did not have the lyrics completed until I had the track completed and that would be true of most of the songs on that record.

That song has a lovely, poetic lyric.

It's important to me that my lyrics have a certain poetry to them, and the only way I can make that happen is if I have a full understanding of what it is I'm trying to express. This is why I don't sit down right away and start jabbering out lyrics as soon as I've got a glimmer of an idea about what the song is. That's only the start of it for me if I think I know what the song is about. Once I think I know what the song is about, I have to exhaust my own thought processes on the topic because the first person that I have to provide for in a musical sense is me. I have to be able to listen to the stuff afterwards and not say to myself, "What the hell were you thinking?" [laughs]. Because I've listened to records that I've done, especially early on, when I didn't take the process as seriously, and I say, "What the hell were you thinking writing words like that? You couldn't have spent an extra five minutes and completed that thought properly?" Now I put off the finalization of the lyrics until right before I sing. That's the only way I can come up with my sort of poetry. I'll have fragments of lyrics laying around all through the process. One-liners, as it were. And they can grow into more elaborate ideas. Usually, if I bother to write something down, I consider it a breakthrough. I've somehow reached a moment of clarity in a topic. In particular, if it's something that people have written about before, why should I write the same thing? I have to come up with some new insight on the subject, or what's the point of me beating a horse that somebody's already beaten to death?

"Bang the Drum All Day."

When I start immersing myself in a soup of musical and conceptual ideas, I will begin to actually dream fully completed songs. They may be completely unrelated to everything else I'm doing. It isn't necessarily during the recording process. "Bang the Drum" was something that just popped into my head one night. I don't know that the song I dreamed was called "Bang the Drum All Day," but the musical part of it was fairly complete. The title lyric must've been in there too. Songs like that, I can't deny them. In other words, I have to finish them, and I have to put them on the record, even if they don't sound like they belong to me. If a song comes to you completely realized, then that's really your muse at work. If it comes to you completely realized and you don't know what it's about, and you have to figure it out, you think, "Where did it come from?" Well, it came from inside me somewhere. So there must be something in me, yet another thing that I have to uncover and examine in order to fully understand myself. For me, that's what I have to get out of the music. A greater understanding of myself. Why I do the things I do. Why I think the way I think.

Are there any songs from your catalog that are favorites of yours that you feel were overlooked?

Oh, hundreds [laughs]. Not any one in particular. I'm always surprised about the songs that do reach people sometimes. Like I say, "Bang the

Drum" is not really a song that I characterize as stylistically mine. But there's something undeniable in the response to it that's taken it to a whole other dimension. When it gets played at all these sporting events, and everyone knows the song, but nobody knows who they're listening to. In that sense, as a musician, there's probably no higher goal to aspire to than to have your music transcend you and penetrate the culture in a way that very few people are able to consciously do. Consciously create something that becomes a cultural icon in one sense or another. So it doesn't bother me that nobody knows that it's me they're singing along with. It pleases me that I'm connected to something that connects me with everyone who just gets off on singing that song. Me and them have something in common. I don't feel so separated from them now [laughs].

Any final words for songwriters?

I have to advise songwriters all the time, because when I get involved in record production, the first thing that I always make a determination on is whether the material is ready to be taken in the studio. I tell them, because I have to tell myself the same thing all the time, it's like anything else in life—the first ninety-five percent of it takes ninety-five percent of the effort. And then the last five percent takes another ninety-five percent of the effort [laughs]. People are often in a hurry to get done. At least for me, if you want to write songs, they get written when they're ready. You don't just say, "Okay, today I'm going to finish this." For me, it's all about a state of mental equipoise and it's all about the poetry of it. If it doesn't sound like poetry to me, then I'm not done. I still have more work to do. Songwriters, automobile manufacturers, anybody—it all applies. People get most of it done, and then they're just in a hurry to finish up. Where the real remarkable aspect of anything is is in the detailing. A painting looks like one thing when you're standing far away from it, but when you get up close, you can see the real difference between a master painter and somebody who's just sloshing paint around on the canvas. It's in those little brushstrokes. My advice for songwriters is to take more time. I have to say that all the time. "Couldn't you have just spent another five minutes on the bridge?" [laughs]. In a sense, you could say, it's never done. There's always room for improvement. I'm always looking to change a word here, a word there, a note here, a note there, just to constantly push it towards the best that I can make it.

CHAPTER 12

Michael McDonald

Interviewed 2003

Hits: "Takin' It to the Streets," "What a Fool Believes," "I Keep Forgettin'"

Michael McDonald likes to talk about his family. Whether it's writing his first song with his father in the early 60s or trying out the verse of an in-progress "What a Fool Believes" on his sister in the 70s or overhearing his own twelve-year-old daughter secretly listening to his latest record, *Motown*, the subject of family is intimately tied to McDonald's career, past and present. "I can't imagine what I would be doing without them," McDonald says.

Born to an Irish-Catholic clan on February 12, 1952, in St. Louis, Missouri, McDonald was surrounded by music from a young age. After he played the tenor banjo for a few years, his dad bought him an old beat-up piano. It was love at first C chord. By the time he was in his teens, he was gigging regularly ("I was a punk kid," McDonald says, "playing with musicians who were older"). So sure was he of his direction in life that he dropped out of high school to move to Los Angeles.

"My parents weren't too happy about it. I took off with a friend who was the brother of this record producer out there, Rick Jarrard. He signed me to a production deal, and to RCA as an artist. I of course thought that I'd go out and come back a couple weeks later with an album on the radio," McDonald recalls with a chuckle. "But it turned out to be an incredible thing. I worked for Rick and gained a lot of experience in the studio, playing piano for other artists, and working with world-class musicians."

All the networking led to an invitation in 1972 from drummer Jeff Porcaro to join Steely Dan. Then three years later it was on to his starmaking turn in the Doobie Brothers. It was on 1976's *Takin' It to the Streets* LP that McDonald really hit his stride as a writer and singer. Channeling his Motown and R & B roots through a more relaxed West Coast sensibility, his songs had a laid-back groove that record buyers and radio embraced. And then there was that voice. The dark chocolate tone, the slight sibilance, the keening falsetto that always seems to carry the ache of unrequited love. McDonald belongs to that elite group of American blue-eyed soul vocalists—Bill Medley, Donald Fagen, Todd Rundgren—whose sound is recognizable after a mere two notes.

In the late 70s and early 80s, he was also the most sought-after session singer in the country. Aside from his hits with the Doobies, he appeared on scores of albums as a guest vocalist. His vocal presence could elevate a good record into something hitworthy (think of Christopher Cross's "Ride Like the Wind").

For the past ten years, he has lived in Nashville with his wife Amy Holland (a terrific singer herself) and their two children, Dylan and Scarlett. In 2003, he enjoyed great success with *Motown*, an album of cover versions honoring Motor City's finest.

Your father played a big part in your musical development.

My dad was a singer. He had a beautiful voice. And he and my mom both really admired great songwriters. In our house, that was a noble profession. Not just the people who sang the songs, but the people who wrote them. Irving Berlin, Rodgers and Hammerstein, people like that. So I grew up with this incredible respect for the profession of songwriting, and how it spoke to the average guy. A great song meant everything to them. They always sang the same songs over and over again, and they wanted me to learn this song and that song. I played tenor banjo as a kid, and I used to entertain my family—the troops, so to speak [laughs].

Do you remember writing your first song?

It was a song I wrote with my father. He handed me a lyric and I wrote music to it. It was called "My Heart Just Won't Let You Go" [laughs]. It was probably not a very great song, but we thought it was incredible. He had this great line in there—"If it was up to me, I'd bring you down, down, down." And we thought that was just so clever. And of course, I wrote the appropriate music, which was a circus-like melody. We were thrilled, and played it for everybody we knew. And that really got the ball rolling for me, as far as, "Hey, I can do this." I started to write songs. Some very forgettable songs, hopefully [laughs]. But right away, it became a passion. It wasn't long after that that I was in bands, and we started to write our own music and play it, whenever we could get away with it. And it wasn't that great even, but we enjoyed more than anything working it up in the garage. This was all very thrilling, heady stuff for us when we were thirteen, fourteen. They're great memories for me, and I have no doubt that they're the reason I do what I do today for a living.

Listening to one of your first recordings—the Del Rays version of "Always Something There to Remind Me" from the late 60s—I can hear a solid pop-soul voice, but it doesn't yet have the distinct sound you'd have a few years later singing with Steely Dan. How would you say your voice evolved in those years?

A large part of it was working in clubs. I realized that there was a stamina part of it. If I was going to be able to sing five sets a night, then there had to be kind of a head voice part of my singing, something with a lesser dynamic than just the full-on rock 'n' roll screamer voice. And I had to be able to pace myself. And that's really come in handy in later years. Back then, I was sharing the vocal responsibilities with someone else in the band. Even in the Doobies and in Steely Dan. It wasn't really until I went off as a solo artist that I actually had to sing the whole night by myself. That's when I realized I had to pace myself and learn to sing in ways that would give me stamina to do a whole night.

You spent a few years on the road with Steely Dan, and then a few more doing background vocals on some of their most memorable records. Did you get any insight into Becker and Fagen's writing process?

Something I learned from Donald Fagen was the incredible simplicity of chord voicings. They used a lot of what we called the two chords. It was basically a regular triad but without the root in the right hand. It would just be the second, third, and fifth. Then the root would be in the bass, and by changing the bass around under those voicings, you'd create other kinds of harmonic tensions. It was like a light went on when I discovered that. It sounded so lush and great. And yet it's very physically simple. I started to use those voicings in my writing.

Let me mention a few of your songs to find out what inspired them— "Takin' It to the Streets."

The lyric came from a conversation I had with my sister, who was an angry college student at the time. In her sociology classes, she really had her eyes opened by the fact that our society was less than perfect, and that trickle-down economics was probably just a lot of BS. People were falling through the cracks at an alarming rate in the inner cities. In our conversation, we were talking about that and I remember thinking, "Where does it finally give?" It's going to unless we become a country whose administrations actually look at these problems seriously and stop worrying about controlling the world at large and believing that freedom is something that is really only for wealthy Americans and not citizens who find it difficult to live in this economy. In certain ways, we're seeing that every day now. I was driving to a gig and thinking, "This idea would make for a great gospel tune." Gospel music, to me, is music of the people. It speaks to workaday people who get out there and make the whole machine roll. For all these people who can afford to buy the government party line, no matter what it is, we're not them. We have to get out there and live in this world. All of a sudden, the intro came to me in my head, and I remember thinking, "I'm not sure what that first chord is, but I can't wait to get to the gig and try it on piano." I was relieved to know the chords actually existed. The rest of the song unfolded from there.

"What a Fool Believes."

It started with a piano riff that I had literally for over a year, but I could never make anything of it. I think I had it all through the *Livin' on the Fault Line* album. I remember I played it for Ted Templeman every once in a while and he'd say, "Man, I'm telling you, that's a hit song! You've got to finish it." He'd always ask me if I'd finished it. I'd say, "I haven't gotten around to it." I'd written some of the lyric on a plane flight from New York to LA, on a napkin. Just some verses. But I really didn't have a bridge or a chorus. Then I was going to get together with Kenny Loggins, so I was playing little things I had, piano riffs, and that was one of them. Then I hear a knock at the door and there was Kenny. We'd never met. The first thing he says is, "I don't know what it was you were just playing, but if you haven't written that song yet, that's what I want to work on." I said, "Well, sure." I was relieved. We worked for the better part of the day. We were stuck on the chorus. It wasn't until the next day on the phone that we wrote it. Kenny actually recorded it first about a year before the Doobies. I've always found that with certain people you're able to do so much more than you can do on your own, and I think my experience in writing songs with Kenny, I always felt like that. There was a certain chord I was able to strike with him. The songs we wrote are some of the ones I'm most proud of.

"I Can Let Go Now."

I know it sounds like a very personal song, but believe it or not, I wrote it about a friend of mine who I was watching go through a difficult time. She had, in so many words, expressed to me that those were her feelings. It was really a song about her. It was almost verbatim to what she said to me. More in her own words. She kind of expressed to me that feeling of "I'm better now and I can deal with things now and I can let go, and I can be around this other person." She had crossed that line where things were better for her at this point. I thought, "There's a song in there." It was one of those rare songs that kind of come in twenty minutes. Sometimes I wonder if that wasn't some dead friend of mine sending me that song. You wonder if you actually wrote the songs like that. Sometimes I think they're gifts from somewhere else.

"Matters of the Heart."

That's one of my favorites. It was another one that arrived quickly and felt like a gift. The song is about that experience I think we've all had with love where one bad experience causes a whole chain of choices and reactions to love that kind of entrap us, and we kind of spin out of control like a top, and we bounce into other people's lives and wreak a little havoc as we go. Not meaning to, but it's all because of this great devastation that we're trying to live through and the fear that it creates in us of ever having to go through it again. So we tend to look for love in the wrong places and we tend to call something love that really isn't love because we just feel so alone. I think so many people have gone through that. It's kind of that ricochet effect that unrequited love can have on a life.

You once said you moved to Nashville to learn more about songwriting. What has living here taught you?

I'd always held the belief that some of the best songwriters live in Nashville. In the back of my mind, I always had a fantasy that maybe I'd go down there and try to see if I was worth my salt as a songwriter. That would truly be a feather in my cap to be accepted in that community as a songwriter. I love living there. I don't know if I've ever made it into the clique of songwriters, or that I deserve to, but I really enjoyed my experience of working with other songwriters. One of the hardest things for me, and one of the things I'd hoped to learn when I went to Nashville, was how to write from a more personal place. That was always a chord I had a hard time striking. I always found it was difficult for me to tap into very personal feelings. It seemed it was always much easier to observe other people and their human nature and their dilemmas than it was to grab a hold of my own feelings and write about them.

One of the hardest things about being a musician, no matter what level you're at, is keeping cynicism at bay. You've said that even at height of the Doobies' success, you felt cynical. How have you learned to deal with it?

I think I've learned, like most people do, that it's not the better part of my nature. When it comes along, I try not to take it seriously. I remember that I have way too much to be grateful for to let cynicism become too big of a part of the landscape of my perception of what's going on in my life, and that to get cynical about the music business really only means that you're taking it too seriously. The things that really are worth taking seriously are the same for all of us—is my family healthy? Are my friends happy? Is my health good? Those are the things you can afford to take seriously, and even at that, you've got to be grateful for what you have. For me, my greatest source of pride will always be my kids. Moreso than any song I've written. The music business is a cruel encounter at best [laughs]. It's about the same for everybody. I have so much to be grateful for as far as people who've helped me along the way and been there for me. But I think like everything else, you find that they love you when you're winning and they can't remember your name when you're not. That's just the facts of life in the music business. You have to know that you're playing a game and those are the rules of the game. You have to be able to know that going in, and know in the end that whatever good experience you got out of it was worth it.

There's a lot to be said for the camaraderie you feel just being a musician.

Yes. To me, one of the greatest lessons I ever learned that helped me with that whole cynicism thing is bottom line, there's nothing better than when I'm up on stage playing music with my friends. Whether it's in a smelly club or sitting backstage with guys that I've worked with for years, I'm as happy in that moment as I ever will be in this music business.

When I'm in the studio sitting behind a mixing desk and I'm listening to something play back and all the guys are there, we have this kind of collective zoom in our hearts that that was a good take, that there was something special there that we're listening to. That's the happiest I'm going to be. I think when you try to measure your success by any other standards, you wind up expecting too much and you disappoint yourself. You have to learn that it's the simple thrills that matter. I'm as happy in the music business today as I can possibly hope to be. I'm as happy as I was in the back of a van sweating my ass off on the way to a stupid gig at a VFW Hall in Illinois. Back then, those were heady days for me. I was playing with older guys. All these guys were eighteen and I was fourteen. Me and Chuck Sabatino, who was a great songwriter and a guy I grew up with in this business, we often talked about how we never believed we'd be doing this in our forties, and that it would never be more thrilling than it was back in those days when we were playing little joints around St. Louis. Those were really the greatest moments of our lives, and if we could feel that way in our forties, we'd have made it.

If you were to teach a workshop on songwriting, what would you tell your students?

Be completely flexible and approach a song from every different angle, to give yourself the luxury of approaching a song from a lyric angle, even if it's only as much as a sentence or a thought. Approach a song from a chord progression, from a melody, from a rhythm pattern. Approach your music from every conceivable angle, and use every conceivable key to unlock what might potentially be a song that you're grateful to have written. Also, never buy into the idea that you're not good enough, or that you're losing some edge. I think I've been around long enough to realize that the music you're making is not always going to speak to a mass audience. That doesn't mean it's not good. I found in some cases, later on, people that you really respect will go, "Gosh, that was the best thing you ever did." And it might've sold the least. You have to trust your own intuition. If you don't start off with that, you're never going to go anywhere. I think songwriting is all about following your own intuition to say something that only you can say in this moment. If you don't put any more pressure on yourself than that, I think it keeps it within the realm of possibility.

CHAPTER 13

Stevie Nicks and Lindsey Buckingham of Fleetwood Mac

Interviewed 2003
Stevie's Hits: "Rhiannon," "Dreams," "Landslide"
Lindsey's Hits: "Go Your Own Way," "Big Love," "Never Going Back Again"

Stevie Nicks calls it "the chaos." For Lindsey Buckingham, it's "the soap opera." Over the last thirty years, it has taken many forms, from shouting matches and onstage feuding at its worst to silent standoffs and uneasy truces during more peaceful times. It drove Buckingham to quit Fleetwood Mac in 1987 and Nicks to depart in 1993. It's a landslide of jealousy, resentment, suspicion, and deceit, tempered by a big love, deep and enduring. It's at the core of what makes Fleetwood Mac such a compelling band and it's the emotional center of their most enduring songs.

As Nicks says, "It's not easy for us. It never will be. Whenever we get back into a room together and start working, we don't agree on a lot of stuff. Especially now, because we're really settled in our ways. It's no different than it was in 1975 when we went into rehearsal for Fleetwood Mac. We were fighting then. And we have fought all through every single record we have ever made. So I think if it wasn't like that, we'd probably all be walking around going, 'What's the matter with us?'"

Buckingham adds simply, "Our real lives have been laid bare in vinyl."

A little history: When Stevie and Lindsey joined in 1974, Fleetwood Mac was a rickety blues-rock band. Though drummer Mick Fleetwood and bassist John McVie were one of the tightest rhythm sections around, they'd been plagued by years of personnel changes and were struggling to find a new direction. Fleetwood heard something special in the *Buckingham Nicks* record that his new recruits had made (in his autobiography,

Fleetwood says, "Nobody ever auditioned for Fleetwood Mac . . . people were *meant* to be in this group").

By 1977's landmark *Rumours*, the Mac's retooled sound—a swirl of pop, blues, and folk filtered through Southern California cool—made them the biggest band on the planet. Buckingham, Nicks, and Christine McVie were writing hits—"Go Your Own Way," "Rhiannon," "Don't Stop." The future looked bright. But there was always that volatile core, threatening to implode and take the whole beautiful dream down with it.

The turning point in many ways came with *Tusk*. It was a bold step forward, experimental and defiant in its production and style. Though it sold over four million copies, it was perceived as a failure in the wake of *Rumours*. As Buckingham says, "I had been through quite a battle just to get that album made in a post-*Rumours* environment. It was exciting for me, a feeling like I had gotten to something that was more challenging and that was going to confound expectations. But the politics after *Tusk* dictated that we weren't going to do that as a group anymore. So we kind of backtracked into some sort of vague no-man's land a little bit."

The classic Mac lineup released two more albums, *Mirage* and *Tango in the Night,* before things fell apart. By then, Nicks had a strong solo career going and Buckingham was close behind. Mick Fleetwood and the McVies soldiered on into the early 90s with new members. Then in 1996, the classic lineup patched up their differences for a tour and a live album, *The Dance.* A handful of new songs pointed the way to what was, six years later, surely one of the unexpected events of 2003—a new studio album from Fleetwood Mac, *Say You Will*.

LINDSEY BUCKINGHAM

What kinds of feelings do you go through in the weeks before a new Fleetwood Mac record is released?

With this record, I'm actually euphoric. This project, for me, has been kind of an epic effort, more than anything I've ever done in terms of length of time involved to keep the eye on the ball, the ways in which it could have come out as a solo album, and finally what it ended up being, and somehow still maintaining its integrity, in terms of my songs and Stevie's songs. In many ways, I feel like I've been working for the last twenty-five years of my life for this. Not just the last six years that it's been literally worked on. A level of maturity, a level of creativity, and a vision that I've been trying to get to have now infused into the whole thing, with a great rhythm section, and Stevie, who I've known since I was sixteen, and it's just a very exciting and profound thing.

What impressed me right away about the record is that you sound like you mean it. There's a commitment that you don't often hear with bands who've been around for over thirty years.

I think the sense of a band who is all fifty-something coming up with something like this *is* a little bit profound. I think it breaks a lot of the clichés about rock 'n' roll. A lot of artists in other forms, whether they're novelists or moviemakers or composers or painters, a lot of them maybe hit their stride at fifty. It's only this rock 'n' roll cliché that you burn out by the time you're a relatively young age, and it is just that—a cliché. So all of that informs the way I feel about not just the release of the album, but this whole year. Hopefully, if things go the way we pray they will, next year we can do another album. It feels like a whole open-ended thing that's happening here.

Listening to your songs on the record, one theme I picked up on was the idea of taking responsibility. Has your songwriting changed since you've had children?

It has certainly affected the way I feel. I think I've calmed down quite a bit [laughs]. I think that these are the best lyrics that I've ever written, without getting specific. You always work towards trying to improve your weaker points, and possibly a sense of safeness that now is part of my life, in the sense of a larger picture. Things that are more important than writing a song have made it easier to write better lyrics. And I think also that it's a skill that gets better the more you work on it, and I've tried to work on it. In terms of the theme you're talking about, taking responsibility, I think you're right. I think there is a kind of subconscious element that has kind of worked its way in, that makes it less about the neurosis of me and my needs, and more about an overview. It's still about me or us, though maybe a small group of us. More concern for trying to do the right thing, and not just a neurotic, selfish point of view, which was a lot of what Fleetwood Mac's dialogues to each other were always about [laughs].

What are the most mysterious parts of the songwriting process to you?

It's an interesting thing. In many ways, I still don't think of myself as a songwriter. I know I've written a lot of songs. I tend to think of myself as a stylist. I think that the way a lot of people do it is they come up with a tangible thing that you can call a lyric and a melody. Then they take it into a situation where it might evolve as a record. I might go in with fragments or ideas that are not particularly well fleshed out, or they're as well fleshed out as I'm able to make them. And then I start to work the painting.

What do you mean by that?

I make that analogy because I can sit with a tape machine and use that as a canvas. You commit to a certain melody, then you commit to a certain guitar part, and one affects the other and maybe the melody begins to change. It's kind of an abstract expressionist way of doing it. At some point, that starts to lead you, as a painting would. Then when you get to a certain point, suddenly you're on automatic. It's hard for me to divorce the process of the songwriting, because I'm not Burt Bacharach, unfortunately, who can sit down and have a complete overview and understanding of so many things that he's been taught, so many European principles and all that. I have to find a different way to do it. So the actual record-making side of it affects to a great degree the writing and vice versa. And I suppose that is the mystery right there, is that it comes in little fits and starts, and it's maybe like making sculpture. You have to really pat it around quite a bit and change it, and lop off the nose and start over again, and there's a kind of abstractness about it.

Let me ask you about a few of your songs to get your reaction—"Go Your Own Way."

That came very quickly. I remember sitting down and putting that together when we were taking a break in Florida. We rented a house to start rehearsing before *Rumours*, and it was an immediate song. It was a very present thing in terms of the response it got from the band. The drumbeat that Mick did in the verse was actually his version of trying to do something that I asked him to do that he couldn't do. What he did was better. I'd been listening to "Street Fighting Man," and Charlie Watts does this kind of offbeat rhythm. Mick, either he didn't want to do that, or he couldn't get it, so he came up with his own version.

"Never Going Back Again."

That's a very naive song. Never going back again? Sure [laughs]. I think the guitar work was inspired by something I heard by Ry Cooder. The lyric as I recall was very much a miniature perception of things. I had broken up with Stevie, and maybe met someone. It could have been someone who really didn't mean a thing. Maybe someone who had kind of resisted getting to know me, and then finally broke down and let me in. But I don't remember who it was now. In the days after Stevie and I broke up, in the days before we started recording *Rumours*, there were a lot of women who would just come and go in a very short time. So in that sense, it was one of those people. The lyric seems not very deep. "Been down one time, been down two time, never going back again." There really is nothing particularly definitive about it. You think about how naive that was and very much in the context of not particularly being about something that was even important. And maybe that's why it's sweet. It was just a frivolous little thing. Of course, it seems to take on more sweetness and a deeper feeling when it's placed on the album with all the other songs [laughs].

"Peacekeeper."

I wrote the song about two and a half years ago. It was, in a very ironic way, looking at the kind of thinking that is matter-of-fact and desensitized towards certain actions that go on in the world, and the kind of blankness and conformity that goes along with that. And then trying to look at what does that do for a married couple trying to work out their problems. How does it affect them? What is peace really? The whole idea that there can be any static condition is obviously an illusion. So can there ever really be peace? There can be moments of peace, or long periods of peace, possibly, whether it's in the world or whether it's in a relationship. But it seems to me what peace really means is valuing the ideal of that, and just being mindful of it. Working towards the maintenance of it, even though you understand it will not always exist. By the irony of sort of being matter-of-fact about not thinking that way is really what the song is doing.

I've always admired your guitar playing, especially your right hand, which is so fluid and precise. Can you talk a little about your technique?

I never really used a pick very much. When I was seven I was listening to Scotty Moore, who had a fingerstyle in which he used a pick along with

his fingers. When rock sort of took a dive for a while there, I started
tening to folk music and bluegrass. I never really got any serious chops ι
banjo, but it helped my speed. But the Travis picking is the basic tem
plate for everything I do. It's just something that evolved. I think a real
breakthrough for me in terms of translating this thing that you're talking
about to the studio and record-making beyond the level of, say, "Never
Going Back Again" was when I started playing "Big Love" live. That was
before *The Dance*, when I did a tour after *Out of the Cradle*. I started doing
"Big Love" very fast, in a Leo Kottke-meets-classical-on-acid [laughs],
whatever you want to call it. It got such a strong response and it got
me back to reminding myself that whatever I can do as a producer, this
is the center of what I do, and it's not something to be taken lightly.
This is somewhere I want to go now, to take that element, the energy of
that, and the singularity of that, and build it on in a much more sub-
lime way.

**I read an interview with Christine where she said how much she
admired your abilities as a producer. She mentioned how you took
Stevie's "Gold Dust Woman," which has a repetitive chord sequence, and
made each section distinct. Since Stevie isn't really an instrumentalist,
how do you approach an arrangement for one of her songs?**

You are in some ways adding to the writing process on the set, so to
speak. "Okay, this doesn't work, let's try this." It's very much like that. If
I am able to do that for Stevie, it doesn't mean I'd be able to do that for
everyone. Maybe that's part of what makes Fleetwood Mac what it is. We
just happen to have a set of cross-references where I have what she needs.
I don't know how it would work if I were to try to do [it] with another
group or artist. In many ways, you might say that was more of the profound gift that I had for Fleetwood Mac, more than as a guitarist or a writer
or a singer. I was someone who could make all that stuff into a record.

Is there a certain thing about Stevie's songwriting that you like best?

I understand the primitive aspects that she has going. I understand what
she's trying to get at. She may not even articulate it herself, but I see what
it is. I can understand the potential. What I like about her songwriting
is her sense of rhythm. It's superb. Obviously, you have to like her lyrics
and her voice, but she does a lot with a very little. Sometimes if you
examine her melodies, they are not particularly elaborate. She can do repetitive phrases, but it's just how she does it and where she stops doing it,

and where she makes a little changeup and how I seem to be able to move sections across that, change what's going on beneath it.

Can you think of an example?

"Gypsy" is a great example. If you were to just pull the melody out from that without any of what's going on beneath, it wouldn't hang together. Without having the instrumental parts [hums counterline in chorus] that allow the potential of what she's doing to come out, it wouldn't make it. So, she needed that. Maybe that's my favorite example of it [Stevie's writing and Lindsey's production] coming together. If you sing, "You see your gypsy, you see your gypsy, yeah," it doesn't really depart anywhere at the point it needs to. It just sounds like someone kind of jamming with their voice, but it allows the openness for me to do things of my own. It's a real collaboration, even though I'm not writing the song.

There's always a soap opera element in Fleetwood Mac where listeners are tempted to interpret the lyrics as a dialogue between the members.

I think we always were doing that, and probably still are in quite a few of the songs [laughs]. We are in a more peaceful place than we were in terms of a functional working band, not just a band who's doing a re-statement of their body of work as in *The Dance*, but a band who's in the trenches doing something new and vital to what's going on with them now. We are much more at peace, but it's tenuous still. And then how *that* relates to the worldview of things enters into some of the songs. Who knows how much of that element was responsible for the phenomenon that was *Rumours*? At what point did the music itself, which was very good music, sort of give over to the musical soap opera element? If you want to look at it in a cynical way, that's part of the gimmick of the band and always has been. It's a hook. There's nothing wrong with that, because it's not a pretense. It's not something where we sat with a PR person and said, "Well this would be a good thing to try" [laughs]. Our real lives laid bare, not just in terms of the media, but in terms of the vinyl. There was a great appeal to that, not just in terms of the voyeurism of it. It was a very touching thing. The fact that we would go through all forms of denial in order to push forward as musicians and really allow ourselves to become quite dysfunctional as people. Not that the whole rock genre doesn't make you that way eventually anyway [laughs]. Living in the subculture of drugs and all that at that time, but I think with us, it was bitter and it was sweet and it was tender and it was brutal all at once.

And now it's going to be a stage musical.

[Laughter] I've heard that. We haven't given anybody our blessing yet, but I wouldn't doubt it at all. If not this year, then next year. We'll see.

Which records influenced you most as a songwriter?

The Beach Boys, *Today.*

John Lennon, *Plastic Ono Band.* I think it had a lot to do with me thinking it was okay to be that rude in my own songs [laughs].

Any collection of Elvis Presley stuff. I wouldn't be here at all without Elvis Presley and without my older brother, who bought the record of "Heartbreak Hotel." Before that it was Patti Page [laughs].

Any number of Beatles albums, maybe *Revolver* or *Rubber Soul.*

Laurie Anderson, *Big Science.*

STEVIE NICKS

In Fleetwood Mac, there's always an added layer of intrigue with your songs and Lindsey's in that listeners wonder if you're singing about each other. Are you still dealing with unfinished emotional business?

Of course. It's not a lot of fun, but it certainly does lend itself to great writing. And it really is back to that old adage that tragedy makes for great art. If everybody's happy and everything's going along, then you have nothing to write about. So Lindsey and I write about the chaos of our relationship, which is ongoing. It's never easy for Lindsey and me.

At the same time, you have to put a lot of trust in Lindsey because he's the producer and arranger on your songs.

Well, he doesn't do a whole lot of things with arranging, because my demos are pretty much there. That doesn't mean that they're not a hundred percent more terrific after Lindsey works on them. I'm very territorial about the way my songs are arranged. What he does is take the skeleton and then he goes in for hours that we never see him and he plays parts and parts and more parts. He arranges right underneath my little skeleton. It's like I laughingly said to him when we first started this new record, because his songs were pretty much done, I said, "Your songs are like beautiful, handcrafted Russian boxes with enamel and cloisonné and they're all incredible and sound like you've worked on them for seven years, and my little songs are like pine boxes" [laughs]. I said, "You've got your work cut out for you, because you have to somehow make my songs compare a little bit to yours." He said, "Don't worry. I'm going to do it."

"Thrown Down," "Say You Will," "Running Through the Garden"—
I think these new songs are some of the best you've ever written.

Thank you. I agree with you. How conceited am I to say that? [laughs]. But they say, you are supposed to get better as you get older and they say if you keep practicing your craft you have to get better. So I'm not one of those people who is ever going to accept the fact that I can't write a song that will appeal to somebody who's twenty because I'm in my early fifties. And I'm never going to accept that when I'm like seventy that I can't still write something that is current. To me, we just have to get better. That's how we all looked at this record. This wasn't going to be just a dumb, stupid album. It's not going to be because we just felt like doing a record. This is because we needed to do this and this musical entity needed to come through all of us, and we are serious as a heart attack about this.

I've read that you're very dedicated to keeping journals. How does
journal writing relate to songwriting for you?

Sometimes I pull my lyrics right straight out of my journals. I'll show you [she gets journals from the next room]. I write prose on the right-hand side, then on the left, I'll write poetry and lyrics. This is from the anniversary of 9/11: [reads] "The murder of innocence cannot be explained, only endured. And I who went to sleep in tears woke up in tears. And I who never said good-bye, said good-bye again. I did go to sleep in tears last night, and I woke up in tears about an hour ago. I laid in my bed and that moment before you really wake up and the tears just started streaming down my face. Fleetwood Mac is mixing our first song from the record today. We start at 3:30. Today, half of me wants to call in sick, the other half of me knows that the people who died one year ago would want me to finish this music in their honor, and not give into this feeling that makes me want to put the TV on the Design Channel and hide away..." This is "Illumé," the song, that's right where it came from. In another two years, I will go back through what I'm writing today and I will pull out stuff, and they will become poems on this side of the book. I'll go through and make the prose into poetry, and that's how I get my songs. I very seldom write just straight poetry or lyrics. It will usually come from me writing about what's going on in my life.

Do the songs you write for Fleetwood Mac feel different than what you do for a solo album?

My solo career is very precious to me, but it's nothing like Fleetwood Mac. It can *never* be like Fleetwood Mac. For each of the members of the band and everyone surrounding us, it's so much more heavy. When I'm working by myself, it is by myself. I'm very inward and very much a loner and I live here by myself, but Fleetwood Mac just overwhelms everything, takes everything. Everything you do is completely built around Fleetwood Mac. So I don't know what else to say about that. It makes my whole face turn red. I get a fever.

I couldn't help noticing that picture of you and George Harrison up on the mantle. Where was it taken?

Isn't that wild? That is probably in 1977, in Hana on the island of Maui in Hawaii. Me and a couple of my friends had gone over there. I don't remember exactly how it happened, but we drove up to Hana, where George lived, and we hung out with him for about three days. We stayed in his guest cottage and we sat around and wrote. I don't think anything really came out of the writing session, but we had a great time, and you can kind of see we were very serious. I took the picture to the studio, so it was on the fireplace for the whole recording of *Say You Will*. It was very much like he was looking out over us the whole time. I liked George very much. He was really a nice man.

Was he or Lennon and McCartney a strong influence on your songwriting?

Yes, absolutely. More the folky stuff.

Who else would you consider an influence?

If I go back to when I was little, my granddad was a country-western singer, so he brought a lot of music to my house. Everly Brothers, a lot of rockabilly stuff, a lot of country rock stuff. Not super country stuff, but crossover stuff, that even then in the 50s was a little bit country but very rock 'n' roll too. That's when I started singing harmony, when I started singing along with the Everly Brothers. Which is so wild that Lindsey ended up working with them. They were a huge influence on Lindsey also. A million miles away from each other, we were inspired by the same thing. As I got older, strangely enough, the music that I listened to was R & B. I listened to "Be My Baby" and all those Phil Spector kinds of things, Motown, the Supremes. That's where I really learned to sing. Then I get into high school, I'm a sophomore in high school and along come the Beatles. I'm very influenced by how good their early songs were. By my senior year, I was standing in front of the mirror with a brush, singing "Take Another Little Piece of My Heart," frizzing up my hair and wearing the little tunic and the really tight bell-bottoms and the high clogs. Then I was going to college and walking through San Jose State like I was already a star. I was Janis Joplin.

You and Lindsey were both Hendrix fans too, right?

He was a huge influence on me. Just the way he sang and played and was so soulful but yet was so rock 'n' roll. He was such a dichotomy, being a black man and a black musician and being so rock 'n' roll. We were so in awe of him. [In one of our early bands,] we opened for Jimi Hendrix. I got to stand on the side of the stage and watch him for two hours. He died not long after. I saw Janis too. But I got the essence before they left. So that was the most amazing thing. That's when I really decided that I wanted to be a rock singer and not a country singer, and that I really wanted to concentrate on songwriting. I was not going to be a stupid girl singer. I was going to be way more than that. Lindsey will laugh, but I was not going to carry equipment and not going to have my salary docked because I didn't. You will pay me as much as you guys get or I quit. So that's when I gained my strength and my confidence. And that confidence never went away. It became part of me and I have it still today, and I'm very grateful for that.

Another musician who's had an influence on you is Tom Petty. In the liner notes on Trouble in Shangri-La, you thank him for an inspirational lecture he gave you. Can you share a little of what he said?

That was in Phoenix in about 1996. I had been in and out of rehab for the Valium and Klonopin that I'd been taking for eight years. I went back to Phoenix and I was really down. It was like, I obviously didn't create anything worth talking about in the last eight years, so am I going to be able to create now? Am I still going to be able to write now? And Tom was playing in town, and I went down to dinner with him the night before, and I asked him if he would help me write a song. And he just flat out, in the Tom Petty swamp dog way, said, "I'm not going to help you write a song, because you are, in my opinion, Stevie, one of the premiere songwriters of our time. I don't need to help you write a song. You just need to go back to your house and sit in front of your piano and start writing." And something about the conversation really hit me. I walked out of the Ritz-Carlton with a new lease on life. If Tom Petty thinks I can do it, then I guess I can. So I went home and I started writing, that night. Sometimes a really good friend is the only one who can say to you, "I know you may not want to hear this but I need to tell you . . ." Whether it's something bad or something good, they get through to you finally.

One of your signature songs is "Rhiannon." How did it come about?

I read a book called *Triad*. It was just a stupid little paperback that I found somewhere at somebody's house laying on the couch. It was all about this girl named Rhiannon. She had a sister whose name was Branwyn. These were Welsh names. I was so taken with the name Rhiannon that I just thought, "I've got to write something about this." And I sat down at the piano, and I started writing this song about a woman that was all involved with these birds and magic. Come to find out years after I've written the song that in fact Rhiannon was the goddess of steeds, maker of birds. She whittled birds, and they came alive and flew and she could turn into a horse, so she was a horse goddess also. Her three birds sang music, and when something was happening in war, you would see this horse come in and it was Rhiannon. This is all in the Welsh translation of the *Mabinogion*, their book of mythology. When she came, you'd kind of black out then wake up and the danger would be gone and you'd see the three birds flying off, and you'd hear this little song. So there was in fact, a song of Rhiannon. I had no idea about any of this. Years after, somebody sent me a set of four books that are written by a lady whose name is Evangeline Walton, who is now dead. She spent her whole life translating the *Mabinogion* and the story of Rhiannon. She lived in Tuscon. I went there in 1977, right after "Rhiannon" had been a big huge hit. I went to her house, and it was totally Rhiannon. On her fireplace was a massive lion that said, "Song of Rhiannon." She spent her whole life on the story of Rhiannon, she never married, she in essence had almost become Rhiannon. And it was trippy. She had heard about the song. She told me about her life and how she had been entranced by the name, just like I had, and it's so interesting, because her last book was 1974, and that's right when I wrote "Rhiannon." So it's like her work ended and my work began. Rhiannon was this incredible character. She married a mortal king, and she was a goddess and they couldn't have any kids, and she had to sleep with his best friend who was a magician, and then she could have a baby, otherwise all the people were going to kill her because they thought she was a witch. It's an amazing story. *Lord of the Rings* move over! Rhiannon's story is much more fascinating.

How about "Edge of Seventeen"?

It was written right after John Lennon died. A week later, my uncle died, and this was a very close uncle. He got very sick very fast, and I was at his house when he died. Just a freak thing. My cousin John and I, we were the only people there, and he was in his bedroom and we were sitting with him, and he just slipped away. Between John Lennon and my Uncle Bill, whose name was actually Jonathan also, "Edge of Seventeen" came out of that. "Oh I went searchin' for an answer/Up the stairs and down the hall/Not to find an answer just to hear the call of a nightbird singing." And the nightbird is the bird of death, really. So I can get up on stage and sing "Edge of Seventeen" and still feel just as traumatized today as I did then, when I first sang it at my piano. It's just so heavy. I use that word "heavy" a lot, and I know that it's an old hippie word, but it just really seems to be the right word. Some of the songs are so heavy. John Lennon being shot to death in front of his apartment for absolutely no reason, when I was a rock star also, so immediately that transfers to, "Is somebody going to shoot me? Is somebody going to shoot me because I didn't write back a fan?" And that's why I wrote the song.

"Silver Girl."

That's written about Sheryl Crow. In the song, where it says, "She would have preferred the last generation," Sheryl absolutely would've preferred to be my age and to have been in our generation and to have been in her own Fleetwood Mac, more than to be in this generation. We all love her and try to take her along with us because we know that. It was very fun when she came to record with Fleetwood Mac. Lindsey likes her a lot and Mick loves her and John loves her, and she's one of our little adoptees. So the song is like an ode to the girl rock star, an ode to the question, "Is it possible to find somebody to love?" When you're rich and famous, it's very hard to find somebody. That's not taking away the hope, but it is stating that it's difficult. I kind of made a choice when I was Sheryl's age, when I was forty, that I didn't really want to be tied down. There are many times during my life that I could've been married and I could've had children and I made the decision to not do it. So I don't know, with her, the only advice I can say is that "You live in the same realm of romantic possibility that I do."

And "Landslide."

It was written in 1973 at a point where Lindsey and I had driven to Aspen for him to rehearse for two weeks with Don Everly. Lindsey was going to take Phil's place. So they rehearsed and left, and I made a choice to stay in Aspen. I figured I'd stay there and one of my girlfriends was there. We stayed there for almost three months while Lindsey was on the road, and this is right after the *Buckingham Nicks* record had been dropped. And it was horrifying to Lindsey and I because we had a taste of the big time, we recorded in a big studio, we met famous people, we made what we consider to be a brilliant record and nobody liked it [laughs]. What are we gonna do now? I had been a waitress and a cleaning lady and I didn't mind any of this. I was perfectly delighted to work and support us so that Lindsey could produce and work and fix our songs and make our music. But I had gotten to a point where it was like, "I'm not happy. I am tired of this. But I don't know if we can do any better than this. If nobody likes this, then what are we going to do?" So during that two months, I made a decision to continue. So "Landslide" was the decision. "When you see my reflection in the snow-covered hills"—it's the only time in my life that I've lived in the snow. But looking up at those Rocky Mountains and going, "Okay, we can do it. I'm sure we can do it. Okay, Lindsey, we're going to the top." In one of my journal entries, it says, "I took Lindsey and said, 'We're going to the top!'" And that's what we did. Within a year, Mick Fleetwood called us and we were in Fleetwood Mac making eight hundred dollars a week apiece [laughs]. Washing hundred-dollar bills through the laundry. It was hysterical. It was like we were rich overnight.

How do you feel about the Dixie Chicks covering it?"

For them to have done it and brought it back is a great honor to me. I am very good friends with them, and hope very much to do a record with Natalie at some point in my life. I have to show you what they sent me [brings out a lovely painted bowl engraved with the lyrics of "Landslide" in a spiral]. It's all perfect. The neatest part of the song is all inside the bowl. So beautiful, and so special. When I'm a hundred and one walking around the house, that will still be just like that. It will be an inspiration to me, to see that somebody cared enough to do this. These girls are very precious to me. I think sometimes if I'd have ever had a daughter, I would want her to be Natalie. She's very special to me. I love her and I care about her in a way that's very motherly. I think she's about the best singer out there. I thought that the first time I heard her sing. I was in Phoenix, and it was the middle of the night, and I had FM radio on, and on came "There's Your Trouble." I wrote it down, and went straight to the record store the next day. So I made the decision then, and it was years before I ever met them, that I wanted to work with her someday. So it was very karma-inspired that they would pick up "Landslide" and want to do it. I think that Sheryl Crow is the one who suggested it to them.

The Dixie Chicks, Sheryl Crow . . . they are all like your spiritual daughters.

They *are* my daughters, and I love that, because since I didn't have any daughters, I feel like I have them now. And I have Norah Jones. I love her. Can you believe, eight Grammys? Norah, this is your *Rumours*. Your life will never be the same, ever again. And I love Michelle Branch. And I adore Gwen Stefani. They are all a delight to me. They are all multi-talented, and I feel very grateful that these women care about me and care about my music. They make it all so very worth it for me. To know that I have reached out and gotten each one of them and maybe made them be a little better, be a little bit more profound, work on their expertise a little bit more, work on their songwriting a little bit more, work on their stage performance a little bit more. I see little bits of myself in all of them, and it makes me cry.

It's almost like your songs are helping to keep you young.

Whenever I do a record, I'm able to go back, way back, and pull some really interesting songs out that were written when I was really young, and then mix them in with what I'm doing now. I feel very lucky that I don't listen to all these songs and go, "Oh, that's from 1976, that's from 2003." I don't see that. That's why I tell you that I will be ninety years old someday and I will still be writing things that are relevant. I think if you keep that innocence, if you try to hang on to that innocence and believe that there is love and there is God and there is beauty, then you will be able to be relevant. I think when you start to become really jaded, that's when you can't write relevant stuff anymore. People that are in their teens and twenties and their thirties don't really want to hear you write about stuff that is so miserable that they can't even deal with it. I think that, for me, because I haven't been in a horrible marriage and I don't have delinquent children that I'm trying to get through college, I haven't had a lot of those bad experiences that really twist people's minds. Then you stop writing about love, and you stop writing about the possibility of love, and when you stop writing about the possibility of love, you are no longer relevant. I don't really care if I get married at this point, I'm quite happy by myself, but I do live in the realm of romantic possibility. Mr. Right. It's possible that he's around the corner, that he could just be driving up the street and I could have a flat tire and there he is. That allows me to write with hope, and I think that's what happens to people when they get older. They stop hoping.

CHAPTER 14

Billy Joel

Interviewed 1996 and 2001

Hits: "Just the Way You Are," "Honesty," "We Didn't Start the Fire"

Like the comedian Rodney Dangerfield, Billy Joel has a respect problem. Despite thirty-two years, fifteen albums (many of them multiplatinum), thirty-three Top 40 hits (including four number ones), and legions of fans who will still pay big bucks to hear him sing "Piano Man" in concert, he has never quite convinced critics and rock snobs that he belongs.

It could be because Joel, though he's a versatile singer with an impressive bag of rock tricks, is not actually a rocker. And this is not meant as a slight. As a songwriter and musician, he has more in common with the suit-and-tie crowd of the 1930s Brill Building. Or if you hear him talk these days, more with the ruffled-shirt crowd of nineteenth-century romantic music. You can hear it in his songs: beautiful melodies, unabashed in their emotion and longing, complex counterpoints and piano accompaniments. In some of his recent concerts, he has even revealed his true roots by playing a quasi-classical version of his doo-wop–style hit, "The Longest Time."

But whatever respect he hasn't gotten—and it's made Joel a curmudgeonly interview subject in the past—it's safe to say that time will prove him to be one of the preeminent songwriters of the late twentieth century.

Billy Joel was born May 9, 1949. When he was four years old, growing up in blue-collar Hicksville on Long Island, he started classical piano lessons. Not long after, bored with reading the dots of centuries past, he began to make some minor changes to the works of Schubert, Brahms, and the like, improvising his own versions. "I found reading to be intrusive to the musical process," Joel says. At fourteen, the budding songwriter saw the Beatles on *Ed Sullivan* and there was no turning back. There followed the standard training program, with a few twists—garage bands, first recordings, poor business decisions (some of which haunted him for years), and a stint as Bill Martin, piano man, on which he based his break-through hit. Once he achieved liftoff, Joel never looked back.

Though he's currently on hiatus from pop songwriting (he released an album of classical piano pieces, *Fantasies and Delusions*, in 2001), the fifty-four-year-old Joel has stayed in the public eye over the last three years with his Face to Face tours with fellow piano man Elton John.

You've said that the prospect of writing songs scares you.

Whenever I start a writing project, there's a great deal of trepidation. Where I used to approach it with absolute white-knuckle terror, now I just have the everyday ordinary jitters. So I must be extremely compelled to write because I find it to be a difficult process, excruciating sometimes. That's the difficulty factor. I'm not terrified because I've proven to myself that I can do it if I set myself to do it and I have the proper amount of input and motivation and all the emotional necessities.

Do you write every day?

I'm what they call a cold-start guy. I don't write every day. Some people, to keep themselves in the flow, will write a song every day. Everybody's got their own rhythm and their way of doing it. I do it by not writing for a long time. Like a novelist. I write when I feel like I have something to write. I don't write because of record company schedules or because I need money or because I want to be more famous. I write purely out of a compulsion to write.

In the in-between times, what kinds of things do you do musically?

Sometimes I stay away from the piano for weeks at a time. I have a big beautiful Steinway in my living room, but a lot of times I feel like it's waiting for me with these eighty-eight teeth [laughs], just sitting there, this big black beast in the living room, hunched with this big cape on it, waiting to bite my fingers off when I put my hands on it. But I find it useful to not work. I feel it's like letting the field lie fallow, so that you can be receptive to input rather than putting out. And I realize that a lot of composers that I've read about did the same thing. There were some people like Mozart, who wrote all the time and was constantly in a state of composition. Then there were composers like Beethoven who went long periods of time without writing anything and then would write this titanic masterpiece. So whatever works for you.

Your melody writing has always been so consistently strong. Do you think if songwriters want to improve their melody writing, that going to the classics is a good thing to do?

I don't think you can really beat classical music, especially the romantic era, for melodic composition. For the use of chords in conjunction with melody, I think composition reached its height. I also have a theory about this. Now, I'm not going to advise people to listen to classical music so that it'll help your songwriting. I don't think it can hurt, although some people may not find it inspiring. My theory about classical music is that it—especially the melodic, ultra-romantic music of the nineteenth century—evolved into the popular music of the 50s, 60s, 70s, and 80s. I don't how much of it is left in the 90s. Not necessarily the blues-based hard rock, but melodic songwriting. Even before the 50s, with composers like Richard Rodgers, all the way back to Gershwin, Cole Porter. These people get lumped into Tin Pan Alley. I don't think that's a fair comparison or analogy. I feel that classical music became popular songs. Take a song like "I Will Always Love You," by Dolly Parton. If you play it as a classical music piece, it could be something by Schumann.

You've always kind of played down the importance of lyrics in pop music, even calling your own lyrics "coloring" to the melodies.

But that's how I hear popular music. I remember my first exposure to popular music was probably at a beach listening to a portable radio or at a party listening to somebody's little dinky record player where they played the 45s where the speaker was about two or three inches big and you really couldn't hear lyrics. What you heard was a melody, some chords, a rhythm. The drums were always prevalent in rock 'n' roll and pop music. You heard the sound of the singer's voice and you heard the production of the recording. One of the last things you ever heard was what the hell they were saying. Maybe you could catch something, and as a matter of fact, a lot of songs that were popular, teenagers, especially in my era, made up dirty lyrics for them anyway, which we always liked better than the originals [laughs].

Once you have a melody, how do you go about setting words to it?

It's this tortured process of having a melodic phrase with a pentameter to it, with a definite conclusion on each phrase where an actual rhyme would have to go. I hate the tyranny of rhyme too. But if you're going to be musical and you're going to make something work, nine times out of ten you do have to rhyme because it would be as if you ended a musical phrase in a different key with no relation to anything else that had happened before. It needs to have a harmony. So I have this tortured process of here's the mold, it's all shaped already, and I have to look through my vocabulary, my pitiful words, and jam them onto this musical phrase and make it match the emotional feeling that the music has. Now if you listen to a piece of music, how does that make me feel? What was I thinking when I wrote that? What was going through my mind? Why did that music get written? That's where you start to look for the words, and then I find, "Oh, it makes me feel this way. Is it about love, is it about life, is it about work, is it about death, fear, happiness, sadness, loneliness, joy?" So there's something encoded in the music and I have to figure out what that is and then drop the right words in. It's like trying to put together a jigsaw puzzle and the pieces aren't premade. You have to cut them yourself. Sometimes you have to smush the board a little bit and bend the frame and make up your rules as you're going along.

Let me ask you about the inspiration behind some of your songs— *"Captain Jack."*

That's what I call one of those "look out the window songs." I was living in an apartment across the street from a housing project, and watching these suburban kids pull up, and they were scoring drugs from a guy who lived in the project, and that was Captain Jack. I was sitting in my apartment, thinking, "What am I going to write about? Well, I guess I'll write about that." There it was, right in front of me. But I didn't get it. What's so horrible about an affluent young white teenager's life that he's got to shoot heroin? It's really a song about what I consider to be a pathetic loser kind of lifestyle. I've been accused of, "Oh, this song promotes drug use and masturbation." No, no, no. Listen to the song. The guy is a loser.

"Say Goodbye to Hollywood."

That was a celebration song. I was moving back to New York, and I was really happy to be getting out of LA. I didn't like living in Los Angeles. The first year I was there, I was kind of seduced by the nice weather, the palm trees, and the views from the Hollywood Hills, the Pacific Coast Highway, and all that stuff. That wore off after about a year. Then I realized there were a lot of phony people there. I didn't make many friends. The sense that I got was that people wanted to get to know you because of what you could do for them. I wanted to get back to New York. It wasn't meant to be a taunting song. It was just a celebration, like, "Okay, thank you, Hollywood." I did it in a Phil Spector style. I was thinking of Ronnie Spector and the Ronettes when I did it. And she actually ended up doing it.

"New York State of Mind."

It took me about a half an hour to write. I got back to New York, I moved into the house, literally had my suitcases with me. I got off a bus that I took up the Hudson and then dropped my bags. There was a piano in this house, and I went right over to it and played "New York State of Mind." I love it when it happens like that. Thank you! Tony Bennett and I just recorded a duet on this song.

"She's Always a Woman."

I remember the melody started being written as "The View from the Thirty-Fifth Floor." I was living in a high-rise on the east side of Manhattan and it was one of those "look out the window" songs. As I was writing it [sings "The view from the thirty-fifth floor"] I thought, "Well, I know it ain't gonna be about that." But it was a bailout lyric. I just needed a lyric to carry a melody until I decided what the lyric would be. It was really written as a folk song. This was during a time that my ex-wife number one was managing me in the music business. In those days, if a woman was too aggressive or too effective in business, she was looked on as a bitch, and I wanted to comment on that whole syndrome. You know, a woman can be effective and it doesn't make her any less of a woman. That was the point of the song, but some people took it as a misogynist song. They kept referring to it as "She's Only a Woman." I said, "No, no, no, that's your title. My title is 'She's Always a Woman.'" Misogyny is in the ear of the beholder, I guess.

"My Life."

I wrote that one night when I was thinking about a young person leaving home and telling their parents, "I don't care what you say anymore, this is my life." And the parents turning right around and saying right back to the kid, "Well, go ahead with your own life and leave me alone." It's kind of a mutual, see you around, don't let the door hit you in the ass [laughs]. There's a line in there that I still strongly believe in. "Sooner or later you sleep in your own space/Either way that's okay you wake up with yourself." You still have to be able to look at yourself in the morning. You're the one you wake up with first.

"We Didn't Start the Fire."

I started doing that as a mental exercise. I had turned forty. It was 1989, and I said, "Okay, what's happened in my life?" I wrote down the year 1949. Okay, Harry Truman was the president. Popular singer of the day, Doris Day. China went Communist. Another pop star, Johnny Ray. Big Broadway show, *South Pacific*. Journalist, Walter Winchell. Athlete, Joe DiMaggio. Then I went to 1950, Richard Nixon, Joe McCarthy, big cars, Studebaker, television, et cetera, et cetera . . . It was kind of a mind game. That's one of the few times I've written the lyrics first, which should be obvious to why I usually prefer to write the music first, because that melody is horrendous. It's like a mosquito droning. It's one of the worst melodies I've ever written. I kind of like the lyric though.

"Scenes from an Italian Restaurant."

It was actually three different songs that I sewed together. One song was called "The Italian Restaurant Song," because I wrote "Bottle of white, bottle of red," and from there I went "perhaps a bottle of rosé instead." I'd never write that now because I can't stand rosé [laughs]. But at the time I was just being introduced to rosé. So obviously, it's in an Italian restaurant, there's a couple talking, there's some kind of reminiscing going on, it's a little slice of life.

The second section—that was actually another song I wrote, a little piece of a thing called "Things Are Okay in Oyster Bay." I was living in Oyster Bay and it was one of the first apartments I ever had. It was like a hippie crash pad, but I really dug it. It was one of these dopey little songs. So I said, "Ah it's just this cutie-pie little tune, it's not worth anything." So then I needed to get from the instrumental section and I recognized we're going somewhere with this. You know where we're going? We're going to Brenda and Eddie. That's what they're reminiscing about. The story just told itself to me as I was going along.

The third part was a song called "The Ballad of Brenda and Eddie." It was sort of my ode to the king and the queen of the high school in Long Island, New Jersey, New York environs—the legendary popular couple in school, which I think is a universal concept.

I didn't sit down and have this whole organized chart. I started playing one, then the next part, then I just thought, "Okay, now where am I?" It's kind of like painting yourself into a corner. Well, how do I get out of the corner? Which is where really true compositional ingenuity comes in. You made the mess, now you clean it up [laughs].

"Just the Way You Are."

I didn't like it very much. Liberty [DeVitto, Billy's drummer] hated playing it because he felt like a cocktail lounge drummer. I listened back to it and I thought, "Ah, it's all right." It just goes to show to you what musicians know really about what's going to be a hit or not. I tend to like the really obscure stuff that nobody ever hears. We were in the studio listening back to it and I was not even gonna put it on the album, and then Linda Ronstadt and Phoebe Snow showed up at the studio and they said, "You've got to put that on the album!" I said, "Yeah, you think so? We didn't like it that much." And women just pleaded with me to put it on the album. So I'm going to listen to what women say. I put it on the album.

"Uptown Girl."

"Uptown Girl" is a joke song. It's a tribute to Frankie Valli and the Four Seasons. I did it in that style. I even tried to sing like Frankie Valli. That strained falsetto. It's a joke, but if you listen to it in the context of the album, you get it. You go, oh, this is like the Four Seasons, which were a hugely influential group in my youth. But taken out of context, it's like, "What kind of pop silliness is this?" So I don't set out to write a hit single. I write songs in response to other songs I wrote.

"Only the Good Die Young."

The song came out on *The Stranger* album and it was no big deal, and then Columbia decided to put it out as a single. That's when there were some problems. There was a radio station in New Jersey—they banned it. Then it was banned by the archdiocese of St. Louis. And then it got banned in Boston. All these archdiocese areas started putting pressure on radio stations to ban it. And the record as a single had been out a short amount of time and it wasn't doing that well. The minute they banned it, the album starting shooting up the charts [laughs], because there's nothing that sells a record like a ban or a boycott. And I speak from experience, because this record would have died out, nobody ever would've heard it if they hadn't tried to cut people off from it. As soon as the kids found out that there was some authority that didn't want them to hear it, they went out and bought it in droves and it became this big hit. Then I did it on *Saturday Night Live* and everybody was all freaked out about it, saying you can't do that on TV. I said, "Why not?" I think some people took offense at it, but there were all these novels written about Jewish guilt, so why not a song about Catholic guilt? Every Catholic I know is still recovering from this incredibly guilty upbringing they had. It was supposed to be light-hearted. It was taken out of context with the rest of the album. People who only heard that single might've thought, "Oh, Billy Joel the anti-Catholic guy" [laughs].

"Honesty."

A lot of times Liberty will get me to write stuff, because I won't have lyrics, and he wants me to have good lyrics. And he won't record with me unless I have lyrics, because he plays to the lyrics. Or he wants to sing along. That's how he remembers things because he doesn't read music. So what he'll do to motivate me to write lyrics, he'll make up the filthiest possible lyrics he can think of, which are really good and the song will live forever like that unless I come up with some lyrics real fast. When I wrote this song "Honesty," originally it was called "Home Again" [sings "Home again, get me out of here"]. We were in Europe or on the road for a long time and I just wanted to go home again. And I didn't write any more lyrics, so Liberty started writing his own lyrics—"Sodomy, it's such a lonely world." Everybody started singing that whenever we'd play that song, and I realized I better come up with some lyrics pretty quick [laughs]. It's a good way to motivate somebody. Humiliation is a terrific motivator.

"Zanzibar."

There was an Ali fight, I think it was one of his last fights in the 70s. I don't know whether it was Joe Frazier or George Foreman, but there was an accusation that he took a dive, that he went down too easy, which is where I got "Ali don't you go downtown." Going downtown means you took a dive. I just came up with that word Zanzibar. Do you know Keith Richards' theory of songwriting? He has this theory and I subscribe to it—it's called vowel movements. When you write certain combinations of notes, certain chords, the rhyme and the sound of the words that came before it have to have a certain sound to it. Like if I wrote a song like, "I love you just the way you ARE." It's a good way to end that phrase. ARE. You can't say "da da da da da FRED." FRED wouldn't have flown. So that vowel sound, "ah(r)," is soft. So Keith says when they write their songs, that's what they do. They just go "ah, ee, oh," what sounds right, and then they figure out what word it's gonna be. I do that a lot. Just the way you are. Zanzibar. I like that "ah(r)" thing. And I had this word Zanzibar, and I mentioned that I had this idea to Phil Ramone, and he said, "Oh, it sounds like a great place." I thought he was talking about the country Zanzibar. So I go, "Well, what do you think when you hear that word?" He said, "I think of all these guys sitting around watching TV in a bar." I said, "Zanzibar, oh yeah, a sports bar. This is a song about a sports bar. Thank you Phil," and I went home and I wrote the song. A lot of times I don't know what the hell I'm going to say. Somebody just throws out a little suggestion.

"Scandinavian Skies."

I like the *Nylon Curtain* album a lot. That would probably be the album I'm most proud of making, as a labor of love. What I realized after I made it, and it was just after John Lennon was killed, that I even found myself singing like John Lennon. I didn't realize I was doing it and I was writing these songs that I pictured John Lennon singing. Like "Scandinavian Skies." I remember Phil Ramone, who was the producer at the time in the studio, saying, "You're really singing it like John Lennon too much" and I didn't realize it. Then when I came back and listened to it, it was weird. And then I said, "Okay, I'll try to sing it more like whoever Billy Joel is," who I'm still not sure what he sings like. And it didn't work. I had to sing it as it was written, as it was conceived to be sung.

Have you been approached by companies to turn your songs into commercials?

Yeah. I haven't done it, not because I'm a snob and not because I think my music is somehow sacrosanct, but just because I thought it was kind of cheesy and I didn't like the whole idea. I didn't want my music to be perceived as a huckster for somebody's product. If I believed in something and I thought that it was a compatible campaign, and they paid me gazillions of dollars [laughs], I'd consider it, absolutely. But if they come to me with deodorant for "Matter of Trust" and "She's Always a Woman" for feminine hygiene spray, I got a problem with that. Now I'm fortunate—let me be clear about this—I'm fortunate that I can afford my conscience. A lot of people can't. I can afford to sit and judge, I don't want to do this, I don't want to do that—most people can't. So I don't want to appear like I think I'm so great because I haven't done that. And I'm also, again in the press, somewhat typed as somebody who's commercial. There's this whole image of me as well, he's had so many hits, he's sold out. Look, I didn't make 'em hits, I just wrote the songs and recorded them. You made them hits, not me. So why shouldn't I sell my songs, if I'm going to be perceived as a sellout anyway, what the hell do I care? Frankly, I really don't care what somebody thinks of me. All I care is what I think of me.

What do you hope longtime Billy Joel fans get out of your classical record, Fantasies and Delusions?

Obviously, I'm not doing this for the money. This is purely a labor of love. I'm not expecting it to be a huge commercial success. What I wanted to do was open people's ears and maybe open their minds to listening to a music that they might not have listened to before. A lot of people are intimidated by what's called classical music. I don't even refer to this as classical music. I refer to it as instrumental piano music. But if they're in any way interested because of the work I've done before, maybe they'll give this a listen. Perhaps they might be motivated to go to the classical section in a music shop and pick up some of the works of Chopin or maybe give a Beethoven a listen. I think that it will open up an amazing world that they've kind of shut themselves off from. I think we've lost the whole baby boomer generation in terms of classical music. The classical world is kind of running out of an audience now. They're dying off. They didn't reach out enough to the boomers. The powers that be were pretty much promoting late twentieth-century dissonant, atonal, modern twelve-tone compositions. They were scoffing at melodic composition.

I don't know what the inspiration for your song "Vienna" was, but it occurred to me that the couplet, "When will you realize/Vienna waits for you" is almost a message to your future self.

That's true. I've become clairvoyant. You know my song "Miami 2017"? Somebody just pointed that out to me. It describes the apocalypse happening in Manhattan. It describes the destruction of the city, where the mighty skyline falls, the bridges blow, and they send a carrier out from Norfolk. I was reading these lyrics and I thought, "Oh my God, I didn't realize this was prophecy." So I've got to stop writing lyrics, man [laughs].

Fantasies and Delusions *is being released simultaneously with a two-CD set called* **The Essential Billy Joel.**

That's all Sony and their marketing. I don't really have any control over that. I assume that what they're doing is piggybacking on the fact that I'm going to be high profile, promoting *Fantasies and Delusions*, doing TV, radio, and interviews, so they think, "Oh, this is a good opportunity for us to sell some old used cars." I'm not going to disown the songs. I'm proud of them. I wrote them and recorded them and I'm not going to distance myself from them. However, it wasn't my idea to have these things come out simultaneously. Or to put out another compilation at all. I think there's plenty enough of them to go around. But to be fair to Sony, I haven't given them a new recording in eight years, so they've got to sell something.

What's next for you?

I want to continue composing instrumental music, at least for the foreseeable future. If I get ideas to write songs, I'm not going to stop myself. I'll certainly sit down and write songs. I haven't closed the door on that altogether. I just don't feel compelled to write lyrics these days. I'm actually very comfortable writing in the abstract. I was always a literal lyricist anyway, and it used to bother me, how literal I was. I always admired lyricists like Paul Simon or Bob Dylan who were comfortable in an abstract vernacular. That's what writing instrumental music is doing for me. It's allowing me to express myself in an abstract way. But if I come up with some song ideas, I'll write them. I'm not going to censor myself. With my instrumental music, I'll probably be expanding from solo piano to piano with a solo instrument, like piano with violin, piano with cello, piano with clarinet, and from there moving into ensemble arrangements, possibly quartets, and then maybe onto chamber size, and then maybe onto full orchestral-size works. It's going to take a while, and I'm going to do this slowly, so I feel like I'm comfortable with the idiom. I'm still learning.

What advice would you give to songwriters who are looking for their own original sound?

I have a theory that the only original things we ever do are mistakes. The only thing that we can really attribute to ourselves that is purely original are our screwups. Because you can be taught to do everything the way it's been done before, the right way, but only you can exquisitely fuck something up in your own unique way. That goes along with that theory of painting yourself into a corner. Okay, well you got yourself in there, now get yourself out. That's where ingenuity comes in. Everything that I think I've ever done that was good was done purely by accident, purely by total serendipity. I recognize it to be something good after I did it. That takes talent to do. But to screw up I don't think takes that much talent. It takes humanity to do that. It's good to be a human being.

CHAPTER 15

Jimmy Jam and Terry Lewis

Interviewed 1999

Hits: "On Bended Knee," "Human," "Someone to Call My Lover"

Over the years, there has been a handful of songwriter-producers whose names have become synonymous with hit records. Holland-Dozier-Holland, Phil Spector, Burt Bacharach, Gamble and Huff, Barry Gibb, and Prince all come to mind. But if you're talking about modern pop and R & B, no one comes close, in terms of consistency and longevity, to the team of Jimmy Jam and Terry Lewis.

Look at their resume. First, there's the who's who roster of artists they've produced and written for—Janet Jackson, Boyz II Men, the Spice Girls, Michael Jackson, Rod Stewart, George Michael, TLC, Sting, Robert Palmer, the Human League, Gladys Knight, Mary J. Blige, Aretha Franklin, Patti LaBelle, Mariah Carey—the list goes on and on. They've also contributed to the soundtracks of box office hits such as *How Stella Got Her Groove Back, The Prince of Egypt, Poetic Justice*, and *The Nutty Professor II*. Second, there are the statistics: over a hundred albums that have exceeded gold, platinum, and multiplatinum status with McDonald's hamburger–level sales, sixteen number one pop hits, twenty-five R & B chart toppers, two Grammys, and countless other awards, from ASCAP to NARAS and everything in between.

There's also that highest form of audio flattery, sampling. Rap and hip-hop artists such as L.L. Cool J, Jay-Z, Bone Thugs-N-Harmony, and Fatboy Slim have all dipped into the Jam and Lewis catalog with big-selling results. Jimmy Jam says, "In the wake of an era of new producers, it's particularly gratifying for us that our music is being used so much either in samples or remakes."

What's the secret of their staying power? Terry Lewis says, "When we first started out, we had to play everything just to get work. To market yourself as a musician and get paid, you had to have flexibility. You can't do the same thing with everyone. I think if anything has been the mainstay of our longevity, it's the fact that we've adjusted as music has evolved and changed."

Jimmy Jam (real name James Harris III) and Terry Lewis met in Minneapolis in the late 70s. Jimmy says, "I'd known Terry for four or five years, and we had both played in a band together, bands apart from each other as friendly competitors, and then finally, there was a point where I was deejaying, and I was upstairs in a club, and he was downstairs in the same club. He convinced me to join his band, after a lot of arm-twisting, and the band that resulted from that became the Time, with the addition of Morris Day and Jesse Johnson. That was the turning point. We were joined at the hip ever since."

The partners complement each other perfectly. In their cowriting relationship, Terry handles the lyrics, and brings a love of rock 'n' roll and raw funk to the mix. (He says, "I put the dirty bottom in the songs.") Jimmy is a natural melody writer, with a formidable command of chords and harmonies. In the studio, Terry is, in Jimmy's words, "the vocal master." Pulling out hit performances from some of the best voices in modern music is his specialty. Jimmy is an arranger and keyboardist extraordinaire. And from their years of working under the disciplined hand of Prince, both men are facile on any number of instruments and recording consoles.

When you were in the Time, you worked with Prince a lot. What kinds of things did you learn from him that influenced your production and songwriting?

Jimmy: The first thing that I learned from Prince was that I wasn't shit, to be perfectly honest. Growing up, I thought I was pretty talented. Then I got into a piano class with him. I remember Prince was just wearing the keyboard out. I thought, "Man, he is really good." There was another thing, a school band, where he played guitar. He's wearing out every song on the guitar. So I was blown away by him. That was the earliest influence he had on me. Then when we actually worked with him in the Time, it was about work ethic. We'd rehearse six hours a day, then hang out and have fun. He'd come to our rehearsals for five or six hours, then go to his own rehearsals for his own band, then he'd cut all night in the studio, and the next day, he'd show up at our rehearsal with some new song that he just wrote. And it would be "1999" or something, and we'd be like,

"Wow, that's dope." The other thing he'd do, he never wanted you to have a free hand. When we would be playing the keyboards, if my left hand wasn't doing something, he'd say, "What are you doing with your left hand?" I'd say, "I don't have a part there." He'd say, "Well, find a part. Fatten it up. Your hand should never be free." Then he would want you to sing a harmony note. Then it would turn into, "They're hitting choreography out there, you guys need to hit choreography." So by the end of the day, you're all crossed up and you're going, "Man, I can't sing this note and play both hands and dance." After about a week of him drilling that into you, all of a sudden you're doing it, and you're not even thinking about it. It just teaches you that you can be so much better than you think you can be, if you just apply yourself.

Terry: Another thing Prince told us was that we should always make records visually. You should be able to see images in your head when you make records. That was before music video. That's something that we've always tried to do.

When you start a project, say Janet Jackson's latest, All for You, how much of a road map do you have of what the record will be, and how much is left to chance?

J: I think it all eventually ends up to chance. Janet is different because we have a sixteen-year relationship with her. We set a general tone at the beginning of what we think the album will be. We knew at every point. We knew the *Control* album was going to be about her growing up and experiencing new things and taking control of her life. She didn't know that, but we knew that, because in talking to her, that's what she talked about. It was very simple because she's very expressive. We wrote songs about what she was feeling. That's always been the trademark of working with Janet, but it's sort of been the trademark of working with everybody. The album really takes the shape that the artist wants it to take. We kind of have a good overview of what we, as fans, would like to see. If we went to the record store, what kind of album would we like to hear? Hopefully, those ideas are compatible with what the artist wants to do. On *All for You*, we had already done a precursor to what the album would be when we did "It Doesn't Really Matter" for *Nutty Professor*, which was a very upbeat, happy song—very much a pop record. Number one, huge around the world, and we all kind of felt like the side of Janet that the public seems to really like, and that was the side that she wanted to showcase. It ended up being a very happy album, with a few edgy songs like "Son of a Gun" and "Truth." For the most part, the feeling of the album is the way she felt during the time she made the record, which is very happy.

Tell me about the songwriting process with Janet.

J: She usually has a bunch of lyrics, and sometimes has an idea of what the song should be musically. One of the first things we do is have a listening session. You see from looking around that we have racks and racks of CDs. We'll play her a bunch of stuff that we like, that we're excited about, and she'll have a bunch of stuff to play us. Old Motown records, stuff that she might not have heard like "Ventura Highway." It was very interesting. We often end up having the same idea to do the same thing. It's just from working together for so many years. It's all very organic. She's gotten very good at expressing herself lyrically. Earlier, she would know what she wanted to say, but didn't know how to say it, and we would help her.

Terry, what would you say are Jimmy's strengths?

T: His number one strength is melody. He likes pretty chords. I've been working with Jimmy a lot of years. Even before we formed a partnership, he would always play the pretty chords. When I got him to play on any demos I would be doing, he would always put those pretty chords on there, and I would be skeptical, because it wouldn't work at first. It would always be like oil and water, then after a while it would seem to work its way through. The timing was right for that type of song. Chord structure, song structure, melody. Melody is king, the most important part of any song. If you can strip everything else away and just sing the melody, you've got something.

Obviously, you're both at home in the studio. Is it part of the songwriting process?

T: The songwriting process starts more in the car [laughs], or just at home in the bathroom or whatever. When you're totally relaxed, free, and not thinking about anything.

J: The writing and producing we tend to do hand in hand with each other, but it's kind of a seamless process. It's hard to tell where the songwriting ends and the production begins because for us it's always sort of been one process. We've had songs that we've produced and haven't written, and vice versa, but the combination of us doing both has always been the most successful, for whatever reason.

T: I think we're songwriter-producers. We produce because we write songs.

I'd like to mention a few of the hits you've written to get your reaction—"Someone to Call Your Lover."

J: We started with a sample from America's "Ventura Highway." Why didn't we just write a similar riff? Well, there's nothing better than "Ventura Highway." I grew up listening to pop radio, and I loved Seals and Crofts, America, Bread, and all of that harmony-laden pop with major seventh chords. It influenced my writing style. My feeling about sampling is always that it's sort of like redoing the song, but it's redoing it and making it for today's audience. I think in a way it's a good thing because what it does is make people go back and listen to the old record. I ran into Gerry Buckley from America on a plane after the song came out, and he was like, "Oh man, thank you. I loved it." He said that it was turning on a lot of new listeners to America. I think in that way it's very cool. Also, I was a DJ, so to bring a record back in a new way to a new audience is cool.

"Human."

J: The rhythm track started off as an accident. We were using a Linn Drum at the time, and we had this beat programmed in there for what we thought was going to be an S.O.S. Band song, and the drums were tuned really high. The beat had a kind of light, mallet-like feel. But somebody messed with the drum machine. When we turned it on, everything had been tuned really low. So the same beat had this crashing sound. At first, we were like, "Who messed with the drum machine?" Then we said, "Hey, that's kind of dope." We started playing some chords with it, and that's how the track happened. The title just came from the fact that we were working with the Human League. We just thought it would be cool if they had a song called "Human." Terry came up with the whole lyric concept. In songs, one of the things we've always tried to do is put a different spin on something. If there was a song where someone was basically confessing to doing wrong, that would be the normal thing to do. "Human" does that, but then the twist is when the girl goes, "I forgive you, now I ask the same of you. When we were apart, I was human too"—meaning human, as "I fucked up." I think that's brilliant for two reasons. One, it puts a twist on the song, and two, because it allowed the Human League to sing as a group in a provocative way.

"Thank God I Found You."

J: Mariah [Carey] tends to bring more finished ideas to the table. With "Thank God I Found You," that was a much more finished idea when she brought it in. She had, conceptually, the chorus to the song. All we did was put the chords to it that worked. Obviously, there's a million ways to take the chords and the melody. Then she had no idea [what] to do with the verse, or where to take it from there. When we were writing the song, we were intending it to be a duet. We were thinking about Kaycee and Jojo at the time we wrote it. They had had a big hit with "All My Life," so we thought, "Let's do something that's a little reminiscent of that, so that way, when they sing their parts, it'll totally fit exactly what they're doing and work nicely as a duet." The bridge section was very much a Mariah-type thing, but using the sort of Jam-Lewis classic chords, the major sevenths. We thought it was a good combination of all the writing styles. She likes it the way she first hears it. We know now to try to get the demo [as] we see it, because she won't want it to change a lot. Where with Janet a lot of times, we'll put a track down for her, just good enough for her to sing it, and then build the track around the vocal. We do that a lot, because that way, if the track needs something, we put it on there. If it doesn't need anything, we just leave it. Janet knows we're going to do that, and she's a little cooler with that than Mariah. I remember one song we did with Mariah where we changed the drums and we did some stuff, and we thought it was great. She said, "Oh no, it was better as it was originally."

"I Didn't Mean to Turn You On."

J: We did it originally for Cherrelle, and her version was a Top 5 Urban record. Robert Palmer is a huge Urban music fan, and he actually called us and said, "I want to do a remake of 'I Didn't Mean to Turn You On.'" He sent us the demo of what he wanted to do. To be honest, we couldn't make heads or tails of it. We didn't get it. It was so different than what we had done originally. We didn't say no. We just didn't respond. Then, about nine months after that, "Addicted to Love" came out and was huge, and had that great video with the girls. Then, one day I was hunting around on the TV at the studio and I came across this Canadian music channel, Much Music. The sound was off, and I look up at the screen and it's Robert Palmer with those same girls in it. I thought, "Hey, that's dope. He did another video with those girls. I wonder what the song is." And it was "I Didn't Mean to Turn You On." We had no idea that he did it. Musically, we were very influenced by the System at that point, and it's kind of a System-meets-the Time, or Minneapolis sound, Prince type of thing. Lyrically, it came from the fact that we were hanging out in clubs like everybody else, and you'd always meet people, and they'd be all into you and you'd be like, "I didn't mean it like that. We're just hanging out. We're just friends." We wrote it from a female point of view. Robert flipped it around, and it was perfect for what he was doing at the time with his playboy image.

"On Bended Knee."

J: Boyz II Men were finishing their album, and they'd been asking to work with us for a long time. We kept running into them at different events, and we would say, "You don't need anything from us. You've already sold six million records. What do you need us for?" But they wanted to work with us. So they came to the studio, and we said, "Just play us your record, and if we don't feel like you're missing anything, then we don't need to do anything." So they played us the record and we thought it was great. They said, "Is there anything missing?" "Well, the one thing missing is a begging song." Remember how "End of the Road" was a begging song, all "boo-hoo" and "I'm down on my knees" and "oh, please, girl" [laughs]. That was what was missing from the record. They said, "Why don't you write us one of those?" Actually the title of "On Bended Knee" came from Steve Hodge, our engineer. We were having a conversation one night and that phrase popped out. And me and Terry have a thing called the book of titles, so anytime we hear a phrase or anything that catches our ear, we write it in that book. When we started writing the begging song for Boyz II Men, that title said it all. That's the last resort when you're trying to beg somebody to come back or make amends. You get down on your knee. Musically and melodically, we were going for classic chord changes. Those changes have been in about fifty records, but we tried to spin them a little different way. In our demo, we tried to sing it like they would sing it, and we can't sing [laughs]. But interestingly enough, if you compare their version to our demo, they sang it pretty much the way we did. We got across the feeling and the melodic sensibility. It obviously worked.

As a team, you've had an amazing string of hits, platinum records, and awards. How do you measure success?

T: You have to be really careful about how you measure success. Are you basing your success on what someone else thinks or what you really feel? I always tell people that I'll always feel successful if I set out to do a thing, or if we set out to do a thing, and we do it, regardless of anybody liking it or not. Then if it sells, it's nice [laughs].

J: We tell that to a lot of the new artists we work with. When we're done with a project, we say, "When you walk out the door in the back of the building, are you happy?" When people leave here, they're happy. Down the road, who knows? A record company may screw up. Radio may not like it. Bad timing. Whatever. It can be all kinds of things that happen. After it leaves here, it's out of our control. So you concentrate on doing the best job you can do in here, and it's interesting the amount of artists we've had—because we've had long relationships with artists—where we've sent out a record, and the record hasn't worked, then a year later we get a call and they're like, "Hey, let's get together and record." And we're like, "Really? The last record didn't work." And they say, "It wasn't your fault. We made a great record, it was a great experience. Let's make another one." That's what Terry is saying about success. It's successful when it's done and we like it and we've done what we set out to do. It's successful at that point. If you remember that and you remember that feeling, that's the important thing. The success is when you finish it, you like it, and you feel like you've come up with a good one. The rest is all gravy.

What advice could you offer to songwriters?

T: Don't be afraid to try new things. Don't be afraid to try what everyone tells you won't work. That's another thing we learned from Prince. Always try. Don't be afraid to write a song, then rewrite it, then rewrite it. Retry, retry. It's so easy to get caught in the mode of what works until what might work never gets a chance. We've always been willing to do what might work or could work, and ultimately get to see if it does work.

J: My advice would be—find a partner. There's nothing like having someone to bounce ideas off of. As we like to say, we have no slack. If I can't come up with an idea, Terry does. Sometimes we both come up with ideas. Sometimes we both don't come up with ideas [laughs]. Then we go golfing.

And then we come up with ideas [laughs]. I think collaboration is really important. There are exceptions, like Prince, who is someone who can pretty much write on his own, although the grooves that he wrote a lot of times were grooves that came from jamming with other people. Songwriting should be a passion. Once a song comes out, people are going to judge it. We have great songs that have never come out that probably never will. We feel they're great, but we don't feel they're necessarily ready to be judged yet. To us, they're great songs. Maybe the right artist will come along and it will be a perfect fit. We write many more songs than ever come out. Just kind of sit on them. It's a personal thing. We love to write, and we write songs every single day. It doesn't mean that they're hits or it doesn't mean that they're great songs. It's just that we write songs. If you have the passion to do that, you should. If you think your song is ready to be judged, then send it on out there and be prepared for rejection and no's and all of those things. But still know in your mind that if you love it and it's your passion, then by all means, continue doing it.

CHAPTER 16

Amy Grant

Interviewed 1996

Hits: "Baby, Baby," "Every Heartbeat," "The Lucky One"

Thanks to *American Idol* and our current national obsession with all things teen, it's not unusual these days for high schoolers to get record deals. But back in 1978, things were different. For a kid that age to get signed was almost the equivalent of one of them being asked to join the space program.

What makes Amy Grant's story even sweeter—she was in her third year of high school when a label came knocking—is that she didn't really have any ambitious designs on a career in music. "I wanted to marry by the time I was eighteen, have children, live on a farm and play guitar," Grant says.

She eventually got all of the above and then some. And unlike most teen singers, who have all the staying power of a prom theme, Grant survived.

After her self-titled debut in 1978, she matured steadily alongside the burgeoning new genre called contemporary Christian, becoming its most popular artist and spokesperson. Albums such as *My Father's Eyes, Age to Age, Straight Ahead*, and *Unguarded* defined her style in melodic, heartfelt songs of faith, devotion, and love. By the time of the excellent *Lead Me On* in 1988, Grant was in full bloom as a singer and songwriter.

Her next album, 1991's *Heart in Motion*, with its number one smash, "Baby Baby," was a decisive step into the secular pop market, a move that confounded some of her staunch Christian fans. At the time, Grant commented, "Sometimes artists change direction because of hard feelings. Somebody goes from a pop career to a gospel career or vice versa because they've got bad memories of the earlier thing. I like both of them, so I'm not really looking to close the door either way. I'd like the freedom to do both."

True to her word, Grant has continued to pursue both successfully, with all the attendant accolades and credits—megaplatinum sales, Top 10 singles, sold-out concert tours, five Grammy awards, countless Dove and GMA awards, TV appearances and movie soundtracks.

In 2003, she released her seventeenth album, *Simple Things*. A mother of four, she is married to the country singer Vince Gill.

Does songwriting come naturally to you?

Yes. I'm not really prolific, but I don't think quantity of songs is what makes you a songwriter. I started writing when I was fifteen, and since then, I think that I've just been compelled to keep writing.

Living in Nashville, do you feel affected by the work ethic of the Music Row songwriters?

I feel a little bit intimidated by it, because I don't really have push-button inspiration like that. I can go weeks without writing anything and so it kind of makes me nervous if somebody says, "Hey, I want to set up a songwriting date," and I go, "Oh no, what if I don't have any good ideas or a succinct thought? I'm just going to be wasting their time" [laughs]. But I think the older I get, I realize that everyone deals with a certain amount of insecurity in taking the risks to write something. Another thing is, part of what makes songwriting so exciting is it's all about working with your limitations. I don't claim to be a great musician by any stretch of the imagination, but I think sometimes that works to my advantage. I was talking to some of the guys in the band I'm working with right now and we were going over a song, and I said, "Don't suspend that chord until on the and-beat of three," and I got tickled, and I said, "I guess it's that same thing I do every time" [laughs]. I said, "I wasn't really aware of it until I was trying to make sure you played it the right way." We all sat around talking afterwards, and Andrew Ramsey, who's playing guitar on a couple of gigs I'm doing, said, "You know, Amy, for those of us who understand all about theory and we hear a song once and play it, there are ways that music can lose its magic. If I were you, I would celebrate your limitations." I just fumble and fumble, trying to approximate chords, even on songs that I've written and recorded, going, "Oh God, I can't remember what the chord was."

A lot of songwriters I've interviewed have talked about that fumbling, and how the discovery part of the writing process is the most satisfying.

I tend to feel a real thrill when a line pops into my head that captures what I'm feeling. It's so exciting. It's almost like throwing your line out into a deep pool and actually getting a bite. You can throw the line out again and again after that and nothing comes back. But once you've gotten a bite, you know what it feels like. So sometimes writing a song is not a matter of just hammering yourself in the head until you complete the rhyme scheme. A lot of times, it's a matter of walking away from it for ten or fifteen minutes, and waiting for the next line to present itself. And it will eventually, if it's something you really want to say. It just takes a while for your mind to put words to it. Then another line will come and you'll think, "Oh good, it wasn't just an accident" [laughs]. That process has helped me learn to be patient with myself as a writer. I'm not fast, but I know people who are really good and really fast. For those of us who are slow, it's the old tortoise and the hare. You're going to get there, you're just not going to wow anybody with the speed that you do it.

On Behind the Eyes, *were you more involved than usual with the writing of the music?*

I feel like I personally regained confidence in what I bring to the table musically. I quit playing guitar for so long that I slowly became delegated just to being a lyricist. I got my first album deal because I played guitar and wrote songs. Then once I made enough money to hire a guitar player that was actually good, I did, because it seemed liked the smartest thing to do. Then when I could afford to have two guitar players, I did. I realized very quickly, at that point, that I didn't have the time or the energy to get my playing up to speed to participate. So I quit playing. But I found, in an attempt to meet what I felt like were people's musical expectations, I kind of cut off my nose to spite my face [laughs]. About two and a half years ago, I thought, "I've just lost the ability to share my music, unless I find myself in a setting where there's some musician that I've worked with before." So I called J. T. at Taylor Guitars and I said, "I want you to make me a guitar because I'm ready to bond again" [laughs]. What I found is that you don't have to be proficient on an instrument to perceive what moves you. Even if I'm stumbling to find the right chord, I know the feeling of singing a line and having the little hairs on the back of my neck stand up. Not because I'm wowing myself with technique. I think that with this album, I fell in love again with the beauty of a simple song.

Which are the hardest ones to write.

They are, because you're just kind of standing there, emotionally naked, with no gimmicks. It better be a payoff, it better mean something, it better connect, or you're running the risk of it being one big yawn. There's a fine line between something falling on the side of the fence of being half-baked or boring, and just on the other side is profound. And I wrote both [laughs]. I probably do yawn better than I do profound [laughs], but I just didn't leave those on the record.

You've said that you wanted to go "below the surface" on this new album. How did that affect your writing?

Until now, I think that I've never really allowed myself to feel free of the expectations of the people and the music that I represent. And don't get me wrong, it's not that I choose to be a spokesperson, but I feel like I represent Christian artists. I feel like I represent women. I feel like I represent moms. I feel like I represent wives.

That's a lot of responsibility to carry.

But it was never even a conscious thought. There was a little meter in my head that registered "acceptable" or "unacceptable." I guess I would have to go to a lot more counseling to understand all that, but I decided to step outside of all of that and say, "I'm going to give myself the gift of assuming that no one will ever hear these songs." Because that's where real freedom comes. I have a safe in my bedroom, and I write down things on scraps of paper and put them in that safe. The beauty of it is, I know that I'll write down what I really think, because I know that no one will ever read it. It's so important to be able to write down what you really think. People that write in a diary or a journal, you take on a different tone if you feel like somebody else is going to read it. You fill in all the blanks. You try to create the framework for whatever emotion you're trying to write. If you're really writing a journal that no one's ever going to see, it can almost be stream of consciousness because you know it all. I don't know how that relates to songwriting exactly, but it does somehow. I felt myself trying desperately to capture real feelings and it had nothing to do with presentation. As I started playing them for the record company, it wasn't like I was writing these things and throwing them in a safe. I gave myself the freedom of saying, "I don't have to explain this." That was my way of just letting it out. I've done some interviews where people have said, "I'd like to talk to you about this line in that song." And I've thought, "Please don't cheapen the experience or undermine the safety that I feel as a songwriter, by trying to hang this song on some framework of time or details, because that will ruin the whole thing." All I know to say is, "Everything I wanted to say has been said."

Do you write to please yourself first?

At the end of the day, the goal is to write something that truly connects with another person, but you're only going to connect with another person if you connect with yourself.

Jackson Browne said he often writes about things "to get past them." Can songs about your personal life take the place of angst or tears?

Or suicide? [laughs]. I think that writing a song can settle a feeling. I relate to what he's saying. It doesn't make it go away, but it brings about a certain amount of contentment. As an example, the song "Missing You" successfully captured that sad feeling. It doesn't bring an end to that feeling, but it said it and there's a huge sigh of relief. Every time I have that feeling, instead of letting my head spin out of control or just that kind of wandering—my wheels are spinning and I'm in mud—I will pick up my guitar and sing that song. And I'll feel like, "Amen" [laughs]. There's an ability to move on.

That song and "The Feeling I Had," which you wrote by yourself, are my two favorites.

You know, I wrote thirty-one songs total for this album, and it was such a great process. David Anderle at A&M and my manager Mike Blanton and a few others were my sounding boards, and it was like being yelled at by great coaches [laughs]. I would show up at A&M and play something for David Anderle, and he would be very polite at the time, then later on he would say, "I never want to hear you even mention that song again" [laughs]. He would let me chase an idea, and then he would go, "I know this has great sentimental value to you, but it's not making it for me." But then I remember, on the song "Missing You," he came by the studio and listened to it, then he turned around, grabbed me by the ears and planted a big kiss on my mouth, and said, "Thank you. That's why I'm so critical of the things that don't nail me, because every once in a while something does."

If a singer-songwriter says to you, "I want to make a career out of this," what do you tell them?

I've had people come up and say, "I would like to be a singer-songwriter," and my first advice is, "Then stop saying 'I would like to be' and start saying 'I am.'" Because that perception of something eventually happening is just as elusive as a cloud. If you are a singer-songwriter, then you start looking for ways to be that where you are. I always tell people that there is no guarantee that this will pay the bills, but if it's who you are, then it's who you are and go on and admit it.

What are your desert island discs?

Joni Mitchell, *Blue*
Carole King, *Rhymes and Reasons*
Marc Cohn, *Marc Cohn*
Don Henley, *The End of the Innocence*
Aretha Franklin, *Greatest Hits*

CHAPTER 17

Jane Siberry

Interviewed 1998

Hits: "Mimi on the Beach," "Calling All Angels," "Everything Reminds Me of My Dog"

Eccentric. It's a word that's often applied to those female singer-songwriters who blend styles with Hamilton Beach vigor and pour their quirky hearts out in sounds that defy categorization. Kate Bush, Laurie Anderson, Bjork are all charter members of the club. Fiona Apple and Tori Amos are too. But no one waves her freak flag with more pride and panache than Jane Siberry.

From the moment she surfed in on her buoyant first single, "Mimi on the Beach," through the free-form jazz creations of her album *Maria* to her latest vocal renditions of Bach and Handel, Siberry has always been part serious artist, part lovable kook.

"Eccentric is a compliment to me," she says. "That means you're more yourself than most people."

Jane was born forty-five years ago near Toronto, Canada. When she was a student studying microbiology at the University of Guelph, she began singing and writing her own songs. Her first record, a self-titled, self-released collection of acoustic-based stories, was financed with tips she received from her waitressing job.

Three years later, she left the restaurant business behind, releasing her major-label debut, *No Borders Here*. In 1985, she followed with *The Speckless Sky*, a gold record that garnered two People's Choice awards in her native country.

Over the next decade, she honed her artistic sensibilities with three more albums—*The Walking*, *Bound by the Beauty,* and *When I Was a Boy*—while taking her spellbinding show from America to Europe to Japan. She also contributed songs to two motion pictures, *The Crow* and Wim Wenders' *Faraway, So Close*.

In 1998, she started her own label, Sheeba Records, which is dedicated to "all things Siberry" with a credo of "no hype, no bullshit." "I'm much better suited to putting out my own records than a large corporation because it interests me to do a lot of small spinoff projects and I have direct contact and access to my audience," she says.

When it comes to songwriting, Siberry is also her own person. Channeling nursery rhymes, poetry, voices of souls lost and found, a love of color, and a distinct interest in all things carnal, she improvises songs in a language that's hers alone.

During our conversation, she even used the word "blowing," a jazz cat's term for "improvising freely." "Words come out and I'm not really thinking about anything," Siberry says. "The songs tell me what to do. The less my brain is involved, the more I trust my music."

Were you less self-conscious as a young songwriter, before you made records for major labels and had to think about creating things for mass consumption?

I think a lot of writers might be like that, but fortunately or unfortunately I've never had a lot of airplay to have that standard to work against, that fear of not writing something for airplay. I just sort of followed my nose. I think when you're starting, there's another kind of self-consciousness that is there though, because certainly you don't know if you're a good songwriter, so there's a different kind of pressure on yourself to make sure you exist. You tend to match yourself against other songwriters. I think now I'm much less self-conscious, because I'm sure I exist as a songwriter.

When you sit down to write songs, do you still feel like a beginner sometimes?

Yes, especially when I *have* to write a song. As soon as my brain kicks in, I feel like a beginner, because I don't know how to do it. If I write naturally, it just comes to me and I sort of take dictation. So right now I'm working on a song that k.d. lang wants for her record and I can't really remember how to write a song. So I'm fuddling around and wasting time because it's not really in my heart to write it. So I do feel like a beginner when I'm coming from that part of me.

You say you write naturally. How does that usually begin for you, if not with a deliberate notion to write a song?

You see something or hear something and it activates a drive in you to capture it, and it usually has an emotional charge to it. You know, you're moved by something and you see the shape, how it could be captured in a beautiful way. It comes from such a visceral part of the body that your brain isn't involved in. Usually, if I have enough time, the song just gathers like a magnet. I rarely sit down to write. I just do dishes and stack towels. Songwriters are often an antenna without even knowing what they're attracted to. Most people don't know why they're writing about things or why they use either muted colors or bright reds in their songs at different times in their writing career. That's why I think I trust in myself—the writing that I do that is not brain driven. I'm not forcing myself onto it. It comes from more of the gut, or what I see in my head, and I'll just write it down.

I've talked to a few writers who've cited you as a direct influence on their songs. For instance, Shawn Colvin on "Kill the Messenger" and Everything but the Girl on "Frozen River"—they refer to your song "Hockey."

Oh yeah. I love that they feel free to refer, because I always refer. I ran into problems with it on *Maria*. I said, "I think I'd like to approach the person to tell them I'm referring" and then they say, "You can't have permission for it." You go, "What?" Well, that's how I work. I think it's a freedom that everyone needs. You're a songwriter and you synthesize the world around you and put it down in some sort of personal order, then we all get to see how everyone else is seeing the world. That's how we learn. We need help growing and understanding things. There's less help nowadays than there's ever been. So I think that's an important freedom to be able to draw from famous songs. Like on "Maria," I wanted to used the line [sings] "Maria, I've just met a girl named Maria" [from *West Side Story*], and that was all I was using from it. But it was sort of a key reference even though it was a fun, thrown-off thing. It was hooked up to all the other imagery in all the other songs, but I was denied permission for that. It's so familiar that it's almost like part of our language. It's like cutting off part of the alphabet. For me it was. So there's a gray area copyright-wise that I think has been messed up.

Some of your songs, such as "Everything Reminds Me of My Dog," reflect a great love of pets, and I've read that you've spent a lot of time observing animals. Has that influenced your writing?

I would have to associate cows with the ability to let a song take as long as it needs. I always found animals fascinating, any animal. Like you can have a great actress on stage and beside them you can have a cat sitting there licking itself, cleaning itself, and everyone will watch the cat [laughs]. There's some inherent trust that what you're seeing is the natural universe reflected in this little being and isn't it ever mysterious and wondrous. When I was young I would go up to a relative's farm. I had no one to play with and the mothers and aunts spent all their time sort of depressed but acting cheery and all day long preparing meals, eating them, and cleaning up, morning to night. Not much joy, you know. So I'd go stand at the fence and watch these cows, and that was my first understanding of what it means to be in the moment. Words I'd use now, but not then. But there's something incredibly profound and beautiful about it, and I'd watch it for a very long time. And they would watch me for a long time and they'd keep chewing . . . it's hard to explain really.

Is it just a patience?

Patience, and an acceptance of all that happens. No controlling. Whatever happens, they deal with it. Why is that different than another animal? I don't know. I think maybe I'm not getting the essence of what a cow is, but another part of me does understand what it is, even if I can't explain it. I learned a lot from my dog, who I don't have anymore. He taught me so much. I never would've been so tuned in to the minute nuances of the everyday light except I had to walk him all the time, so I got out. Now that I don't have a dog, I notice how much less connected I am with the outdoor world.

How has moving to New York City affected your work?

You get lots of ideas because you can record a guitar and vocal, then you play it in your living room in New York City, and you hear horns honking right across the chromatic scale [laughs], which is very exciting. When I was young, often when my ears would perk up and I'd say, "Now that is interesting, that's the kind of music I like," it would take me about ten seconds till I registered that the record was skipping, that the sound was coming from the problem. The same sort of thing, that amazing happenstance, that chemical experiment is there, if you're open to seeing it. Also, New York's been very good for me because I've come into contact with lot of different musicians, and people are getting to know that I live here now, so I'm being invited to work more with other people, which I really love. If this city has been attracting some of the most artistic people in the world for years and years and years, there must be something happening here. I believe it is, just on a subtle level. There's something about the makeup of this city, on this particular part of the planet that is concrete.

What's the most difficult thing for you as a songwriter now?

The hounds of self-doubt are always at your elbow when you write. That's always been a struggle, probably with most people. It's much easier now than it was before. Mostly I just listen, so if things get in my way it's because something's stopping me from listening, some kind of distortion—like how you see yourself won't allow the voice of the muse to come through, so you control things and you end up with stuff that sort of smells like a rat. Then you feel it and the listeners feel it. That's part of it. You can't shoot a hundred every time, but I think that's the goal.

You've always impressed me as a writer who has a clear channel to her muses. Are there things that you find helpful to keep that connection strong?

One is just seeing the quality change when I don't trust the muses. When I allow my brain to interfere, the quality goes down. It takes on a sort of self-consciousness or preciousness or something that I really don't like. I hear that in my music and I know exactly when I was afraid or changed it. It's just seeing that difference in quality. And you have to be where you're supposed to be. I know that when I went to Real World, Peter Gabriel's collaboration week a few years ago, my writing changed. The vibration in the valley was so powerful and spiritual. It was too much for me. My lyrics became a bit too highfalutin, like they had messages. I was so uncomfortable with that. It wasn't natural to the state of wisdom that I'm in right now. So I could see clearly that it's not for me to write that way. Maybe other people. The best stuff I do is just who I am, you know? But coming from a sort of intuitive level. Something else about songwriters that I want to say: I have this thing about what's happening today where there's not much structure. People are sort of having to find their own religions, you know? Sort of lose them and find them. You can't just count on being brought up in a Catholic household, being satisfied and dying a Catholic, or Judaic, or Hindu. Nothing quite fits our times. Everyone's sort of having to form their own philosophy of what a good life should be. It's really more important than ever to write about what you know. Not to have answers, not to teach, not to have a mission, but to say how you're finding it is to be alive. That's how we learn and that's the most valuable thing that I read or hear or see in film. How that person is finding being alive, and how to learn from each other. For me songwriting is about that. That's one of the most valuable things someone has to offer as a songwriter. Just to say what you're experiencing.

CHAPTER 18

John Rzeznik of the Goo Goo Dolls

Interviewed 1996

Hits: "Name," "Iris," "Slide"

John Rzeznik set himself a deadline for success. If he didn't have some tangible sign that his group the Goo Goo Dolls had made it—a hit song, or at least a record that didn't end up in the cutout bin—by the time he was thirty, he was going to pack it in. "I didn't want to embarrass myself," he says.

After forming in 1986 in Buffalo, New York, the Goos soldiered on for nine years—endless cross-country touring in a van, thankless opening gigs, bad business moves, records that were critically acclaimed but commercial fizzlers. Rzeznik's deadline was looming. Tensions in the band were high. They canned their longtime drummer. Then everything changed, thanks to a song called, appropriately, "Name." It made the band's.

While this moody ballad about aging didn't quite fit with their established punk-pop repertoire, it took off on the radio. In the years after, Rzeznik embraced his inner McCartney and penned a steady stream of melodic smashes for the group, including "Iris" (which stayed on Triple A and Modern Rock charts for a staggering ten months), "Slide," "Broadway," and "Black Balloon."

Though the Goo Goo Dolls have become hugely popular, Rzeznik says, "In the end, it always comes back to the music. For us, success—real success—is one song at a time."

I read that you started writing songs when you were fifteen. Over the last fifteen years, do you feel like it's gotten easier for you?

No [laughs]. After you've been writing for fifteen years, you start to wonder, "What if I run out? What if you're only given a limited number of songs?" Some guys may have a thousand, and other guys may have four-teen. Maybe I only have eighty-six. I get really terrified every time I have to write a record because I think, "What if I can't do it? What if it sucks?" But they come. When they don't, I guess that'll be when it's time to give up.

When you were writing songs for this new record, do you feel like you made any discoveries about the writing process?

I got a little closer to the bone than I ever thought I'd get. It got a lot more personal than I thought it would be. It's kind of a weird thing, writing. You can sort of drain all the poison out of your soul, or you can really use it as a tool to better yourself emotionally, maybe understand some things about yourself that you never did before.

When you sit down to write, is there the intent to work through a problem?

I'll sit down with the guitar and start to play and the music will start to influence a mood, and it will take me somewhere. Things just start to come out of your mouth, and then later on, they get put together in cohesive ideas. Things lay around on tape for a long time that make absolutely no sense. It'll be some slurred gurglings and then one or two words that will come out [laughs] that make sense.

When you're in the initial stages of writing, do you have more of a sense of leading or following?

I think I'm just sort of sitting there watching, and if I decide to follow, I'll go. Whenever I try to lead and bend something into what I think a song should be, it usually winds up slapping me in the head and sucking [laughs]. It's so weird. There are songs you have sitting around for five or six years and they just never seem appropriate at the time, but there'll be one line that you'll remember. That's part of it too. If I sit down and play something and I remember it after I put the guitar down, if I come back to it the next week or month, if I remember it, it's worth being pursued. If I don't remember something, it's not even worth bothering with.

Does it help you when you're writing a lyric to have a specific person in mind?

Sometimes I'll write a song for a friend or I'll be thinking of something I did when I was ten. It does help to have something specific in mind to focus on. Most of the time I just let it flow. Sometimes six months later you'll look at what you wrote and you'll go, "You know, I think that's what that's about."

Let me ask you about a few specific songs. What was the inspiration behind "Flat Top"?

It's about being completely disgusted with the way mass media is destroying us. It's turning us into a bunch of scared little rabbits that are afraid to come out of their hole because of a big, bad scary world.

Do you play off the TV much when you're writing?

Sometimes I find myself sitting in front of the TV at four in the morning doing a lot of writing.

"Ain't That Unusual."

That's about a friend of mine I hadn't talked to in years, and wanted to, but didn't get the chance to.

How much do your songs change from the time you write them to the time you put them on a record?

Not much. Sometimes I like to record demos just to hear a musical arrangement. I like to have an arrangement together before I get in the studio, but then I like to hear it with a band playing it, with a real drummer instead of a drum machine. A real bass player instead of me. Then I'll take it back home and listen and see where it takes me.

You used an open tuning for "Name." Is that something new?

No, I do that a lot. I was never brave enough to do it with this band, because you know, up until "Name" broke, we were expected to be one thing, which was a power punk band with three goofy fun-loving guys that just wanted to scream and entertain you. Which is cool, but it gets a little thin after a while. I've always played with open tunings. I sit at home and play with my guitars. It just seemed appropriate for me as a writer to do this song. All this stuff on the new record, about three or four months after the record was done, we decided we needed a different drummer and we couldn't work with our old drummer anymore. It was a scary experience. I also remember going out to play our first show with our new drummer and really listening to the songs and going, "Wow, this is the first time in my life I feel like a writer." I felt enough freedom to actually feel like a writer.

Was it weird that "Name," the first Goo Goo Dolls song that gained mass acceptance, was atypical of what the band is known for?

Yes. I have this huge body of work that is largely ignored. I feel so lucky to have had a hit, you know? I feel really blessed about that. I could never bemoan having a little success. It's great. It's a lot of fun. People return your phone calls [laughs]. But people are slowly starting to come around to the rest of the music on the album, and I don't think I'll ever write another song again that's as big as "Name." I just wish that people had a chance to listen to some of the other stuff before they got "Name." It's a funny thing when you're out there. We had only sold fifty–sixty thousand records every time we made a record, before this one. And I don't know what we've sold with this one, but it's a lot more, and it's based on the strength of "Name." I tend to worry that that may limit the size of my palette as a writer. But I'm ignoring all that. I'm going to write exactly what I want to write, and hopefully people will dig it.

Are there people in the picture, businesswise, who are now wanting you to come up with another song like "Name"?

No. We've made a lot of fucked-up business moves, because we were kids. We wanted to play, we wanted to keep our band going. And every time the thing was dying, somebody comes along and says, "Here, sign this piece of paper and we'll do this." So we basically sold out a huge piece of our own ass just to keep making our records and go out and tour in a van. We never thought anything about that. All roads lead to where you are and here I am. I regret having signed some of those stupid pieces of paper but I don't regret the fact that it kept the band alive. People say, "Oh, you had this big hit and you sold out." That's the one thing that bothers me about "Name," because it is indicative of me as a songwriter but not to the general public what the Goo Goo Dolls are about. But when fans who've been with us for a long time say, "Fuck you, you sold out," it's like, "Fuck you, no I didn't. I wrote exactly what I felt." There are two components to selling out. A, you need to do something that you normally wouldn't have done and B, you need to make a lot of money. And I haven't done either of those things, so how could I have sold out?

It's a stupid reaction, but it seems inevitable that fans do that. Maybe they feel like they're losing their exclusive hold on you.

The critics and press are the worst. They root for you and root for you, then the second you get some success it's like *bam*, they just crank on the disdain machine and fucking try to grind you into little pieces through it. I've really learned. Every piece of bad press I've ever gotten stings. It still stings. The bigger you get, the more punches you have to take. Sort of weird. But I guess if you walk into a room of two million people, five or six of them are not going to like you. That's the way life is. But generally, I think the press has been positive. A friend of mine gave me an insight about critics. Critics fancy themselves music aficionados. They consider their taste to be better than that of the average Joe on the street. So if the average Joe on the street is going out and buying something en masse, it must suck. So it's not the critics' disdain for you, it's for the public at large [laughs]. You just happen to take the bullet for the public at large. That was a really unique insight.

Tell me about cowriting with Paul Westerberg.

It was like a correspondence course in songwriting. It was like I answered an ad in the back of a magazine—"Learn how to write songs from a real songwriter." He's always been a big influence on my songwriting, and when our band started, all we wanted to do was kick ass as hard as the 'Mats. Because they were the only band around in 1985 that didn't completely suck [laughs]. Those guys and Hüsker Dü. All the bands that we were really into had broken up by that point. He was always so honest and such a brilliant writer, and he always downplayed it. He was always so humble and honest about it. He was so fucking brilliant. He could just fire you up in a frenzy or make you cry your eyes out in a span of six or seven minutes, and that's the thing I admire about Westerberg the most. Of course, he was someone, in the early stages, that we really tried to emulate, as much as possible. You're eighteen years old, writing songs for a band—you don't have a fucking clue. So you try to just imitate people, and then you grow beyond your influences. I think on the last two or three records we've really done [that]. To write a song with him was a dream come true. It's like when Keith Richards finally got to jam with Chuck Berry. It was a dream come true.

What five albums were the most important to you as a songwriter?

London Calling, The Clash
My Aim Is True, Elvis Costello
Hot Rocks, The Rolling Stones
Let It Be, The Replacements
Flip Your Wig, Hüsker Dü

CHAPTER 19

Tori Amos

Interviewed 1993 and 2001

Hits: "Silent All These Years," "Cornflake Girl," "God"

Visitations, messages from other worlds, contact with strange beings...
no, it's not a vintage episode of the *X-Files*. It's the songwriting world of
Tori Amos.

As a songwriter, Tori has always been very colorful in her descriptions
of her creative process. The first time we spoke, she described her songs
as female visitors.

"Some of them aren't even human looking, but they're a form that feels
kind of female," Tori said. "And they come and say, 'It's time for you to
put down in music my essence and what I'm trying to tell you.' So I feel
the essence of a song and then it completely leaves me, then I have to start
again. I don't know if you've ever had a dream where you've written a
song and you really love it. It's great, then you wake up and you can't
remember it. This is kind of the same thing except I'm awake."

Tori was born Myra Ellen Amos on August 22, 1963. The daughter of a
Methodist preacher, she was pounding the keys when she was a mere two
and a half. By age five, she'd won a scholarship to Baltimore's Peabody
Conservatory. Six years later, she was expelled for playing by ear and
improvising. As a teenager, Tori gigged continuously, playing everything
from Gershwin to U2 in hotel lounges and gay piano bars. All the while,
she was honing her writing skills.

Following her love of music, she eventually moved to LA and released *Y Kant Tori Read*, a heavy metal album that unfortunately was more
about image than content. It stiffed. Four years later, after intense self-
examination and a move to England, she reemerged with a newfound
confidence and a whole bevy of strong songs. She was signed, and her album *Little Earthquakes* shook the British charts with a seismic jolt, bringing

a flood of popular and critical acclaim. Since then, she's released albums and built a worldwide following. Like Dave Matthews Band and Phish, Tori is an artist who connects with millions of devoted fans without getting much radio play. In some ways, she's like the prog-rock artists from the 70s—ELP, Genesis, Yes—in that she makes heady, complex music that invites listeners into a richly imagined world. The main difference between Tori and Greg Lake is that Tori has sex appeal. Lots of it.

Her erotic persona is carried even further in her mesmerizing concerts. By her own admission, she "makes love with the audience." Whipping her bright red mane in a frenzy, undulating against the piano keys and singing in a voice that can rise from a velvet whisper to a tempest's raging howl, she often appears to be approaching orgasm on stage. Of her performing approach, Tori comments, "I have a responsibility to give all of my being, which I make a commitment to."

Are you a disciplined songwriter?

Well, I've been doing it since I was a little kid—almost before anything else. I can't even remember when I started writing. I was always making up my little ditties. So it's kind of a part of my day. As far as the discipline goes, I'm a pretty disciplined person anyway, and I'm pretty ruthless, as far as what stays and what goes in a song. I always listen to my tummy.

Can you explain that?

Beyond the logical mind there is the tummy. And I really believe this, because we can overthink everything. Hey, I'm not writing things for some genius that's sitting trying to criticize. I'm writing from the tummy, because that goes beyond what somebody else's concept of cool is. I'm so sick of cool. If this world has one more megameter of cool, we're just gonna explode. So it's about allowing yourself the freedom to express. When you allow yourself the freedom, that's your first step. Then the other step is the craft of it, the skill. Okay, so if I don't have a very big music vocabulary, it's not about big. It's about how you use what you know. I think you can stay on one chord for five minutes and make it incredibly interesting, if you know what you're doing. The more that I open my mind to different possibilities musically and lyrically, then the more places I can go. Whereas if I'm going I-IV-V-I all the time, it's gonna get a little sweetie pie [laughs]. So that's the other end of discipline. It's like running a marathon. You can't run it unless your muscles and heart can take the distance.

I remember reading how you prepared yourself for one writing session by sitting in the center of a kind of circle of lyric fragments and song titles. Do you always do meditations like that to conjure up a song?

Yes. For this album [*Under the Pink*], I was in New Mexico for the writing and recording of it. And I would go out into the desert and just sit until really the soul of the song came and visited me. When it would come, I would just start to get to know who this being was and what they were trying to say to me. Of course all these beings are just parts of me, parts of you. Anybody that comes to visit you is a part of you somewhere, somehow. So I would sit and try to just feel what I was feeling. So many times, I think I'm supposed to feel a certain way, and that's not good. That's not very interesting, in your normal life or your creative life. So I would sit by the Rio Grande and try to stop all the voices. I still had to deal with it as much as last time. "Silent All These Years" was just a beginning, but the outside voices didn't get any quieter, they just got louder. The whole last record was about finding my voice again. So it was kind of different because I had just stumbled onto things that I hadn't dealt with in fifteen years, whereas this record, it's about how to... struggle to stay awake, if you know what I mean. To stay conscious, to be present...because once you go, "Yeah, this happened to me, yeah I was violently held hostage and sexually and emotionally violated; yeah I was a minister's daughter and I denied how I buried my true beliefs for all those years, yeah, yeah, yeah." When you first deal with those realizations, it's kind of like the whole earth opens up. A week later, a year later, you don't have the firecrackers like you did, but you're still healing and dealing with things. So this one was a bit trickier, because when you first come to a realization, it's like a kid in a candy shop. We've talked about these subjects before, so obviously I can't write "Me and a Gun" again, because how can you write that again? This record is working through not being a victim anymore. I had to sit out there in the desert and listen to what my inner being was really saying, not what I wanted it to say to me.

Do your lyrics arrive in a stream of consciousness?

Lines here and there do, but there's a lot of reworking that I do. I'm pretty ruthless with lyrics. I don't let anything slide. The music is more stream of consciousness and it's always done first, with a line here and a line there. Again, a line of lyric will come for a verse, then I have to craft around what does this line mean? What needs to support it? Okay, it's a very interesting line, but how I set it up or how I pay it off is where it really means something or doesn't mean diddly. Then it comes back to what I am trying to say here and it gets tricky because I'm not in that trance anymore. I'm just sitting, me and my chair, me at the piano, going, "What is this girl trying to tell me?" Even though this girl is me. So I'm sitting there by myself and I have to try to go into the inner world. It's all about the inner world, songwriting is. Even if you're talking about the outer world, you have to go into the inner world to see the outer world with any interesting viewpoint.

Is it important for you to rhyme?

I like assonance myself, close, but not a true rhyme.

The reason I ask is that your lyrics are kind of free verse, yet by not having perfect rhymes, I think they hit you harder in a way.

Yes, I agree. I'm not a big believer in rhyme. Who decided that rhyming was the way to do it? Who was that guy? Let's go find him and have a little chat, because this has really cramped writers for a long, long time. It's about content, it's not about the rhyme. Everything is tone to me, like what a word feels like. There's certain words that I love, like "lemon pie." How it feels in my mouth.

What's the happiest accident that's ever turned into a song for you?

I don't know if this is happy, but it's kind of worth mentioning. The song "Pretty Good Year." I got a letter from a guy named Greg. He's a fan, and this letter just happened to get to me, because a lot of times I don't get them. But he's from the north of England and he drew this picture, a self-portrait of himself. It was a pencil drawing and Greg had glasses and long hair and he was really, really skinny. He had this drooping flower in his hand. And he wrote me this letter that touched me to the core about how at twenty-three, it was all over for him. In his mind, there was nothing. He just couldn't seem to catch the kite by the tail. You know, sometimes you see that kite flying and bloody hell, you just have to grab the tail, bring it down and see what's on that kite. Well, he just couldn't find a way around putting his desires and his visions into anything tangible, except this letter. Many people today, before they even reach thirty, feel this way—it's a functional exercise waking up, brushing your teeth, going through your day. People have just numbed themselves. I don't know the answer why. I think there are loads of answers. It's not my job to come up with an answer. Nobody wants to hear an answer from me. The point is, what I tried to come up with is the feeling we all feel. Shaking us out of the numbness. I was just telling Greg's story and Greg affected this singer so much that it brought my own stuff into it, and that was kind of a neat surprise.

Once I read that you said that you tried to write like a camera. That's an intriguing notion. Can you elaborate?

If I can't see and smell and taste what's happening, then I'm not doing my job. I can't write something where I'm not tasting what the wall is made out of. I wanna know if there's smokers in the room. I wanna know if this person washes or only kind of washes twice a week. It's okay, no judgment, I just have to know, because that's the thing that shakes me out of my sleepy pie, is the senses. When I'm listening to the songs, I have to feel like I'm living them with this girl that's singing. That's my director point of view. And yet being the writer of the play and also the actor, sometimes it gets a bit self-involved [laughs]. Then some of the songs, like "God," I'm just so in the middle of, that I'm not really the director. When I wrote that I was having a complete conversation with the concept of what God is. Not necessarily what I think God truly is, but what the institution, whether it be educational or what have you, has made of God. To me, it's the root of all problems, that song right there. For me, one of the most important things I've ever done. You can call it my prayer if you want.

What are the top three things you wish you could do as a songwriter but haven't been able to?

The biggest one is, I don't think you can ever feel like you're finished as a writer. There's always so much else to say. There are pieces I've written that I'll never be able to write again, like "Me and a Gun" or "God." Once you say it, you say it. But I think that as songwriters, we have to say, hey, we did that. When you're dealing with a rape subject, you got some pretty serious guns loaded there. It's a deep subject. It's very different than when you're dealing with a song like "Cloud on My Tongue." So I try and compare, I just wish I could stop comparing my different songs, because I'll never write "Me and a Gun" again. I can't. I can write about the aftermath, and that's what I do. All my songs, whether it's "Pretty Good Year" or "Yes, Anastasia" are about the healing process. I don't think that

I'll ever have written enough work to feel like I can die now. But I will die and it'll just have to be enough. I guess that's one, two, and three all in one.

You've called your performance style "confrontational." Do you think it's necessary to be shocking in some way these days to get people to listen to you?

I don't know. Shocking can be a bit boring. My performance style is more based on my relationship with the songs and what I need to express that night and the energy in the room. If I walk into a room, I can't tell you right now how I would handle it, until I'm in the situation, but I play the piano in a pretty passionate stance. My right leg supports my whole body. That's one big reason why it's swung back behind me. And the left foot on the pedal because it supports my diaphragm and my whole body and I can play with ten times the power while I'm singing than I could in any other way. The deal is that I have a responsibility to give all of my being, which I make a commitment to. I go into a meditation and a trance to expose myself. And if you come there to just be a bit of a sneaky Pete, then you know, it's not only me up there. I call a lot of energy into the room. I'm not alone. There's like thousands of spirits hangin' out. So I'm usually pretty supported when I walk out there and the whole live performance is about transformation of myself. I go and find different parts of myself each night that I need to deal with. Sometimes it's joy. Sometimes it's my violent side or whatever, and we work through it. The audience dictates to me what I'm going to deal with, because I tune into them and everybody there that night is changing the atmosphere. But if there's some energy that's disrespectful, it's not just about paying a ticket price. I don't make money off the tour. It's not about that. It's about honoring each other, and I honor my audience and they're pretty wonderful people. They're all interesting characters, they all bring stuff to the party.

How does a songwriter shed layers and expectations and find their own sound?

First of all, songwriters need to understand what is their intention and what is our role. We are documenting a time. That's what we're doing. Music can do that in a way that nothing else can. We love painters and we love dancers, totally groovy. But sound goes into the being. I think it changes the DNA, I think it can shift somebody's whole molecular structure. I really believe that. When they hear something, the kind of emotion that it can stir up, the memory or what have you. So what is our job? Our job is to get in touch with ourselves. If we're not in touch with ourselves, how can we possibly give something to the people out there. My big worry is that we as songwriters aren't doing our job, because we're letting these people who run the industry, who run critics' sheets, that run the radio stations, dictate what we're going to talk about. Now hang on a minute. If all of us got together and had a little powwow and said, you know, we have a commitment first to ourselves and out of that I'm sure each one of us can come up with something a bit catchy. But what are we talking about? There's no excuse for this schlocky shit out there, there's no excuse. Anybody that's writing shit, they know. I'm not talking about sentimental, but we all know when it just doesn't do what even it wants to do. Hey, I can hear something—and it's not just me. C'mon, loads of us can go, "That person wrote something to please somebody." This is not about an inner experience or even somebody else's inner experience that they stole. This is about listening to another song on the radio that was a hit and formulating it. Formulated songs. Hey, if that works for you as a writer and you make lots of money, go knock yourself out. But what is our role? If we could remember who we are. We are the poets who are going from town to town, and trying to remind the populace, with all the stuff going on, information, whether it's television, movies, or what have you, all this media, everything is straying away from the heart. Everything is really straying away from what's inside of yourself. And that's what people are starving for. I don't like the word "documentation," but in a sense, songwriters are the mirrors, just like the poets were in another time. The poets of the late nineteenth century especially. The French poets, they were the voice of their time. So what are we? I think there's a lot of us who are trying to remember why we're doing what we're doing. We have to put our hands, as writers, on the 220 voltage and say, "Well, what do I want to write for?"

As an artist, you don't fit neatly into any kind of format. How did you get around that?

I just kept honoring myself. I said, "This is what I do. I'm a girl who plays the piano." This is what I do. So if nobody comes to see me, guess what, I'll be in my living room playing the piano. Now I hustled and I got my work out there and it's not like I didn't take it to the street, because I did. I played for as many people as I could and I keep honing my craft and I keep trying to just explore myself and explore my writing and share it. Sharing is why we do it. I don't think we're writers if we don't want to share. But if nobody wants to hear it, I'm still going to do it. I'll share it with myself. And then I go listen to other people and they share with me, and it makes me feel much better.

Any final words of advice?

I do want to support the writers out there. Our job is a real special one, because we're either supporting a media that would like us to forget about our feelings or we go against the media and say "no," we want to remind people that they can form their own belief systems. It's about encouraging each individual to be your own bird. You got to be your own song. That's our job.

CHAPTER 20

John Linnell of They Might Be Giants

Interviewed 1997

Hits: "Birdhouse in Your Soul," "Guitar," "Boss of Me (Theme from *Malcolm in the Middle*)"

"Purple Toupee," "How Can I Sing Like a Girl?," "Till My Head Falls Off," "James K. Polk," "Exquisite Dead Guy," "Hovering Sombrero," "Mink Car." A brief sampling of some of their titles tells you that the New York–based duo They Might Be Giants are definitely not writing generic you-and-me-baby love songs.

John Flansburgh and John Linnell, friends since their high school days, have, according to Linnell, always wanted to do work that's "inspiring and culturally interesting." And what began as four-track experiments in their Brooklyn apartments has sprouted into a cottage industry supported by a large network of fans. TMBG have released ten albums (as well as side projects—Flansburgh's group Mono Puff and Linnell's album *State Songs*), toured incessantly, made groundbreaking videos, composed the theme for the TV show *Malcolm in the Middle*, and written a children's book with accompanying CD (*Bed, Bed, Bed*). They even have their own Dial-a-Song service.

That's right. If you dial 718-387-6962, you can hear, depending on the week, demos of new songs, unreleased tracks, and greetings from the two Johns. They started the service fifteen years ago. Linnell says, "We didn't have any records out, and it seemed like a good way to get our music heard."

Aside from their obvious talent as pop artists, I think their inclusion in this book will make it clear to readers that in the world of songwriting, there is still much uncharted territory. Though it may seem like it's all been said before, one listen to the songs of They Might Be Giants will tell you that it hasn't.

What made you want to write your own songs?

I don't know, that's pretty difficult to figure out. I guess both John and I, whatever we've done, the point of it has been to do the creative work. I wrote a lot of instrumental music in high school. I didn't really get into writing songs exactly until a little later.

What were those early pieces like?

[Laughs] This is very embarrassing, as you can imagine, talking about the work you did in high school, but they were kind of inspired generally by Frank Zappa. In other words, things that were combining composition with recording techniques and psychedelia, things like that.

Are you a schooled musician?

Not especially. I think that most of the stuff that both John and I do is founded on the things that we taught ourselves. I took a little bit of theory in high school and college, and I went to Berklee for a summer. But that was pretty much just piano lessons and ear training.

Who besides Frank Zappa influenced your writing?

Now, the more important influence, maybe for John too, is the Beatles. Even in the 70s when the idea of the mainstream was much less appealing to us, we wanted to do work that was kind of individualistic, and at that point there was this clear feeling among us and our friends that mass culture didn't speak to us as individuals. That was the step we all took from preteens to teenagers, was realizing that there were individual cultural things that spoke to one as an individual, and therefore, the idea of being only interested in the Top 40 was the anathema to doing original work and so on. That was a very kind of knee-jerk feeling.

Did you and John know early on that you wouldn't be writing normal, you-and-I-style love songs?

Yeah, I think we were much more into that idea at the time, that we were not normal. I think now we've completely turned around and feel like we're as normal as anyone else. One thing I realize, looking back, is that the idea of normal in our high school was completely abstract. Nobody felt like they were the normal ones. Everybody felt like an outsider in the whole school, and it just was not something we were aware of at that time.

Did you guys start the group in high school?

No, but we started working together in high school. We started doing this band about ten years ago in New York. We'd both moved to New York from different places the same year, so we started recording and writing together again. Within about a year, we started performing.

Are you and John at it all the time or do you just write for specific projects?

I think we would be at it a lot more, but we're touring a lot with the band, and I find it impossible to write on the road. I really need a clear schedule and a lot of peace and quiet. That's my own particular neurosis, that I can't really work with other people around or in the room, or if I have other things to do on the schedule ahead of me.

When you and John cowrite, do you actually sit down in the same room together?

No. We've done some collaborations, but we mostly just each write songs. We split the writing about halfway, right down the middle on our records, and then there've been a couple of things where we've found different ways to collaborate. One example is "My Evil Twin" from the last record, and that's something where I wrote a bunch of music. It was all MIDI, and I put it on a computer disc and gave it to John, and he wrote the melody and lyrics over top of it.

For songs coming from two separate writers, you guys are amazingly in tune.

Well, as you know, we've known each other a long time, and that is very important as far as what we're doing. We have a very clear understanding of each other's sensibilities, and we have an enormous amount in common. We have a lot of differences too, but we're very tuned in to one another.

When you write songs on your own, where do you usually begin?

I have the worst writing habits of anybody [laughs]. I always write the music first, which is really difficult. Impossible, in fact. That's just the way I've always worked. A couple of occasions I've come up with words and been able to write music. But for some reason, I really get started with a melody. Usually the melody to me is the interesting thing, and I have to come up with the lyrics to put over it. It kind of maybe explains the kinds of songs that I write, where often the lyrics seem like they're having to fit into a metric structure. It's a chore [laughs]. I think you'll notice with my songs maybe more than John's that the metric spacing of the words is identical from one verse to another. That's because the music was written first, and I can't bear to change the melody.

What makes a great melody?

The thing is, I have a particular kind of melody that I write. I think there are a lot of great songs and great melodies that are very different from what I do. There's this album by this guy Frank Black. He writes really interesting melodies. I find them a little counterintuitive. There's some really odd rhythmic things that happen in them, and they're very beautiful for that reason. I don't think he's trying to write beautiful melodies, but that's the effect they have. My melodies are almost always scales. That's the other thing, I tend to write melodies that move up and down in scales. The large interval that I use is the hook, but the meat of it is all scales, moving up and down [laughs]. I mean, it sounds really dumb, but that does end up being a lot of what I write.

When you have a piece of music that you really like, what kinds of things do you do to get the lyric going?

I really mix it up. I've written a lot of lyrics that are very elliptical, partly for the reason that I was telling you about, that I'm trying to make them fit into the melody. Often, if it's a pop song, I think the lyrics tend to be a little less obvious, for that reason. Another thing about the lyrics is that the sounds of the words are important too. The sounds of the syllables have to fit in with the melody, all the stresses and everything.

Will you write a dummy lyric?

I've done that a bunch. "Birdhouse in Your Soul," that's a really good example of that. It started as a dummy lyric and almost even sounds like a dummy lyric, the song that ended up being on the record.

Do you tell yourself at the outset that it doesn't have to make sense?

Oh yeah, I keep reminding myself not to wring my hands over the fact that it doesn't seem to make sense right away. When you repeat something over and over to yourself, you eventually make sense of it [laughs]. It's really important to relax about the importance of what you're doing and not think of it as earth-shattering. I think you can write good lyrics if you don't take yourself too seriously.

A lot of times when I read about They Might Be Giants, words like "absurdist" and "nonsensical" are used to describe the songs. Do you agree with that assessment?

It's sort of painful, because it sounds very dismissable. Actually, I think whenever you kind of caricature anybody's work as anything, it makes it easier to throw away. The other thing is I think we really do write a lot of songs that are in no way surrealist or quirky or anything like that. We write songs which are pretty straightforward. But if you have a reputation for being one thing, then people could miss out on the fact that you're doing something else.

What's the hardest thing about the whole process?

Once you've gotten the good stuff figured out, it's hard just to make it all hang together. In some ways, it's the necessary thing where you're just kind of plastering up all the cracks and making it smooth. It's the least interesting part of the work, trying to make it be a cohesive song rather than a collection of parts.

When you're writing, do your songs make you laugh?

Sometimes, yeah, but usually not. I think that when you come up with a good idea, sometimes it's something—and this can be when you're doing any kind of work, but this applies to songwriting—when you come up with an idea that surprises you when it pops in your head, that makes you laugh. It's often something that you feel is really good, and it can be the thing to hang the rest of the song on. The good idea that makes the rest of it march in step.

Some of your songs make me laugh, like "Shoehorn with Teeth."

I think some of them have sort of the structure of jokes, and unfortunately, this is getting back to this problem we've had of people considering it to be a novelty or joke. To us, our songs are very meaningful, and interesting, and the whole point is that they're saying something. But they have this structure of some joke maybe. Part of the effect is that it lightens the song up so it's not pretentious. Like I was saying, if you think of what you're doing as tremendously important, you can really drive people away.

I think you and John put your records together really well by placing a funny song like "Spider" after "The Statue Got Me High," which is a great lyric.

I think that the contrast is another important element in what we're doing. Occasionally people ask us what our favorite song is and that's one that really drives us crazy. It's very difficult to pull one song out and say this sums up everything, when really an important part of what we're doing is coming up with contrasts. That's one of the values of having an album, is that you can really say a lot of different things, and they each are heightened by one another in a way. You can allow yourself to do something that's a little more intense than you'd want to have as your manifesto [laughs]. But then if you contrast that with something else, it gives you freedom to do it.

Have you ever used a song by another artist as sort of a springboard for one of your own?

Sure. In fact, when we started that was one of the more common things we were doing. I like the way you put that, because I think that we also gave some people the impression that we were writing parodies, and they really were, I think, the opposite. I really feel like we wanted to rejuvenate the stuff that we liked by referring to it.

"Narrow Your Eyes" has a very British Invasion sound.

Oh yeah, definitely. That was obviously part of the whole aspect of what we were into when we were growing up. If you hear the original music, it sounds fresh, so the real challenge is to come up with something that is as fresh now. Often you hear people remaking songs, doing covers of classic oldies. It almost always fails to capture the thing that was cool about the original.

Let me ask you about a few of your songs to get your reaction—
"Purple Toupee."

I have this friend who likes all of our songs except that one. She said she didn't get it. She thought "Purple Toupee" was like a surrealist toss-off. Then she changed her opinion about it when I told her that the song had used a couple of Prince songs as a springboard, "Purple Rain" and "Raspberry Beret." I guess part of the idea was that, at the time, it seemed like there was this 60s revival in the works. It reminded me of all the other revivals that had taken place that were reviving times that I wasn't around for. They must have been complete shams based on what the 60s revival was. It seemed like it was based on this utterly one-dimensional caricature of the time that it was supposed to [be] representing or reviving. That still goes on now. That's sort of what "Purple Toupee" is about.

"Ana Ng."

I wrote that one after I'd been looking in the Manhattan phone book. This isn't actually the way John and I write. We don't go to sources. But I think for some reason I had the phone book open. I wasn't thinking about writing at that moment. I noticed that there [were] about three pages, which is really a lot of individual numbers, of people named Ng. There are probably thousands of people named Ng in New York, just the letters N and G. And I didn't know what ethnicity the name belonged to or anything, but that sort of sparked my curiosity. Another thing that inspired one of the lines in the song is a Pogo comic book where they're trying to determine the opposite side of the world, and the way they do it is actually blowing a hole through the globe with a gun, which was very funny.

"James K. Polk."

That one I wrote with a friend. We were both interested in the fact that people know facts based on these kind of historical songs with melodies that are catchy. The lyrics aren't in and of themselves something you'd remember. We were thinking of that song "The Battle of New Orleans" by Johnny Horton. He wrote a bunch of history songs, and they're wonderful actually. We picked a president that we literally knew nothing about. We just both knew the name [laughs]. It turned out to be somebody who was really pivotal in American history. He was president during the largest expansion of the country that's taken place. He started this fake war with Mexico in order to grab all the southwestern land. He was just a very kind of hardline character, and he wasn't particularly well liked by anybody. He's just this very peculiar figure for that reason. Noncharismatic, but he did these tremendous things.

"Metal Detector."

Musically, it was inspired by a song on my old 70s Moog. The lyrics were inspired by this book written by this old Yankee guy who spent all his time in the islands hunting for buried treasure. He wrote a book about it and published it on this vanity press that put out these really weird, mentally ill books [laughs].

"The Statue Got Me High."

It's kind of a song about having an epiphany or something. The song actually started with completely different lyrics. That's what I was saying about dummy lyrics. I think the song was called "The Apple of My Eye." When I came up with the line "the statue got me high," it amused me. It was taking two things and putting them together—not a non sequitur but something sort of interesting and odd about the juxtaposition of those two things. Part of it is that it's the idea that the statue would be in a public square, a monument. Not necessarily a work of art, but something that's just utterly immobile and represents something that's in the past—just the idea of that blowing somebody's mind. It seems like one of the least likely things to make the top of your head come off, and that's what happens in the song.

Were all the twenty-second ideas that make up "Fingertips" things that you didn't finish?

No, they were written to be part of "Fingertips." The project was to write a bunch of choruses and nothing else. In other words, I had to restrain myself from writing any other parts of the songs. I wanted a collection of choruses that's something like what you see on TV late at night, like the old K-Tel commercials. I was thinking about how you know a lot of songs from these ads, but the only part you know is maybe one line, which is half the chorus. And yet they stick in your head in the way a whole song would. In a way, these tiny chips of songs seem complete, because you don't know the rest of the song.

What advice could you offer to songwriters?

You really have to want to do it, independent of whether or not there's a future in it. Maybe I'm wrong about that, but that's how John and I got going—we really liked what we were doing. We didn't have a career ahead of us necessarily, so therefore the career consideration didn't affect what we were doing. Except to the practical extent that we had to figure out how to perform the music, things like that. The main thing is we would have done it no matter what. We did do it for a long time without any money. There are bands that come up to A & R people and say, "What can we do to get signed? We'll do whatever you want." And that's not even what A & R people want to hear. They'd be in bands if they knew what to do.

CHAPTER 21

Sarah McLachlan

Interviewed 1994

Hits: "Possession," "Adia," "I Will Remember You"

The first ten songs that Sarah McLachlan ever wrote ended up becoming her debut album, 1988's acclaimed *Touch*. Considering that the typical songwriter's first ten songs are earnest embarrassments better left in the bottom of a dresser drawer, this is quite a feat. But McLachlan's songs didn't appear out of nowhere. She'd laid a lot of groundwork.

Born January 28, 1968, in Halifax, Nova Scotia, Sarah started her classical training in music about the time she was taking her first steps. "I had twelve years of guitar, six of piano, and five of voice," she says. At the same time, as a kid, she was drawn to the sounds of such seminal folk rock artists as Cat Stevens, Joan Baez, and Simon and Garfunkel. Later, as she reached her teens, it was Peter Gabriel's music that touched her most. "The emotional response you get from his songs, because of the honesty, that really inspired me to find my own voice and write from that point of view," she says.

Though her debut and its follow-up *Solace* (1991) made McLachlan a bright new star in her native Canada, it wasn't until 1994's *Fumbling Towards Ecstasy* that she broke through on the world stage. For the writing of that album, McLachlan retreated to an isolated cabin in the mountains for nearly seven months of meditation and soul-searching. This kind of Thoreau-like experience has become her method of choice for creative expression. "It's given me so much, as far as learning about myself," she says.

Since then, McLachlan has become almost synonymous with female singer-songwriter, a star with multiplatinum sales, Top 10 singles like "Building a Mystery" and "I Will Remember You," three Grammy awards, and lots of movie and TV soundtrack appearances. Her brainchild, the Lilith Fair Tour, helped bring long-overdue attention and respect to many of her fellow female artists. In late 2003—after a five-year hiatus during which she had her first child—McLachlan returned with her seventh album, *Afterglow.*

You said that it took about six years to learn how not to edit yourself and remain open in your music.

[Laughs] Hopefully I'll get that back again someday.

What kinds of things can songwriters do to reach that place in their writing?

Well, for me on this new record, it was mainly secluding myself, being away from society and being away from everything. I locked myself up in a cabin in the mountains and stayed there for seven months. It was just an amazing time for me to really focus on a lot of stuff that had sort of been lurking behind the scenes in my brain but never had the time to come out. Or it kept being put aside, because there were so many distractions. Also, I think I got incredibly in tune with the earth, with nature, like I hadn't before. I couldn't write a thing for three months. My brain was eating itself. It was terribly cold out and I couldn't do anything creative. I was just frozen. Everything was churning around inside but nothing would come out. Then spring happened and everything totally opened up. I was blossoming as well. Most of the songs—I had written four previous to going to the cabin—were written then, about seven of them, between April and May. The place that I got to in myself of feeling calm and peaceful and also, for the first time in my life, feeling I'm happy now. Not "I would be happy if . . ." There was always that going on with me. I finally got a place where I was totally happy and peaceful and living in the present tense instead of in the future, you know, and projecting things.

Did you go into that experience with any sort of agenda?

In the process of not being able to write, I kept a journal, these sort of morning pages. I wrote three pages before I'd do anything else, just to try and clear my head. Most of it was totally banal, like "Mm, coffee smells good. I have nothing to say. I have nothing to say" [laughs]. But sure enough, about midway through the second page, sometimes I'd really open up and all this stuff would come out. You know, you're not really awake yet and you're just sort of spewing whatever's on the top of your head, sort of free-form. And there was no editing happening there at all, because no one was going to read this book. I could say whatever I wanted. I didn't have to hide behind anything, and I think that really helped me. To be really open and honest with myself, that was good. I'm pretty good at deceiving myself or I've known myself to do that in the past [laughs].

Did you listen to music while you were there?

I listened to a lot of Tom Waits, and Talk Talk's *Spirit of Eden*, which is one of my favorites.

The opening lines of your songs are always captivating, and they seem to contain the germ of the whole song in just a few words.

I figure the first two lines usually tell the whole story of a song [laughs]. The first two lines are what comes out first when I'm writing, and they basically tell which direction, for me lyrically, the song is going to go. Sometimes those two lines will sit for months by themselves, until they find a completion to the story, or a completion to the stage that I'm in of trying to work through something, until hopefully I'm somewhere near the other side of it when I can be a little more objective and write it down. It's the same with putting titles to the songs. Most of the titles come from the last word in the second line.

Say you have those two lines and the music wants to continue. Will you let it go on without words?

Unfortunately, I often try to fill it in. I'm still a bit stuck to that convention of writing a song with a four-line verse, the more traditional phrasing of a stanza. So if there are only two lines, they usually end up being four lines. I work at making it four before I stop. But there's also this thing when I go into the studio. Pierre [Marchand, her producer] is great at editing. He'll say, "Why don't you just not sing that line? Do you really need to say that? You've already said it." He has done that, which is something that I can't really do, because I'm not objective about it. And I don't see things from the same direction that he does, which is why he's so good to work with.

Do you demo songs before you go into the studio?

I demo them in a very simple way, with acoustic guitar or piano. Sometimes a drum machine. But my sort of restrictions on myself for going into the studio are making it strong by itself in the simplest form. So if you're hiding behind a lot of production, if you take it away, you can still play that song and it'll be strong on its own.

You mentioned a drum machine. Do you ever write with just a groove?

I never have before. I'm pretty lazy as far as technology, and I think it's something I'll probably have to get more into, because I'm sort of exhausting the instruments I'm using, or exhausting the inspiration they give me. I can go back and forth, but I don't have a piano, so I end up doing a lot of stuff on guitar. But when I was in Montreal I did, so a lot of this record came from piano because it was such an exciting thing, a new sound, a new instrument. That happened with electric guitar as well. I started writing with that, because it was a new sound. So maybe I will get into the drum machine. I just have to learn how to use the damn thing first [laughs]. I always fight against technology. I want to be grass roots and I want where it comes from to be organic.

It sounds like you have a good combination with your producer, because he strikes me as a technically minded person.

Oh, he's amazing that way. He's such a techno-head. But at the same time, he totally comes from the organic sense of letting the song happen in whatever direction it goes in. Just following and not pushing the song for any wrong reason.

A lot of your songs have an air of mystery and darkness. Is there something you do during the writing process to conjure this mood?

[Laughs] I just think it's what's in my brain. It's not that I'm really pessimistic or anything—I'm not. But I sort of like the effect of two sides of things—one being really pretty and one being really ugly, like when you lift up a pretty rock and there are all these mites and worms underneath it [laughs]. I think that sort of came from this one poem I read in grade nine. It's funny, the little things that stick with me my whole life. Wilfred Owen, a World War I poet, wrote about being in the field in the war and all the horrors that went on. But somehow, without glamorizing or romanticizing it, he made it incredibly beautiful. In the same breath, he'd be talking about something horrendously grotesque. I just really loved that. That's actually where the title of the record came from too—*Fumbling Towards Ecstasy*. It was taken from a line in one of his poems—"Quick boys, in an ecstasy of fumbling we fit the masks just in time . . ." I thought that was amazing. "In an ecstasy of fumbling." It was so beautiful, and since grade nine, I've been trying to fit that into something [laughs]. I sort of have a little library of phrases and words in my head that I like. Like "murmur." Never been able to use it yet, but it's a beautiful word. I like words that say so many things. Language is such a beautiful thing, and words are so amazing.

When you're writing a song about a relationship, do you keep a particular person in mind?

Yeah, I usually do set up a fairly clear image of who I'm talking about. "Plenty," for example, is definitely aimed at another individual. I tend to switch people in a lot of the songs. Sometimes I'll say "you," and sometimes "I," and I'm not really sure why I do that.

What was the inspiration behind "Good Enough"?

A lot of things. That song has been such an amazing experience for me because I've learned so much from it. There are so many different stories that I attach to it now. But it sort of came from, initially, really missing my best girlfriend. It started out as fiction, about a couple in which the woman was pretty much alienated by just about everybody, because her husband was really abusive and domineering, which sort of somewhat mirrors my mother and father's relationship. And basically, I am the friend coming in, saying, "Hey, you deserve more than this. Why don't you come with me and I'll take care of you?" The video that I'm going to do for that song is the first sort of dramatic narrative that I've done. Everything else has been pretty abstract, trying to find a parallel universe to describe it differently. But we're going to have a little girl, a man and woman, and a friend. Possibly an imaginary friend. We're going to look at the relationship between the little girl and her friends and also, between the mother and the little girl. And there's quite a bit of alienation from the father, who's been behind the scenes the whole time anyway.

Love is usually something that's idealized in pop songs, or expressed in a codependent "I'll die without you" sort of way. What do you try to do with the concept of love in your songs?

In the past I thought it was really a great thing, but it turned out to be really bad, so what does that mean? I tend to try to analyze the mistakes, or what went wrong. Why did this not work? Usually I turn to myself and ask what's wrong with me, or where did I go wrong? Then I turn to them and ask, where did they go wrong? So I guess I'm trying to show that hopefully—and it depends on the song—it's not any one person's fault. It's like there's two people involved. I'm focusing more on the emotion of what people go through when love does go away, or when people break up. The anger, the frustration of why did it go wrong. I tried so hard. Maybe I tried too hard [laughs]. It depends. On this record, on "Plenty," I decided I was in love with somebody. The problem was that I had projected the image of the perfect man onto them. And they sort of played up to it as well. Then it sort of crumbled fairly quickly, and there was a frightened little boy behind that facade. It was wild for me, because it was the first time I'd really deceived myself in such a grand manner. I wanted to believe it, so I forced myself to believe.

Are songs an act of discovery for you?

Yeah, and sometimes long after the fact. Going back to "Good Enough," one of the things I was focusing on was, "Don't tell me why he's never been good to you, don't tell me why nothing's good enough." For a couple years, every time I'd see my mom, I'd say, "You know, you deserve more, you deserve to be happier than you are. Why are you putting up with this?" Basically telling her that the only thing she knew sucked. So she never wanted to see me, and I wondered why. I couldn't understand it, then I wrote that song. Around the same time, I tried reverse psychology and didn't hassle her anymore and just accepted that she accepted. Then she opened up. She completely changed and she started saying, "I'm not going to accept this anymore. I'm changing this and this and this." It was fantastic, because I wasn't beating it into her. She was doing it on her own. That song taught me that. I have a lot of emotional attachment to that song.

Is it difficult for you to keep emotional connection with your songs over the course of a tour?

It does fluctuate, but I've found that with these new songs, it's been really easy to keep the connection. I don't know if it's because they're fresh and new or if it's because they're the strongest songs I have yet. The good thing is that usually I can remember the places that they came from when I sing. I don't remember what they're about so much as the place they came from, the mood that I was in, the strong, quiet place that I was in when I was writing it. And that gives me a lot of happiness. Sometimes I'm going through emotions, singing the songs and not even listening to the words, but having some weird memory of sitting under a tree and feeling happy [laughs]. Other times I'm thinking about my laundry. The weirdest things go through my head when I'm singing. I'll think about what I said five minutes before, like, "Man, that was stupid."

I don't think I've heard anyone talk about what goes through their minds when they sing.

[Laughs] All sorts of crazy stuff. Just life. Like, the Canucks lost, what a drag. And you'll be singing very well and emoting, but little flashes will come in of other things. Then all of a sudden I'll find myself at the end of the verse. How did I get there? I guess I got through, but I was someplace else. That happens fairly often in certain songs.

Sir Laurence Olivier once said that when he was acting Hamlet on stage and bringing audiences to tears, he was sometimes wondering if his shirts would be ready at the cleaners the next day.

[Laughs] It makes sense. You do something like that every night. One night—and I never watch TV—but I've become involved in hockey, and it's really fun. So I was watching a game before a show and when I go out there on stage, the TV had sucked all my memory away. Before every line of every verse and chorus, I was terrified right up until it came out that it wasn't coming out, that I'd forgotten it. It just freaked me out. Not too many people noticed it in the audience because I'd hit most of the lines. But I asked an actress friend of mine and she said it'd happened to her before. You've just got to trust that it's there. You're just blocking it because of your fear. You've got to get rid of the fear, so think about that laundry list, think about mowing the lawn, and it'll be there.

What would you like to accomplish as a songwriter?

I'd like to keep trying to be able to work through things. Songwriting is such therapy for me. It's given me so much, as far as learning about myself. I'd like to be able to keep doing that and that's it. That's everything to me, just being able to work through things. I guess an offshoot of that is other people listening to it and being able to get something for themselves.

Do you have the sense that what you're doing will last?

Yes, it certainly will last for me. I'd like to think I'll keep writing and getting better and better. I hope [laughs]. I'm really proud of what I've done so far, and that pride hasn't diminished in any way.

What advice would you give to someone looking to make a career as a singer-songwriter?

I'd tell them to go read *Letters from a Young Poet* by Rainer Maria Rilke, because his advice is better than any advice I could ever give.

CHAPTER 22

Ben Folds

Interviewed 2003

Hits: "Brick," "Army," "Still Fighting It"

"Every morning, I wake up, I have a song in my head that I've never heard before," says Ben Folds. "It's been happening since I was a kid."

Born September 12, 1966, in Winston-Salem, North Carolina, Folds started making up his own songs at age five. "I remember standing in the lunch line in first grade and having a couple of songs in my head, and I was wishing I could play an instrument so I could get them out. It was ridiculous stuff. I started playing piano when I was eight and the first thing I did was find my songs on the piano. By the time I'd been playing piano for a year, I had a cassette tape with forty songs on it."

Picasso once said that he spent his whole life trying to learn how to paint like a child. Folds has found a similar connection with the preteen songwriter he was. "The songs I wrote when I was nine years old, if I were to sit down and play them for you, you'd be shocked about how much they're like what I write now."

What he writes now are unforgettable pop songs. Musically influenced by everything from the ornate radio hits of the 1970s to Broadway to garage rock, Folds is like Elton John in thrift-store duds—a piano man with heart, humor, and high energy in equal measures. Beyond the zealous outpourings of melody and piano-pounding grooves, what really sets his songs apart is a lyric style that makes you feel like you're dishing the dirt over coffee with the singer. Folds can be raucous ("Song for the Dumped"), insightful ("Zak and Sara"), poignant ("Carrying Cathy"), and at times, downright romantic ("The Luckiest"). But no matter the emotion, he invites you into his world and lets you feel like you're part of it. Not an easy thing to do.

This empathetic gift has earned him a huge following all over the world, first as part of the power trio Ben Folds Five and, since 2001, as a solo artist. Ben currently resides in Nashville with his wife and two children. In 2004, he will release his second solo album.

What do you think made you want to write your own songs?

I've been making up songs as far back as I can remember. Five, six years old. We do that with our kids now. Before we go to bed at night, they make up a song about their day. We sit around with them on their bed and one of them will get up and start singing, "I played with my bike today . . ." That's kind of the way I was. I had songs in my head. Singing wasn't done in my house, or encouraged, or looked on as anything but silly or sissyish. So I never really sang the songs. I just had them in my head. It took me until I was twenty-two, twenty-three years old to even think about maybe singing and have other people hearing it.

Did you take piano lessons?

I took lessons for a year, but I didn't like it because it didn't have anything to do with writing my songs. That's why I played piano in the first place, so I could hear what I was making up.

What do you consider your first fully realized song?

There was an instrumental piece I wrote on the piano that my aunt—who was a music teacher—transcribed for me. I guess because that was on sheet music, I felt like it was fully realized. It was exciting to me to see the notes—that wasn't something I could do at the time—and realize it was my song. I went through a horrible dorky teenage period that lasted from prepubescence to twenty years old [laughs], where if someone was going to hear one of my songs on tape, it was like Frank Zappa. It was just a big joke. Like "Having Two Dicks Is Cool" or some ridiculous, silly-ass novelty shit. Meanwhile, I had these other ideas and I would start to work on them, but I was actually really shy about being expressive like that. The first things that came out in that vein were two songs—a song called "Video" and a song called "Emaline." Those two were serious songs. "Video" I wrote when I was seventeen. "Emaline," [I] was nineteen. It was like, wow, those sound like real songs. I played in bands where we played my songs, but the other songs had to have some kind of flips or twists to make me feel like it would distract people from the song, because [I] was just embarrassed about writing songs. But those two songs kind of remained as the boring ones. Funny, after all these years, the other ones went away and these are two songs I still play in a gig.

When you first came to Nashville in the early 90s, I remember seeing your group Jody's Powerbill and thinking that you already had a strong, original voice as a writer. Did you find that early on?

Yeah. Sometimes I'll think, "I'm going to write a Smashing Pumpkins song" and at the end of the day it sounds like what I did when I was nine years old [laughs]. Initially, that's a bummer to me, because I feel like, "Am I too caught up in the 70s or something that I have to sound a certain way?" No matter how I try to stylize it. I listen to that stuff I wrote when I was nine years old and the shit sounds the same way. It's just the way it goes into my head and comes out. That's what I guess affected me on the radio. Also, I think I had a really good ear at a young age for assimilating what was going on with the music. I can think of a song that I haven't heard since I was five years old and I can probably analyze the chords for you and sit down and play the bass line. I was really listening to it. I was so locked on it as a kid. A lot of things were burned into my head when I was growing up in the 70s that I actually understood so well that they just stayed in. Since then, I don't listen to Billy Joel—I mean I like him—but I don't listen to stuff that people would think I listen to. And when I write something that I feel is inspired by something really new, whether it's Sigur Ros or whatever, it comes out and everyone says, "Oh yeah, that sounds like Harry Chapin [laughs]."

I remember talking to you once and you said that one way you liked to start a song was to listen to a record that you liked and take what you called "an impression" of it. Rather than learning and dissecting the song. Do you still do that?

Yes. I'm listening to it for inspiration. But these days, I find that more in photography or something less literal. I like hearing youth in music, so I like hearing really new shit where they're just going for it. Unlike a lot of my contemporaries, or people my age anyway, I'm not offended by the idea that someone continues to bring up the same symbolism over and over again. You've got your new Jimi Hendrix or you've got your new Beatles. The most important thing is that you hear them busting out at the seams. I worked with Ben Kweller for the Bens CD and he was just busting out. He's twenty-one and he's like, "I wanna do this, I wanna do that!" You can feel that in his music when you listen to it. Technically, the music is okay, but when you hear that, that's what inspires me. If I listen to music, it's just sometimes to remember that part of it. Because I don't feel that way about music anymore, unless I get a jolt from someone I'm working with. That's why photography for me is more exciting. I look at a Bill Brandt picture or something and it makes me remember why I play music. I don't really play recreational music. I only do it when I'm supposed to, and I've been like that for a long time.

On a lot of your songs—"Where's Summer B?" or "Steven's Last Night in Town"—you have a very conversational style of lyric writing, where it's almost like you're talking to a friend rather than addressing an audience. Dropping real names into a song—Tamara Easton. How did you develop that?

It sounds tossed off, but I revise a lot. My method is to end up writing on the floor at some point, where there's seriously ten or fifteen sheets of paper on the floor that are all updated versions of the song as I go along. I'll write it and I'll be singing it, trying to make some sense out of it, and it won't feel right to me. And then that's when I start to write it again on another piece of paper, but change the wording so it doesn't feel so formal. The formality's what bothers me the most. Sometimes you say what you mean but it's so literal that it isn't the way you'd say it to somebody, so I feel really fucking corny singing it. I don't like it when they sound like lyrics. I think what I'm doing is writing it again and I'm hoping as I come to the part that gave me the little twitch, that I just rewrite that in my own words a little more, like I'm saying it to somebody. I might sing that, then write it again and rewrite the twitch a couple more times. I have such a hard time finishing lyrics that even when I'm writing it over and over, three sheets of lyrics might be the same exact thing and never change. I just write it again, then I write it again. If I don't keep moving like that, then I won't do it.

Even your stage presentation, which is very musical and often complex, has that air of informality.

I think the informality is just a matter of not liking the dress-up part of it. It used to fucking freak me out when someone I knew would stand up and sing a church song or something, and all of a sudden, they go into this voice [does big vibrato]. What they're saying and how they're doing it creeped me out. It's like something has taken over their body. Then they sit back down next to you and go, "I'm gonna get a hamburger after this," and you think, "What the hell? It's a different person" [laughs]. That really bugged me. So I never wanted to be the guy who went up on stage and did that. I'm singing my songs like a conversation. I realize it can never be the same thing completely. But if the song is not breaking the law a little bit in the lyric world—it doesn't have to be that much—then it's probably bumming me out, and I don't want to finish it. One of the hardest songs I ever had to finish was a song on the last album called "The Luckiest," because the things I wanted to say in it were so cliché, because they were real. I was trying to find where I would actually stutter over that in person and I finally realized when the old couple next door died within a couple days of each other, I realized that's the sort of thing I would mumble as an example if I was actually saying those things. Then I had my last verse.

It's a wonderful song, and that last verse is more powerful because you almost apologize for the strange example of the old couple.

The song existed with a third verse before that, and I was never even going to show [it] to anybody. It was never going to come out. I'm still really driven by fear of embarrassment [laughs]. Making an album or making a song, I don't want lyrics in there that make me uncomfortable. But I want it to be real and sincere, so it's a lot of work for me. I'm writing lyrics for my new album right now and it sucks. It's a pain in the ass. I hate it [laughs]. What's a white boy to do?

With the way you describe your lyric writing, it sounds like you already have the music in place. Is that the case?

The music usually happens while I'm working on other things. Walking around, sleeping. It morphs in my head. I go back to the piano, and I realize now I've got a bridge, a transition here, then it's all finished. I suppose, to anyone who's with me, it looks like I've been working on the music. I'll sit down at the piano and play it, but it was already there. The music is so easy. The lyrics are so tough. But I know the emotional cadence of a song as soon as the music comes. I know that sequentially, that this is tension, this is release, this happened before this, and this is the point in the song where something is revealed, but I don't even know what the song is about. That makes it really tough. Sometimes I don't find the lines and I don't write the song. I've got a hundred songs sitting around with completely finished music that I can't do lyrics to. And it's because of reasons like that. I take for granted the musical part. Now if I have lyrical ideas, God forbid that fucking happens, I'll run home with a pencil and write it down because it's so precious. It's like they don't come often enough.

I would like to mention a few songs to get your reaction and maybe find out a little about the inspiration behind them— "Jackson Cannery."

I'd never really listened to the Beatles before. I'd heard them, but my parents really only had black records around the house. That's all there was. I guess, like Steve Martin in *The Jerk*, I discovered my white roots all of a sudden. That song has a lot to do with just the saltiness of the dominant seventh chords, moved up, in a very John Lennon-ish kind of way. Lyrically, I wrote what kind of came into my head. There was an example of a guy I knew who kind of lost his marbles on the way to school, and had created enough stir that the bus pulled over and let him out. I always thought that a real dramatic way, whether you're ending your life or having a breakdown, is to make everybody a witness to what you're doing. So "Stop the bus"—that's where the first line came from. From that, I kind of extrapolated from a bunch of things in my own life. I was married at a really young age, and I felt a lot of pressure about that. A lot of the song has to do with wanting to quit. "Seconds pass slowly and years fly by"—that has to do with the feeling I had. I really have no idea what it's about. It would take a shrink to work it out. It's not really all that well written lyrically. The title is the guy's last name combined with a place that I used to work put together.

"Boxing."

I was writing songs and then I wrote that one, and it kind of upped the ante on things, because I knew that it was better than what I'd been writing. I knew it was more unique and that no one wrote like that. It's exciting to be writing and realize that you've hit on something that's your own style. My father is a big boxing fan, and "Boxing's been good to me" was something that he would say. It made me think about resigning and quitting, and then I love Muhammad Ali's story and everything about him. I've read more than half of the biographies on him. He's such a symbol. And really, if I was writing that song now, I'd probably want it to be a little clearer, and I'd probably want it to be more full. I'd probably want to not hint at things, but go for the jugular sometimes. Whether I got to it or not would be another story, but I wasn't frustrated at the time with just tossing out the images and putting things out there like that. I was excited to hear them come back.

Do you find in general that as you get older you want to be clearer in your lyrics?

I think it's a logical progression. It's the place I want to go. It's something that I feel like I don't hear enough of. I'm not really interested in being so literal and simple that there's no mystery to it. But enough clarity. That's shocking to me. I like a little bit of breaking the law. When I wrote the song "Emaline," which was 1986, considering what I was being fed at the time, I was really proud of lines like "for stupid reasons." People were singing lyric-speak, and to have that word stumble into something that was pretty made me happy. Now what makes me happy is to take off the fucking sunglasses, lean over to someone and say, "That's what I'm talking about." I want to be clear. It's something I don't hear enough of. I want to hear it the way you'd say it to your friends.

"Zak and Sara."

That's a thought I'd had for twenty years—the girl sitting on the Peavey amp in the music store having to listen to her boyfriend play "Dust in the Wind" over and over [laughs]. When you're a kid, you have all these ideas, and if you're a girl—at least in the South where I grew up—you've got to listen to your boyfriend's ideas first. In my mind, I used to think, "Maybe she's writing her own song, but she's got to sit there and watch the dude playing 'Dust in the Wind.'" So I thought it would be funny if, in retrospect, she was inventing the entire rave scene. Something really far out. Twenty years from now, would you ever think this was the way people relate to music. She's coming up with all that in her head. But at home, when she brings up things like that, she just gets smacked. I like the Franny and Zooey stories—the way Franny sees so many things that are kind of real, but she's kind of insane. Just to show that Sara was kind of crazy and creative, I imagined that the guy got up to go call his father about layaway plans so he could get his Fender Squire, and then she has to say something to the salesman about how "You're all going to die in your cars and you're working in a submarine." Then the boyfriend comes back, she shuts up, and he keeps playing. That's just the way I saw it. So then at the end, he finishes the song and she claps. She snaps out of it. She's not going to think about rave anymore until it happens. Probably more of a short story than a song.

If you were teaching a workshop on how to improve as a songwriter, what kinds of things would tell your students?

I guess it would depend on each person's particular disease. You can't teach someone creativity, you can't teach them individuality. They need to learn compositional technique. I did a little songwriter seminar thing with Vic Chesnutt one time and I completely didn't agree with him at all. I'm not going to get in a screaming match with a dude in a wheelchair, but I was kind of offended. He's sitting in front of a group of a hundred kids who are aspiring songwriters and he's telling them the best thing to do is not to worry about it, smoke some dope and sit down to write your song. Sorry. That's crap. He learned chords somewhere. Don't smoke pot because Vic Chesnutt told you to. Pot's great, but that's not part of writing a fucking song. I see so many songwriters who give that kind of advice. You know, "Oh, don't worry about it. Let it flow through you." I say, "Fuck that." Learn your technique, learn what Beethoven knew. Beethoven wasn't a sellout. He knew his way around his keyboard and he understood music. The "letting it flow through you" shit—your song will probably last five years that way. As soon as everyone else who let it flow through them at the same time and had the same little life is going to pass on and be working at IBM with you. You should treat your art as a craft and a discipline too. Learn the tricks of the fucking masters. When I get stuck in a song and I don't know where I am, I find myself using concepts of composition that come from studying classical composition. Everyone's going to tell them to be themselves, to write your truth. Well, why else would you be writing? If you have to tell someone that, then what's the point?

CHAPTER 23

Seal

Interviewed 1995

Hits: "Crazy," "Kiss from a Rose," "Prayer for the Dying"

In "Kiss from a Rose," Seal does three things right off the bat that are supposed no-no's for a contemporary hit: he begins with a Bach-like vocal chorale, which is beautiful, but decidedly not "commercial." This gives way to a delicate verse in 6/8, a time signature that's hardly ever heard on the 4/4-dominated charts. Maybe one out of every thousand singles will use it. And then that opening line—"There used to be a graying tower alone on the sea..."—is elusive and wide open to interpretation, as the rest of the lyric is. There's even some question as to what he's singing. Is it "I compare you to a kiss from a rose on the gray" or "...on the grave"?

But Seal balances what could be slightly precious artiness with full-tilt commercial thrills in the melodic chorus (that "Bay-bay!" is worthy of Marvin). It's one of those feats of songwriting that only happens a few times every decade, and even if he never writes another tune as perfect, Seal has earned a corner in the songwriting firmament.

Of Nigerian and Brazilian descent, Sealhenry Samuel was born in Paddington, England, one of six children. His striking facial scars are the result of a skin ailment he had as a young boy. At age eleven, Seal made his first stage appearance, singing "I Can See Clearly Now" at a school talent show. Smitten by that experience, he began his long pursuit of a musical career, which included stints in a funk band that toured Japan and singing for his supper in faroff places such as India, Thailand and Nepal. All the while, he was writing and recording demos.

In 1990, he collaborated with British DJ-performer Adamski to score a hit single, "Killer." With fans and critics buzzing, Seal was signed and released his first record, 1991's *Seal* (Warner Bros.), which was eventually boosted to platinum status by the worldwide smash "Crazy." That song, a stirring fusion of 60s idealism, 70s funk, and 80s techno-sheen, defined Seal's stylistic approach. Since then, he has released three albums and charted with songs such as the aforementioned "Kiss from a Rose," "Prayer for the Dying," and a cover of Steve Miller's "Fly Like an Eagle."

What's your latest discovery about songwriting?

I don't know if I have any blinding new Revelations. I've always had this theory that songs already exist and you just have to open up and let them flow through you, almost like a vessel or a conduit of some sort. Also, it pays not to force a song, which is basically saying the same thing. You have to really open up and allow yourself to be a channel for them to flow through.

To keep the channel open, what kinds of things do you do?

You have to be open to life. You have to allow yourself to think that there are any number of ways to produce a song, that there is no set way. You have to be open to musicians that you're working with, and you have to be prepared to trust your instincts and go with them. At least in a lyrical sense, if something doesn't make literal sense, but it feels good, or the essence of it feels right, that's really what you should go with.

If you believe in the idea that you're sort of an oracle and songs come through you, do you feel that the ones that come really fast are better?

What, because they're less inhibited? Yes, I'd have to agree with you. I think they are the better ones, those that come naturally. The ones that almost write themselves.

How can songwriters improve in that respect?

I think practice, although that sounds like a contradiction in terms [laughs], enables that to be more likely. Not that you can practice writing a great song or even a good one. But I think it's a question of keeping your hand in, or keeping your eye on it. I find if I play the guitar a lot— and I'm not a great guitarist by any stretch of the imagination—but if I play it a lot, when I'm suddenly called upon to deliver something, it will be easier. I think it's the same way with songs. If you want to make your-self available for songs to flow through you, you have to keep playing stuff, keep writing, even if you aren't writing stuff to your satisfaction. I think you have to keep on doing it and then it's almost when your defenses are down, when you're least expecting it, that something will come like that. It's almost as if you'll know instinctively where to go.

Are you pretty disciplined about writing?

No, I don't keep any kind of schedule, but I'm going to have to start because that's probably an area of my work that I'd like to get more under control. Just the discipline to sit down and write.

When you're not feeling inspired, do you ever write just for the exercise of it?

No, never [laughs].

Love is usually idealized in pop songs or sung about in a codependent way. What do you try to do with the idea of love in pop songs?

I try to emphasize the thing of unconditional love. I do sing about love in an idealistic way, but I'm more concerned about unconditional love, other than "I'll love you just as long as you love me back" type of approach.

One of my favorite love songs of yours is "Kiss from a Rose." What inspired that?

I can't remember what exactly inspired me to write the song, but I guess it's a combination of things I was going through. I'm not going to tell you what the song means because I'm not a fan of literally explaining things word for word. Most of my songs tend to be written from personal experiences or from things I see happening to other people or stuff that I'm indirectly involved in.

The first few times I heard that song, I thought you were singing "a kiss from a rose on the grave" rather than "gray." Do you find that a lot of your fans will accidentally mishear your lyrics?

All the time. One of the last things I read on the Internet actually was the line you just mentioned—"a kiss from a rose on the grave." I am singing "gray," which is even more ambiguous. I kind of like the fact that people have read that interpretation into it—"on the grave"—but again it's maybe slightly too literal for me. Maybe it's too much like pointing it in one direction. In my lyric writing, I tend to leave things more ambiguous, so they're left open to interpretation. To me, that's the beauty of song-writing in general, that songs are left open to people's interpretation. It's the vibe of what I'm saying that's important and not the exact literal translation.

Are they left open to yours in that when you write the song, you might not know what it means?

Absolutely. Every song [laughs] is like that. I find consolation in songs that I've written years ago, and they'll take on a different meaning and console me in a different way. There's always something that'll make me go, "Oh wow, that's probably what I meant when I wrote that song." Maybe it was to get me through this moment.

I can even see this idea of open interpretation in the recording techniques you use. Several of your songs have this cool thing where they sort of fade in with you singing unintelligibly below the mix, then fade out the same way.

That's probably because I couldn't think of anything intelligent to say [laughs], more than likely. No, that's not necessarily true, though in some cases it might be. More often than not, it's the texture and sort of phonetic sounds that I'm preoccupied with, I'm concerned with and not so much the literal effect. If you take somebody like Elizabeth Fraser of the Cocteau Twins, it's all about phonetics, isn't it? But there's an order to her sort of made-up language. She's somebody I've actually learned a lot from, and was a huge influence on my approach to singing a song.

Can you tell me what inspired "Prayer for the Dying"?

I really wanted to write a song that served as some kind of comfort to people who were dying of incurable diseases or things beyond their control, and to those people who had lost people close to them. I mean, what do you say to someone who is dying of AIDS or someone who is dying of cancer? What do you say that can offer some kind of consolation? So this was a song where I really tried to dig deep. I really tried to put myself in a position of someone who was losing their life. I don't know if I succeeded, but I thought, what would I want someone to say to me? That's basically how that song came about.

So when you're beginning a song, do you usually have such a clear idea of what you're writing about?

No, it tends to present itself along the way more often than not. Sometimes I'll come up with a good melody over something that one of the guys is playing, then sometimes I'll have to look for some angle at which to approach whatever it is we're doing.

When you're writing lyrics, do you tend to free associate?

Yes, it goes back to what I was saying about each song already existing. You have to just open and allow the song to come through you.

Are there certain environments that you find more conducive to writing?

Yes, and usually they're nothing to do with music at all. When I have time to relax and when I'm away from the business is usually when I write the best music, or the best lyrics. But then, on the other hand, when I'm faced with a band such as I have now, then songwriting becomes a pleasure. It becomes easy in that respect because they're all such great musicians.

So you're writing on the road?

I have been, yeah. Out of jams and out of stuff I've been doing in the hotel rooms by myself. I'd like to mention my band, because I think they're four of the best musicians on earth. Earl Harvin plays drums, Reggie Hamilton is our bassist, Jamie Muhoberac the keyboard player and musical director, and our guitarist is Chris Bruce. Chris and Jamie have been really inspirational in the stuff that we've written on the road.

Earlier you mentioned the Cocteau Twins. Are there other artists that you return to for inspiration?

Marvin Gaye. "Save the Children" is a wonderful song. Marvin is a huge inspiration on my writing and my singing. Joni Mitchell obviously. Hendrix, though I haven't been listening to him in the last year. There are also a few current artists I love, like Alanis Morrisette. She's a girl you'll hear more about. In fact, you should interview her. She's an incredible lyricist. She has a song called "You Learn." I use that as an example because it's not the one that I would immediately like off of her record because it's really commercial and it's the obvious hit, but it's heartwrenching. The lyric really says it all. It's a beautiful song. You should listen to that record. She's going to be around for a long, long time. She has that ability to turn a phrase, just like Joni.

Have you ever gone as far as to use songs by other artists as springboards for your own?

I'm sure I have. My guitarist Chris pointed out to me the other day that he could tell I'd been listening to Hendrix when I wrote "Future Love Paradise," which I was. But it's not like I hear a song and say, "Ooh I must write a song like that." I'll be inspired by many songs, but I don't sit down with a conscious intent to imitate.

If you feel yourself getting into a rut with your songwriting, what kinds of things help you move through it?

New musicians, change of situation, change of environment. A break. Again, not forcing it. Sometimes it helps to leave it, then come back to it later.

Is it important for you to finish everything you start?

No.

Are you pretty good about cataloging your half-finished songs?

No, they just tend to exist on various bits of paper or in my mind somewhere [laughs]. My theory is that if it's good I'll remember it and it will crop up. If it's worth ending up on a record, then it will do [so]. It will find its way back. If the melody is strong enough, I'll remember it at some point.

How did your time in India and Thailand affect your songwriting?

From a spiritual point of view, it opened me up to a lot of areas of my life which were closed up until then. That whole period of my life allowed me to get to know myself better. The songs on the first album were very young: if we only stick together, we can save the world. That's the space I was in. It was an indication of me embracing everything around me. It was also an indication of how idealistic I was feeling at the time. I think I was writing those songs from more of a humanitarian viewpoint.

Were the songs on your debut your first songs?

No, I'd written a whole bunch before that. But when I first wrote "Crazy"—I think at the end of 1989, that's when I felt I had something.

What were some of the obstacles you had to overcome to reach that point?

I was writing from my voice and not writing from an instrument, so the songs didn't have a common thread through them which was identifiably mine. So that was really the changing point. When I started playing the guitar, "Crazy" was the first thing I wrote. "Kiss from a Rose" came from that period, too.

With the success of your first record, did you have to deal with the whole sophomore jinx dilemma?

Well, there is that danger that people talk about of trying to make an album you think people want to hear, as opposed to what you feel. But I'm a firm believer in serving the songs as opposed to trying to curb the songs into a category or context that they don't necessarily fit into naturally. I believe that each song has a life of its own, so I tried to serve the songs as best I could.

If you were going to teach a class on songwriting, what would be three things that you would stress to your students?

God, I couldn't teach a class [laughs]. I wouldn't know where to begin because I'm so disorganized in terms of songwriting. It depends on what you're writing for. I think it's important to write from an instrument or have some understanding of music, however basic it may be. Only because it opens you up, it frees you. Also, I think that whatever instrument it is you have, it has to inspire you. It has to be something you like the sound of. If you don't like the sound of it, then it won't inspire you. Also, going back to allowing yourself to be open so that the songs can flow through you. Don't ever really try to force anything that doesn't come naturally. I've done both. There were songs on this last album that were forced and they're fine, but they don't have staying power to the person that wrote them. Just allow yourself to be open, and don't be afraid to go with something that necessarily doesn't make even musical, literal, or lyrical sense. If it feels right, then pursue it and don't be swayed from it. But at the same time, remain open to outside influences. Take on board everything, select what you want, and dump the rest.

CHAPTER 24

Paula Cole

Interviewed 1998

Hits: "I Don't Want to Wait," "Where Have All the Cowboys Gone?," "I Believe in Love"

There were a few months there in late 1997 when you couldn't turn on the radio without hearing "I don't want to wait for our lives to be over..." Love it or hate it, Paula Cole's song was impossible to escape, and impossible to get out of your head once you'd heard it. It had first been used to dramatic effect as a theme on the TV series *Dawson's Creek,* then jumped onto the airwaves, taking up a long residence in the Top 40.

Though she was one of dozens of female singer-songwriters who rode in on the post-Alanis wave of the mid-1990s, Paula Cole stood out. While she shared some of the common traits of that Lilith generation—confessional, outspoken, New Agey—she had a musicality and range that lifted her above the average girl with a guitar and bruised heart.

Cole was born April 5, 1968, in Rockport, Massachusetts, a tiny resort town that has been grist for the mill of some of her most pointed songs. Her mom is a visual artist, while her dad, a biology professor, plays music part-time. Though there wasn't much money, there was plenty of jamming and harmony singing around the Cole household. "They taught me the most singly important life philosophy," says Cole. "Music is meant to be self-made, to be experienced directly."

After high school, Cole attended Berklee College of Music, where she impressed her instructors as a jazz singer with a bright future. "I learned a lot cerebrally. I was pursuing the virtuosity of my voice and the techniques of music, but ultimately I felt empty. I wanted something a little more personal."

She found it in songwriting. "The river was always there inside of me, but I was very shy," she says. "I could see that this was my path. I felt destiny in my own music."

Once Cole found the right door to knock upon, the opportunities flowed forth: a record deal (her debut was *Harbinger*), critical acclaim, and concert dates with Counting Crows, Sarah McLachlan (Cole was a founding member of the Lilith Fair tours), and Peter Gabriel (she sang background on his tour for *So*). Her second album, *This Fire*, caught on with two ubiquitous singles, "Where Have All the Cowboys Gone?" and the aforementioned "I Don't Want to Wait." It won Cole a Best New Artist Grammy (she got a record-setting seven nominations for the album) and sold millions. Her third release, 1999's *Amen*, despite strong songs and further maturation, fared less well.

Currently, Cole is caught in an increasingly common modern dilemma. She has finished recording a new album that her label, for whatever reasons, is refusing to release. Whether she will go the independent route (Aimee Mann, Jane Siberry, etc.) or battle it out with Warner Bros. remains to be seen. Venting her frustration on her Web site recently, Cole wrote, "I often imagine myself as an artist from the 70's. I just think my music would've been so embraced in that more organic time. I'm so happy I was able to experience the 70's even as a little kid. It felt like a more hospitable time on the planet with *Sesame Street* on the TV, *The Secret Life of Plants* a bestseller, and Crosby, Stills, Nash and Young's 'Ohio' on the radio."

How do you feel like you've changed as a writer from the first album to your second?

I kind of feel like there's a maturation of self, like I'm standing on my own two feet a lot more. I'm more proud and confident about who I am, and I'm more happy about who I am. I've moved through some of my insecurities and fears. Even little things, like playing piano live or wanting to produce the album but being afraid to do so. Big changes in my personal life. Change in a relationship. I just feel like it was a big explosion, a big journey [laughs], with a lot of freedom found.

The first single, "Where Have All the Cowboys Gone?," is really taking off. What are your feelings about the American cowboy myth?

This song is interpreted differently by everybody. That makes me happy, in a way. I think it's kind of beautiful that my little song could be universal and be interpreted by different consciousnesses, different minds. I intended it to be wistful and melancholy and sarcastic, and an examination of our roles. Some people don't interpret it that way at all. They think I'm looking for my gentleman. I have a low opinion of media in general. A lot of the information we're given is statistically false. Even the news. A lot of the roles we're given by media and society are very ill-fitting to our souls and our very natures, and hinder us from potential growth. So it is sarcasm. The Marlboro Man, that image of machismo on the billboard, it's ill-fitting to a lot of men, and it puts pressure on them to be macho. And roles that are given to women are confining and certainly don't express the breadth of creativity and potential that are in a lot of women's voices and souls. I think a lot of people feel that way.

How did the song begin?

I was living in San Francisco, and I was writing a lot of songs. It's an older song, and it could've been on *Harbinger*, but for some reason it wasn't. Back then, it didn't receive a lot of enthusiasm. I was listening to a bit of XTC at the time and I was appreciating the wit and cleverness of their lyrics, which is usually not my style. Usually I like honest, true emotion, but I was in a mode of appreciating what they did. I felt that there wasn't much of an expression of sarcasm from a woman's point of view in songwriting, and it just came out. That question, "Where have all the cowboys gone?," came out on a page and it demanded to be a song. I quickly wrote words, then music to it later. The song was buried for a few years. It wasn't believed in by many people, but somehow it gnawed at me. It tickled my mind. I remember being back there, so I reproduced it, did a new demo, then suddenly everyone was excited. That's a good lesson. Sometimes you do have gems in your old treasure chest. Not every new song is your best song.

On the song "Throwing Stones" you have a line, "Now my anger is my best friend." Do you feel part of a movement with other women songwriters who are expressing their anger in their music?

I'm pretty ignorant about other people's music. I listened to Alanis Morrisette's album for the first time after I'd made my record. I'd heard the single on the radio because you couldn't avoid it. I appreciate what she has to say. I feel like all the power to her. I feel that she's being sincere. But all I do is look inside myself and I draw my songs from my own experiences, so I don't feel like I'm part of any movement. It will all be clearer in a decade or so. I just feel like the world of radio and the world of music is starting to become a little more balanced, and therefore a lot of the good music that's being made by women is able to come through.

Does that song feel like therapy?

Yes. I'm able to express anger. I was nervous about putting that song out. It's very real. It's so autobiographical, and I knew I was making myself very vulnerable by expressing these emotions, and I was nervous to immortalize it on plastic CDs and put it out for sale. But I feel like I didn't want to start censoring myself, and I'm an artist, and therefore the anger or even negativity I'm feeling is safe in an artform, in the pod of a song. It's almost my duty as an artist. The music is stronger than my ego. I feel like I need to be honest.

Once the song was on the CD, how did the feelings change?
Were you able to move on easily?

Yes. Once I had made the decision, then it was fine. Just water moving under the bridge. I don't listen to my albums. Just a rare couple of times.

Is it hard for you to listen to your own stuff?

I spend such a long time with it in the studio, and you have to listen to the songs over and over and over again, and you become incredibly saturated with the work, and I didn't have the desire to listen to it for a long time [laughs]. Then I'd listen to it just to see if it was any good, here and there. But I don't know when [was] the last time I listened to it.

What inspired "Nietzsche's Eyes"?

That to me isn't about anything detailed or analytical about his life. It's more about the metaphor of his blindness and his insatiable need to work, and continue working, even though it was causing his blindness. He was searching so hard for something and yet it was so self-defeating. And that's the way I've felt in a relationship.

I really like the song "Feelin' Love." It's a great vocal performance,
with lots of different colors and tones. How do you build a vocal
performance?

I think I was inspired by Al Green, and it's probably obvious. It's definitely influenced by 60s Memphis/Stax soul. It's interesting, when I listen to *Harbinger* now, I hear that I'm singing mostly in the low part of my range. It's darker, and there's even, I feel now, an affectation in there. It's where I was, so I honor that in a way. But I feel like I'm unlearning a lot of bullshit, and I'm unlearning a lot of the societal things, and I'm getting closer to who I really am. My voice, I feel, has kind of exploded a bit. Between albums, I would just experiment with my voice sometimes, and that's where I've kind of discovered these weirdo things I've been doing [laughs].

As someone who was admittedly shy, how did you get to a place where you could sing a come-on song like "Feelin' Love"?

It's the same place that allowed me to be naked on the cover and do those screaming vocals. I know myself, and I love myself more, and I don't care as much about my ego honestly. I think things can roll off my back. I'm happier, and I'm in a beautiful relationship that totally inspired that song. We're all in a male or female body. There's no mystery, and there's nothing to be ashamed of. I'm comfortable with it, and I think too, as a woman in society, you learn all these veils of repression and shame about the power of sexuality, and men looking at you. I learned to be shy or ashamed or feel victimized, but I don't feel that way anymore, and it's such a freedom. I feel like we're all like this. I love myself the way I am, and I don't feel that sense of shame anymore, so I can express it for me.

Did anything else help you?

I started doing yoga about a year and a half ago, and it started making my body much more of a finely tuned instrument. It's like if I were a violin, it suddenly tuned all the strings. Suddenly this beautiful melody could be played through me. With breathing exercises, I literally found my body and discovered me. Whatever you want to call it—chi, prana, self, spirit—I really came to know that and had a spiritual revolution. I grew up in this scientific-atheistic household and realized that my own sense of spirit in me, my connectedness to God, to spirit, and things started changing. I can't explain it, but yoga caused a huge difference. I had less pessimism, more choice, and it helped me to live in the moment and see the beauty of all things in the moment.

How did "I Don't Want to Wait" end up as the theme for **Dawson's Creek?**

Kevin Williamson [creator of the series] wouldn't take no for an answer. He knew I didn't like TV. But he said, "Just watch the show and help me elevate the state of television." It was such a beautifully eloquent and impassioned plea. So I watched the show and thought it was really good. And I thought, why not?

Having worked with Peter Gabriel, what are some of the best things you've learned from him about being a musician and songwriter?

I'm a really big fan of *So*, and I used to walk around Boston with my Walkman listening, and I knew it inside and out. I made *Harbinger*, and it wasn't released for year, and then I got the gig with Peter. On one hand, it was so huge and incredibly rewarding and moving for me. When I first heard "Don't Give Up," something in me said, "I'm going to be singing this song. I want to sing this song." And then for me to sing that song with him was such a rewarding feeling. And then day-to-day life goes by and you realize, he's just a guy [laughs]. He farts and he burps like all of us, and he's got problems and issues like we all do. He's shy. I appreciated that he allowed me to be me on the stage. He didn't really give me any guidance or analysis or critique or anything. He just let me be me. And that's, I think, his strength. He brings in a lot of talented people and then lets them mix. I was really an observer. An observer to his career and to his show, and I would watch what he would do with his audience and watch what he would do with his success, and I would think about what I would do in that position. I just learned tremendously. I was absorbing so much information, and in the meantime, I was seeing the world, and opening up culturally, and overcoming some shyness.

What do you hope that people will get out of your records?

If they just want entertainment, that's okay. But if they look to me for any kind of inspiration or guidance—which I think some people do—then maybe just the example that I was able to lift my very diffident self out of a small town and persist with something I loved and overcome a lot of obstacles and continually learn more about the world and grow as a soul, and that I'm not unique. This is available every day to everybody. Everybody can persist with their talent and go somewhere fantastic and revelatory.

Any final words?

We are what we think. If we can be objective enough to see what we're thinking to realize that we're thinking about limitations constantly and saying negative things about ourselves, then that's what we will be and that's what we will bring upon ourselves. If we decide to stop that demonic voice and realize we have a choice and starting thinking, "I'm capable of this. I'm going to persist with what I love," then you'll bring love into your life and happiness into your life.

CHAPTER 25

Jewel

Interviewed 1996

Hits: "You Were Meant for Me," "Who Will Save Your Soul," "Foolish Games"

In 1994, a free-spirited twenty-year-old singer-songwriter-surfer named Jewel Kilcher was living in her van, hanging out at the beach near San Diego and existing on a diet of carrots and peanut butter. A mere two years later, she was the biggest star on the planet—her face on the cover of *Rolling Stone*, a mega-platinum CD, two Top 10 singles, a book of poetry, sold-out concerts, and just about all the fan adulation one girl could handle.

Jewel's supersonic ascent had elements of the classic old-fashioned American Dream come true. Consider her beginnings: Born May 23, 1974, she grew up on an 800-acre homestead near Homer, Alaska, and lived a rustic life—no running water, no television, and plenty of hard work. At the same time, her parents, a musical duo with showbiz in their blood, welcomed their young daughter onstage as part of the act while they did the circuit of hotels and bars.

Thanks to her mother's tutelage, Jewel also got an early appreciation for poetry. "Through those lessons, I was given a tool," she says. "After my parents got divorced, I started writing poetry a lot because I didn't always know how to express myself. That, to me, is the real beauty of writing: it makes you more intimate with yourself."

While on a vocal scholarship at Interlochen Arts Academy, the sixteen-year-old Jewel took up the guitar and began writing songs. "It was a natural progression," she says. After graduation, she spent the months soul-searching, traveling, bumming around, and struggling against the nine-to-five routine, which led to her residency in a van parked near that San Diego beach. What began as a weekly stint singing for free at the Innerchange Coffeehouse grew into something bigger, and soon Jewel was the hit of the Pacific Coast, attracting first local and eventually national attention.

Her debut record, *Pieces of You*, was a slow starter. It had been out nearly fourteen months before the first single caught on. Jewel then spun through a two-year whirlwind where she seemed to be everywhere at once. Since then, she's kept a lower profile, exploring different sounds and directions on her subsequent three albums. The dance-flavored *0304* in 2003 was the biggest departure yet, with a glam makeover and urban dance beats replacing her strummed guitar.

This interview was conducted a few months before Jewel's career took off.

When you were growing up in Alaska, what kinds of things influenced you to become a singer-songwriter?

My father's a songwriter, and I started singing with him and my mother when I was six. They played in hotels, and put out two albums. So that was always definitely a factor in my life. It wasn't a weird thing to write songs. It was a very normal thing, very easy for anybody to do. Also, my mom had poetry workshops with us kids—from a very early age, we'd all sit down and write little poems about the clouds and the birds and the sunshine [laughs]. After my parents got divorced, I started singing in bars and clubs with my dad when I was eight. So I had a lot of influence that way. Music was always part of my life, I always sang, and I loved it.

Can you recall writing your first song?

It was kind of a blues song [laughs], and it was a lot of work. I'd noticed that I'd been going around making up songs in my head, but I never really did anything with them. "Well, maybe I'll just pay attention to one of them," I thought. But it was hard, because I'm not a trained musician and I didn't know format or that a verse is four stanzas. I only had an ear and intuition, so I had to kind of invent a method for remembering. I made up a little music chart on how to remember notes [laughs].

Were there people you listened to as a kid that shaped your writing?

I never meant to write songs. I felt like I was a singer, so I listened to Ella Fitzgerald a lot. There was a big potato patch we had to weed every day after school—it was about an acre—and I had this little broken tape player and I'd listen to Ella all day long. To this day, I just love her voice more than any voice in the world. Now that I think about it, something that really influenced my writing was that in ninth grade, I got to take a philosophy class. I never really thought I was stupid by any means, but before that, I never really thought. I realized that so few kids were ever taught to think. Being able to read Plato and Kant really taught me how to think, and it gave me a method to articulate and follow through with ideas so your brain didn't just slip off into whatever little zone it slips into [laughs]. That changed my writing immensely. It made me a very articulate writer at a very young age, and it made me incredibly watchful.

I've read that some of your songs grow out of poems. Is that a way you like to write?

Each song is a mystery. I don't know how I write. I started playing guitar about five years ago and I didn't mean to, but I guess since I've written so much poetry and that kind of thing that it was sort of a natural process. When you pick up guitar and learn some chords, you're naturally going to put some words to it. I'm just getting old enough that I'm starting to see cycles in my life [laughs]. It's kind of exciting [laughs]. I'm noticing that poems I wrote when I was sixteen are now surfacing in my songs. I feel that my better songs are from that, when I sit down with my journal and I really put my brain to work, instead of just rhyming.

When you're beginning a song, do you do a lot of free association?

It's the most mysterious process I've ever been involved in [laughs]. And now so much rides on it, not only my dream, but a lot of people's careers and a lot of money is going into it. It's kind of horrifying because I don't know how the fuck I do it [laughs]. But I do free associate in the early stages. More than anything, as long as I pick up my guitar and start playing and don't criticize myself, then something is bound to come out. I guess that's the hardest part for me, not overanalyzing what I do and just letting it come out.

Do you have any methods to sidestep the critic?

I guess every time I hear it, I just say, "Shut up" [laughs]. I have to tell myself every other thought, which is a lot, "Just be quiet, Jewel." I have a friend who I really respect as a songwriter, and the thing I respect most about him is that he doesn't judge it. Even retarded babies deserve to live, you know? It's true, you have no right to judge your own songs, and it's hard with the pressure that you have to write a hit, or something weird like that. Is this a hit? That's the worst thing you can do. If I just sit down and write, just follow a creative pattern and be true to it, it's going to be its own cool thing. That's the best you can do.

Do you write a little bit every day?

Yeah, I think like that all the time. My brain is always kind of engaged in that, and I'm always watching people and I'm always absorbing.

Tell me about the song "I'm Sensitive."

It was a song that I thought was really dumb. I have this thing about cheesy, like I think cheesy is bad because cheesy is simple—as though simplicity were wrong. I wrote that song for myself, and I write very few for myself. And I started that song off saying, "I think I might die today" [laughs]. I had a really bad experience with this one band member, and things were just getting to me. You know this whole business that they say, the whole cynical, jaded thing. I saw a recycling bin and I remembered that someone once told me that the power of the brain is to recycle thought. Like a water filter, we can take a negative thought and turn it out as something more beautiful. It really just turned the song around. It could have been a really good hardcore song, but it turned right around and I thought, "Well, more than anything we have to keep our faith, we have to keep our hopes up." I thought I'll just write this for me. No one has to hear it. But I happened to play it as a new song just to try it out when I was recording live. When I heard it, I thought, "Wow, I really like it." And people's reactions have been really great, so I find it kind of shocking [laughs].

I like the line "Why does it have to be so complicated?"

It's true. Things can be so much simpler [laughs]. A lot of us just crave simplicity, and we forget that it can be. I'm just trying to take my reality with me wherever I go now and just say, "It's going to be simple."

Where did the song "Adrian" come from?

I don't know if you've heard of a band called the Rugburns. The guy who writes for them is Steve Poltz, who I mentioned earlier—the guy I really respect as a songwriter. He's as brilliant as John Prine, Townes

VanZandt, and Bob Dylan, as far as I'm concerned. I'm very lucky to have him as a mentor and as a friend. He and I write songs together, and that was one we wrote together. I grew up writing a lot of short stories, just making things up about people and really getting into it. So that's all that was. He said, "Adrian came home again last summer and things haven't been the same . . ." and we went from there.

How about "Painters"?

When I was studying philosophy in school, I was really fascinated with the idea of immortality, and what made us immortal and why wasn't I, and how could I be? [laughs]. My favorite reading was Plato's *The Symposium*. In it, he talks about how perhaps through love and beauty we reach immortality. And that's something that really stuck with me, because it was kind of a tangible, believable thing. I guess I believe that through art, if you do it consciously and with enough intent and passion, it will probably not only be the most honest expression of yourself, but if you put that much life into it, it does breathe. That's what the song's about for me, people who put that much passion into their work.

"Angel Standing By."

I believe in angels. I believe that in my loneliest moments, I haven't really been alone. I must have a driving angel, because I drive so bad that I should be dead [laughs]. It's also written for a friend that I'm not around very much, especially if I'm in a relationship or traveling. It's kind of about that. I know that I've gone through much of my life feeling alone and more than anything, I just want people to know that we aren't.

Name a few songs you wish you wrote.

Oh, there's so many. I wish I wrote a lot by Cole Porter. They have such craftsmanship. When kids were listening to Cyndi Lauper and Madonna, I was listening to the *Cole Porter Songbook* by Ella Fitzgerald, and I think of that song "I Get a Kick Out of You." Also, "Too Darn Hot." Those songs were innocent, with really subtle relationship play, but all in a really clean way. It was great writing.

What would you most like to accomplish as a songwriter?

Just to keep writing [laughs]. I want to be better at it, because I don't think I'm very good yet. More than anything, I think songwriting is a vehicle for me. It's a tool. I studied marble carving, dance, drawing, and all that, and I think I was best at writing because I've been doing it for so long. It's like a vehicle to touch people, and it's a very accepted medium. So if anything, I just want to refine the art of it and use it as a better and better tool to just be with people.

CHAPTER 26

Dido

Interviewed 2001

Hit songs: "Here with Me," "Thank You"

Dido (she's named after the queen in Virgil's *Aeneid*) grew up in an eccentric London household, her mom a closet poet, her dad a literary agent who specialized in military books ("There were always these weird old generals about," Dido says). Television was forbidden, so Dido took up the recorder, practicing classical pieces for six or seven hours a day. By the time she was in her teens, she was also playing violin and piano. "I was sort of an odd kid," she laughs.

But after college, it wasn't music she pursued, but publishing. "I had this shining career as a literary agent," she says, "looking after big-thriller writers, trashy novelists, and some well-known journalists. I'd got enough money together to live for a year and thought, I'll try this music thing, and if it doesn't work in a year, I'll take my old job back. So I left, and a year to that day I got a deal."

Her self-titled debut had a folk electronica vibe, downshifted and ethereal, falling stylistically somewhere west of Beth Orton and south of Sarah McLachlan. It was a slow builder. Nearly a year after its release, the song "Here with Me" was picked up as a theme for the WB series *Roswell*. And then came the big reversal of fortune—"Thank You," a tuneful love song, was sampled by controversial rapper Eminem as the hook of his single "Stan."

Of her association with hip-hop's bad boy, Dido says, "It's been sort of a strange thing, but luckily I think what Eminem did with it is brilliant. It's a whole different way of looking at the song."

In fall 2003, she released her second album, *Life for Rent*.

What's your latest discovery about songwriting?

My whole thing is that I wrote a lot of this album on the piano, and it was only recently that I started playing guitar. I'm truly hopeless on the guitar, but since I know so few chords, I can write hundreds of songs. When I learn a new chord, I can write another ten songs, 'cause it's so exciting. This friend of mine who was teaching me said, "Look, don't learn too many chords. Take it one at a time." So that's my new thing, one new chord a day.

You've said that you wrote a lot of your album while driving in your car. What would you say it is about driving that is so conducive to songwriting?

I think you can sort of go mad sitting in the studio looking at the same wall and trying to picture things. Although I like writing that way, it's nice to get out in the car. You see people, they do things that are unexpected. You can look into people's windows and get ideas. It's having all those visual images, more of them than you would get from sitting in one place. I'll take backing tracks in the CD player or the tape player, and another tape recorder on the seat, and then I'll write over it. I'm not scribbling on bits of paper while I'm driving a hundred miles an hour [laughs]. I'm not a dangerous songwriter.

Is there a place you like to begin your songs?

I do it so many different ways. Sometimes people give me backing tracks, which then I start writing over and change what the backing track is a bit, or expand on it. Sometimes I just start with the piano and me, sometimes a guitar. Sometimes I have friends round and they'll be playing something. Sometimes I'll write over an already existing piece of music, then write something underneath.

Do you finish everything you start?

No. It's important to me that I work on them, but I'm crap at finishing them all. I've got hundreds of unfinished ideas. I'm totally disorganized. I just stick them into a big black book.

In the early stages of writing a song, do you have more of a sense of following or leading?

Definitely leading. I'll actually sit at the piano, and I'm thinking about it before the song comes. I'd love to say that songs just came and I wrote them down, but it doesn't work that way for me. It's the carriage before the horse.

Do you feel like songs exist before they're written?

No, I don't think so. I love that idea, it's a brilliant thought. The way I write songs, that theory wouldn't work for me. My whole thing is that I feel lucky every time a song is finished, and you've created something. It's such a nice feeling. I never want to analyze where it's coming from because I think as soon as I do, it'll stop.

A lot of writers say they're at their best when their lives are in turmoil. Is that true for you?

Not really. A lot of songs, like "Thank You" and "Here with Me," I've written when I'm really happy. I'm better when I'm on holiday or when I'm chilled out. If I'm having a rough time, I'll go into the studio, because you do want to cash in on those kinds of feelings. Any extreme of emotion and I'm off writing a song, because you have to exploit it. But I think I definitely write better when my life is peaceful.

Tell me about how "Thank You" evolved.

A friend of mine came round, and he was playing around with this beautiful guitar riff, and I started humming a melody. After he left, I had a bath, then wrote the lyrics in like five minutes. It was the quickest song I've ever written, without a doubt. There were no crossings out, it was blah blah blah, finished, done, which is very rare for me. I knew I wanted to make the verses about having a shit day, and the choruses would be very sweet.

"Isobel."

I wrote that with my brother Rollo. No one can tell the difference between the way we write. Actually there's a massive difference, but it's good because we can finish each other's sentences. He can tell me roughly what he wants to say and I can make it into lyrics, and sometimes he'll come up with lyrics. We wanted to write about someone leaving. We grew up in Ireland, and we were thinking, "What would be one of the main reasons to leave Ireland?" The only reason when you're a teenager would be to go have an abortion, so that's what the song is about. I called it "Isobel" because that's the name of one of my best friends, and I wanted to be singing about someone I cared about.

"I'm No Angel."

I wrote it as an apology to my boyfriend. The whole point of the album is being human and willing to admit your mistakes, never regretting what you've done and learning from your mistakes.

The concept of love is very idealized in contemporary pop songs. What do you try to do with love in your songs?

My whole thought on love is that most of the time we're screwing up, but it doesn't matter and it's part of being alive. I think my songs are trying to say that. Love isn't some big, grand thing. It's just a really small part of life that makes us incredibly happy. That's why I like "Thank You." I feel like I got my point across on that song about what love is. There's the line about "handing me a towel." That's a useful thing to hand me [laughs], as opposed to giving me a big hug or something. I don't want that, because I'm wet [laughs]. It's the very small things, very small moments that matter. A lot of my songs are saying, "Yes, I've screwed up and you've screwed up, but it doesn't matter."

What advice would you offer to singer-songwriters?

Be persistent, and only write what you absolutely believe in, because if your record does do well, you're going to have to sing those songs for a long time. Don't think about your audience, because there isn't one yet when you're starting. Just think about what you want to hear, and make that music. If it works out, that's brilliant. But don't write what you think you should be writing. It's a mistake, trying to second guess what people want to hear. It's almost impossible to do. And the other thing is, don't be too arrogant about it in the beginning and don't be afraid to sort of give things away to get what you want in the future. I signed a lot of bad bits of paper, and I've sung on a lot of things, and I've given a lot away, and I've helped people write things and never asked for anything. But, in the long run, it totally helped me get farther quicker. Don't be afraid to be a bit of slave for a while, then sort out the mess afterwards. I don't regret any of it. My management is horrified by some of the things I've done, but when you start, I think you should do everything to get experience, then worry about it later. That's sort of bad advice, but it worked for me.

What are your desert island discs?

Stevie Wonder, *Songs in the Key of Life*
David Gray, *White Ladder*
Portishead, *Dummy*
All of Beethoven's symphonies
Police box set

CHAPTER 27

John Mayer

Interviewed 2002

Hits: "No Such Thing," "Your Body Is a Wonderland," "Bigger Than My Body"

In 2006, John Mayer will have his ten-year high school reunion. As he fantasizes in the song "No Such Thing," he will bust down the double doors, stand on tables, and run through the halls screaming at the top of his lungs, basically letting everyone know that Spartacus has returned.

But now that his major label debut, *Room for Squares*, has barnstormed its way into high schools from his native Connecticut to California as the official soundtrack for sensitive teenagers, Mayer might have to consider a little fantasy revision. Maybe he could beam a satellite greeting to his former classmates from the stage of a sold-out Madison Square Garden. Or he could just buy his former alma mater and rename it John Mayer High.

Anything seems possible these days for the twenty-five-year-old singer-songwriter. In two short years, he has risen from a coffeehouse troubadour with a homemade CD and a mailing list to a pop star with throngs of adoring fans and a close personal friendship with Elton John. *Room for Squares* is at two million and counting. Mayer has toured the world, graduating from small theaters to arenas. He's had a fling with a Hollywood starlet. He's been nominated for Grammys. He's been featured in magazines from *Rolling Stone* to *Seventeen* to *Guitar Player*. And he has several Internet discussion groups devoted to him.

Back in the early 90s, when Mayer was a high school student, his aspirations had nothing to do with all this fame and fortune. He wanted only to be that most raggedly honest of all musicians—the bluesman.

"I was fifteen years old, with my room plastered with posters of Stevie Ray Vaughan, Albert King, Bonnie Raitt, Jimmie Vaughan, Robert Cray—these were my friends," Mayer says. "Everyone else my age had Nirvana, and I was skipping class, reading the Buddy Guy biography, *Damn Right I've Got the Blues.*"

Like every aspiring bluesman, Mayer went down to the crossroads, which in his case was the family breakfast nook. "My parents were professional educators, so it was pretty hard to walk in the kitchen and say, 'I think I want to play guitar.' They said, 'Well, what's the syllabus for that?'"

Mayer studied the hot licks of his mentors and by his senior year, he was playing gigs in nightclubs around his hometown. His quest to be "the kind of guitarist that made other guitarists go, 'Whoa!'" took him to Berklee College of Music in Boston. He lasted a year.

He recalls, "When I got out of Berklee, I realized that playing guitar in the way that I really wanted to play it starting out would have only reached other guitar players. I wanted to hit people's hearts."

The way to people's hearts, as anyone from Caruso to Coldplay could tell you, is through a song. After relocating to Atlanta, Mayer channeled all his guitar chops and suburban blues feeling into becoming a singer-songwriter. Within a few years, he'd built a huge local following and made his own CD.

He was signed by Columbia Records and, to their credit, they spent time developing him rather than giving up after six weeks, which is the usual major label m.o. for new artists. Mayer toured relentlessly. *Room for Squares* caught on by word of mouth. His style, which appeals to everyone from teenyboppers to boomers, is an updated version of 70s singer-songwriter pop. Centered on the acoustic guitar and his warm, corduroy voice, it's mellow and melodic, but with a little more attitude and rhythmic snap than James Taylor or Jackson Browne ever had.

Despite his success (his second album, *Heavier Things*, went Top 5 as this book was being written), Mayer says, "I'm still a struggling songwriter. The game is the same no matter what you do and who you are. When you're alone in a room, it doesn't matter how many records you sold, how many people you've got around you. It's you and the possibility and what are you going to do to find it."

You've been on the road for a year and a half. Is it hard to stay connected to the songs you're playing night after night?

Yes and no. For instance, playing "No Such Thing" without an audience for a radio station is dreadful, absolutely dreadful. But to play in front of people—I see this movie every night and I know the funny parts, but they're not funny anymore. I know the great parts, but they're not great anymore. But when I watch the audience watch the movie, they wake me up again. So there's that anticipation, and every crowd is different every night. I remember during the last six months of the touring, I really made sure to remember each night—this is another show to us, but for the people watching the show, their tickets had been sitting on their dresser for the last two months. Every time they get up in the morning, they put their underwear on, they look at the date on the ticket and they look at the date that it is and they count. I think more performers need to sit in the car outside of the club or the venue or the arena and watch people go into the show. Because when you see them walking so fast that it becomes skipping, and you see them so elated to be seeing you, that right there is the biggest slap in the face. Wake up! This show is not what you're doing in between video games. This show is the realization of people looking forward to your playing for the last two months. Once I started thinking about it that way, and once I started watching people walk into the show at seven or eight, when I went on at ten, once I realized that I am the culmination of that anticipation, I took everything a lot more seriously. Every single artist knows the feeling of standing in front of the stage, looking at the artist's gear before they're on stage and going, "That's his guitar. Oh my god, that's his drum set. Oh my god, that's his microphone. He's going to be singing into that." To plug in my walking out on stage as an extension of that, it puts everything in perspective.

The songs that you wrote for the first album I would imagine came from a very free place without much ego attached.

No, actually they came from a very egotistical place. I had just come out of Berklee, having been forced to mix with hundreds and hundreds of other guitar players. And I saw what most of them were doing wrong. I saw what some of them were doing right. I remember when I got out of Berklee, I had such a chip on my shoulder about what I didn't want to do. I didn't want to be just a guitar player. I know it's been proliferated in the press—"He wanted to be a guitar player and then he stopped." It's not that I stopped being a guitar player, but I realized that playing guitar in the way that I really wanted to play it would have only reached other guitar players. It's a tradesman's job. So I realized I wanted to hit people's hearts. But at the same time, I wanted to prove to the musicians of the world that I really had my musicality going on, which came from a definite place of ego. Check me out, check out the tricks I can do with these harmonies, check out what I can do with this resolution that you thought was going here but it's going here. I think there were a couple of places where I put that first. The same lyrically. *Room for Squares* for me goes down in my history as an attempt to be very clever. Every facet of that record is trying to be clever, from fourteen tracks and thirteen songs to plays on words to "quick game of chess with the salt and pepper shaker"—those are very cerebral. I wasn't very emotional as a musician.

But obviously, a lot of listeners connect to it emotionally.

It does have emotion, but there's a certain element that's missing because it's so clever most of the time. I've since found that clever goes to people's heads and that's great. But what goes to people's hearts is space and openness and directness. I've seen a lot of songwriters who are clever and I don't remember most of them. But those moments are only really there to help bring about a deeper understanding of a song. Those clever moments now, when I want to use them, I want people to really get what I'm talking about. I don't really care about using the music as a calling card for my ability to write music anymore. *Room for Squares* really was a calling card for my ability to write music. The place that I'm at now is really blissful. People know I can write, people know I can rhyme words. I don't have to throw the kitchen sink in anymore. Now I want to take a kind of honest, heartfelt position on it instead of using it for a sandwich board for what I can do.

Does selling two million copies of your first record and knowing who your audience is restrict your songwriting at all?

You'd be surprised. I need to preface this by promising that I would tell you if I really was pressured. I have no problem saying I'm scared shitless but I'm still going to try to rock. It's amazing to me the confidence that I have when I'm alone in my room and I'm writing. Mainly because I have people in my life to thank for it. There's nothing in my life that reminds me that I've sold two million records other than a plaque on my wall. I don't have yes people, I don't have people exposing the inner belly of the record industry to me. When I'm alone in my house, I feel like I am the John Mayer that's on my driver's license and that's it. So I'm able to leave all of that stuff at the door, and just go back and write another great record that I really feel like is coming along very strong. But who knows? The fun part and the scary part of writing a record alone is that either this idea that you came up with is genius or it is the most insipid thing in the world. And not knowing if it's genius or insipid is scary, but it's really fun too, because it tests you. It's almost like the power of suggestion test. Do you still think this is cool even if there's a chance of someone else not thinking it's cool? I do. So I don't have any pressure at all. My pressure right now is to not let the pressure get to me [laughs].

Let me ask you about a few of your songs to get your reaction— "No Such Thing."

I came up with the chorus without a guitar. Something about the catchiness of the notes—they weren't even in rhythm yet—really turned me on. I was humming it before I picked up a guitar. It's just about learning that all my friends who did what they were supposed to do to appease people around them weren't happy at all. And though I didn't have anything to show for myself on paper every three months, there was something happening. I thought maybe there was a way to succeed in something that didn't have a form, if the person living through it was able to govern themselves and not fall prey to every little thing outside of a structured life. Not drinking, not smoking. Paying attention and remembering what you're here to do. It's very difficult to keep in perspective. You have to remind yourself daily. I'm here in this apartment. I don't do anything but work eight hours a day labeling video tapes. But there's a better reason. I'm not a bum. I constantly had to prove myself. It's a very overcompensatory emotion in the song. I'll show you, I'll show you all. Even though I don't stand in those same shoes right now, it's still a fun song to sing.

"Why Georgia."

It's the other half of "No Such Thing," because they both talk about being on your own. "No Such Thing" is the chest-pounding, "I can do anything—I'm invincible" song that is almost like the daylight hour song, and "Why Georgia" is when you get in the car after you finish pumping your chest and it's just you. It's that lonely kind of reconnecting with yourself and your fears, and being honest with yourself. I think that's probably one of the truest songs on the record in terms of content. It's so true that for a while I wondered if I should really use the word "Georgia" in it because I thought, "How is that going to affect the universality of the song?" I think that the chorus is interesting because it shares a sentiment that is completely universal and then is followed by a very esoteric explanation. Am I living it right? It's an almost Southern gospel approach, which everyone can get into, and then it becomes "Why Georgia why?"

"Your Body Is a Wonderland."

It's perhaps the most misunderstood song on the record. I get women who come up to me and say, "If only my boyfriend felt the way about me that you do in that song, I'd love him so much." The answer to that is, "Well, he does. That's what you hate about him." That song is objectifying women completely, but in the most loving, truest, selfless way. Women, I believe, are ready to get down and dirty and fool around as much as men are, but women want to be sure that there's nothing at stake in terms of shame. They want to be sure that there's love and trust involved. The song is like, "You know what? We've got the love thing. We've got the trust thing. I've been scared for a while of wanting to approach this issue because I'm not sure what you're going to say." For millions of years now, girls have said, "Is that all you think about?" "Wonderland" says, "No, that's not all I think about. But it's all that I'm thinking about right now." It taps into that part of women that makes them feel sure enough that they can get it on. Because women are ready to get it on, but they have such wonderful restraint and such an amazingly great—and frustrating for men—series of qualifications for, "Will I let myself do this?" The song is trying to meet all the qualifications. Let's get this out of the way. It's obvious that I'm with you and I love you. Now I want this song to be exactly about how much I really just love your body. I think the song makes women feel safe. I think the reason they respond to it is that it makes them feel safe, and from that they can think sexually about it.

There's a planned obsolescence built into every aspect of pop culture these days. Last year, The Osbournes *was the hippest TV show. This year, it's stale. The same thing tends to happen with many first-time artists. How do you think you can get around it?*

My first rule, the reason that I've gotten this far, is because I don't get more apprehensive as I get higher. I think what happens when you first start out, you don't pull punches. You swing hard, you're bold, you don't think twice. You do your thing and it gets you where you're going, and then you double think everything. You never go with your first answer. You always go with your fourth answer. Your fourth answer is fucking wrong. But people think as they get higher and higher, they start thinking about every digit on their hand and how it's going to grab onto the next rung, and how that might possibly go hand over hand to the next one. It's not the way art works. It's not the way that decisions based on vital art are made. It is the way that business decisions are made, and there is no business in art whatsoever. But there are a lot of people's dreams coming true at the same time, and everyone has a different instinct about it. You get them all together and they go, "Oh my god, it's happening, it's happening, it's happening! Okay, okay, okay, what do we need to do right now, think, think, think!" I will say that the only person who doesn't really think that way is me because I'm the guy holding onto the hat. It doesn't frighten me. But it's interesting to see how other people around you start to get scared of heights. They want to double- and triple-think everything. It's a very tricky place to be right now because obviously, I wouldn't want to do anything to lose momentum. But you can also lose momentum by not doing anything to lose momentum. Staying around really comes down to being told what you got and then forgetting about it, and just doing your thing. "Hey, you've got this much in the bank." Isn't that fantastic? I guess I can buy a pair of shoes next week. Or, "This is how many records you've sold." Isn't that fantastic? But never parlay that into your next thing by trying to top yourself. That's where boringness sets in. That's where you go into a studio and you go, "Do we want to sit on these chairs?" People make their first record with one microphone in four days and sell a million records. Then they go in with a million-dollar budget and they want to sit around all day and talk about catering. It's not that hard—I got to break it to you. You write a song and you record it. The sound that you're making is going onto a tape and the tape is going to be shipped out to a bunch of people. I think when I visualize recording on that level in that unprecious state, it makes a lot of sense to me.

Any final words?

I wrote *Room for Squares* based on how can I get the world to see that I can write songs. Right now, I don't need to be clever. I just want to say what I want to say. I want to make a record that I'm going to want to play every single song every night.

What records influenced you most as a songwriter?

Pearl Jam, *Vitalogy*. I was heavily influenced by Pearl Jam. That early stuff, the melody was so intriguing, yet in the sweet spot of the song, I don't think anyone's come close. Listen to "Nothing Man"—it's unbelievable. There are a million things you can sing over any given chord progression, and Eddie Vedder always chose the one right way out of a million things.

Ben Folds Five, *Whatever and Ever Amen:* It's the perfect pop record. His lyric writing is so heartfelt and it's also so direct, so conversational. It really tapped into this really intelligent, sarcastic, scared kind of vibe.

Jeff Buckley, *Grace:* It's one of the most important records of all time, because it proves that though it may take a long time, you can write a record with melodies that have never been sung before, and it can still be dead on. It's gorgeous, it's frightening, it's haunting, it's beautiful, and so perfect that it's hard to imagine that that record was put together in the first place. I just get the sense that it just appeared one day. That's the best work that you can do, when you can't hear the work, you just hear the art.

Freedy Johnston, *This Perfect World:* His voice is so pure. His melodies are so simple but so heartfelt. If Jeff Buckley is an Ayn Rand novel, then Freedy Johnston is *The Little Engine That Could.* But in such a way that is so effective that it's scary.

Martin Sexton, *The American:* Great production and moments of just complete release, almost live sounding.

ABOUT THE AUTHOR

BILL DEMAIN is the author of *The Sterling Huck Letters* and *Behind the Muse: Pop and Rock's Greatest Songwriters Talk About Their Work and Inspiration.* As a music journalist, he has written for such publications as *MOJO, Entertainment Weekly*, and *Performing Songwriter*.